Remembering, Repeating, and Working Through Childhood Trauma

Remembering, Repeating, and Working Through Childhood Trauma:

The Psychodynamics of Recovered Memories, Multiple Personality, Ritual Abuse, Incest, Molest, and Abduction

Lawrence E. Hedges, Ph.D.

JASON ARONSON INC.
Northvale, New Jersey
London

This book was set in 12 point Goudy by Lind Graphics of Upper Saddle River, New Jersey, and printed and bound by Haddon Craftsmen of Scranton, Pennsylvania.

Library of Congress Cataloging-in-Publication Data

Hedges, Lawrence E.
    Remembering, repeating, and working through childhood trauma : the
    psychodynamics of recovered memories, multiple personality, ritual
    abuse, incest, molest, and abduction / Lawrence E. Hedges.
        p. cm.
    Includes bibliographical references and index.
    ISBN 1-56821-228-3
    1. Adult child abuse victims. 2. False memory syndrome.
    3. Psychotherapist and patient. 4. Transference (Psychoanalysis)
    5. Countertransference (Psychoanalysis) 6. Multiple personality.
    I. Title.
        [DNLM: 1. Psychoanalytic Therapy—methods. 2. Child abuse.
    3. Repression. 4. Transference (Psychology) 5. Multiple-
    Personality Disorder—therapy. 6. Professional–Patient Relations.
    WM 460.6 H453r 1994]
    RC569.5.C55H43 1994
    616.85' 822390651—dc20
    DNLM/DLC
    for Library of Congress   94-2266

Manufactured in the United States of America. Jason Aronson Inc. offers books and cassettes. For information and catalog write to Jason Aronson Inc., 230 Livingston Street, Northvale, New Jersey 07647.

This book is dedicated to
the many people who live their daily lives
with the damaging effects of trauma suffered in infancy,
who know that somewhere deep inside something is wrong,
that something keeps them from being quite like other people,
that something dark and mysterious
keeps them isolated, frightened, and alone.

Contents

PART III
THE DUAL RELATIONSHIP IN PSYCHOTHERAPY

PART IV
PSYCHOTIC ANXIETIES AND THE ORGANIZING EXPERIENCE

ACKNOWLEDGMENTS

The ideas worked out in this book have emerged in collaboration with the following colleagues:

Bill Cone	Jack Platt
Jolyn Davidson	Linda Reed
Cheryl Graybill	Sandra Russell
Robert Hilton	Karyn Sandberg
Virginia Wink Hilton	Donna Stapp
Ann Huffman	Sean Stewart
Jane Jackson	Gayle Trenberth
Kim Khazeni	Ted Trubenbach
Alita Kullman	Mary E. Walker
Steve Lawrence	Ruth Wimsatt
Jeanne Lichman	William White
Debbie Miranda	Robbie Woods
Dolly Platt	Cynthia Wygal

The manuscript was prepared by Jean Bourns, Breta Hedges, and Jason Keyes under the supervision of Ray Calabrese. Jason Aronson, Judy Cohen, David Kaplan, and Carol McKenna have provided editorial expertise. Thanks are extended to all of these people for their contribution.

Introduction:
The Recovered
Memory Crisis

Recent shifts in public opinion have mandated changes in all sectors of our society aimed at correcting age-old patterns of abuse. People who have been subjected to damaging treatment have felt encouraged to speak up and seek redress for the wrongs done to them in the past. Memories of painful experiences that individuals have tried not to think about for many years are being revived, and abusers are being confronted with the effects of their deeds. This vanguard of the civil rights movement has generated public indignation and a call for more effective laws and judicial procedures to limit widespread abuses of all types.

But along with the revival of painful memories of abuse that people have done their best to forget, another phenomenon has moved into the public arena—"recovered memories"—which emerge with compelling emotional power but exist to tell a story that could not have or did not occur in the exact or literal manner in which the abuse is so vividly remembered. On the basis of such memories, usually recovered in some psychotherapy or recovery group setting, acusations on a large scale are aimed at people who claim not to be perpetrators of abuse. As of February 1994, the False Memory Syndrome Foundation in Philadelphia boasts more than 10,000 member families claiming innocence of the crimes of which they are accused. Highly respected public figures, as well as ordinary, credible private citizens known in their communities to lead basically decent lives, are having the finger of accusation pointed at them. The controversy is heated and, unfortunately, has become drawn along lines of whether the memories of abuse are true or false.

Among this group of otherwise credible people who are being accused are numerous well-established individuals in the mental health field and in all of the other helping professions including nursing, medicine, law, the clergy, teachers, scout leaders, child care workers, and choir leaders – in short, all people in our society vested in any way with caring for others. New laws in more than half the states have changed the statute of limitations to read, "three years from when the abuse is remembered," though it is not yet clear whether such laws will stand up in court. By now, accusations based on memories recovered in hypnosis, "truth serum" interviews, recovery groups, and psychotherapy are coming under sharp criticism, partly because so many of the accusations are so outlandish, partly because a sizable number of memories have proved faulty, and partly because of the witch hunt atmosphere surrounding the recovered memory controversy, which threatens widespread injustice if responsible social controls are not forthcoming.

There is nothing new about recovered memories of abuse. They have been studied carefully for over a century in psycho-analysis and much is known about their nature. What's new is that the public has suddenly taken an interest in recovered memories. The highly suspect concept of repression as used by workers doing recovered memory work is being laid at the door of Freud and psychoanalysis when no such slipshod notion exists in psychoanalysis. Similarly, a naive and faulty notion of "body memories" as used by recovery workers is being laid wrongly at the door of bioenergetics analysis and body therapy in general—schools of thought and practice very carefully and responsibly worked out that never speak of body memories in such a careless or addled manner.

There are clearly many issues to sort out before we can regain our individual and collective sanity on this subject. In the chapters that follow I review a century of study on the phenomenon of memories recovered in psychotherapy, concluding that if memories recovered in psychotherapy are not taken seriously in the psychotherapy context, then we will indeed have a disaster on our hands. I then focus in depth on one area of clinical study—multiple personality—to illustrate the kind of careful and reasoned thinking I am advocating, since abuse is widely assumed to be centrally causal in multiple personality.

I then move to consider the chief cause of lawsuits and ethical complaints against therapists—the so-called dual relationship. Once the potentially damaging effects of sexual and other personal kinds of relating between therapist and client began to be understood, the accusation hysteria began sweeping the field of psychotherapy. A narrow moralizing movement began influencing ethics committees and licensing boards, shifting the focus from issues of exploitation and damage to the concrete details of the therapist–client interchange. The new morality of dual relationships would make it unethical, for example, for a therapist to attend a client's wedding, to send a dozen roses to a bereaved client, to accept a box of Christmas cookies from a client, or to engage in a hug at the end of a particularly meaningful session. One therapist who commutes to practice in an area of California recently hit by a disastrous earthquake brought her patients bottled water. Is this a dual relationship and therefore potentially damaging?

I take the position that the heart of psychotherapy—transference and its interpretation—cannot be accomplished without dual relating. There is a continuum of dual relating that ranges on the one extreme from a fully separate sexual and/or personal relationship to its opposite, the powerful and beneficial essence of therapy – the transference interpretation. If we begin moralistically legislating against all forms of dual relating without regard for interpersonal meaning or therapeutic context, we carelessly and thoughtlessly invade the most valuable and powerful forces operative in psychotherapy. My purpose for reasoning out the problem of dual relationships in psychotherapy is to illustrate how vulnerable therapists and other helping individuals are to accusations in general.

In this book I trace a large class of recovered memories to their source in primitive or psychotic anxieties, left over from the first months of life, that I assume to be operating universally. My thesis is that, while we are now aware of much more real abuse than has ever been acknowledged before, this widely reported class of memories surfacing in psychotherapy today is not new and cannot be understood literally. Memories recovered during the course of psychotherapy need to be taken seriously – considered psychodynamically and dealt with in thoughtful and responsible ways by therapists, not simply believed in and acted upon.

A therapist who takes a simplified recovery approach of encouraging clients to remember the abuse, be validated by being believed, and then confront the abusers, is not only involved in a devious and destructive dual relationship but is actively colluding in the resistance to the emergence of developmentally early transference experiencing with the therapist. Clearly the client has experienced some terrifying and traumatic intrusions – often in the earliest months of life, perhaps even without anyone really being aware that the infant was suffering subtle but devious forms of cumulative strain trauma. Memories from this time period simply cannot be retained in pictures, words, and stories. Rather, the body tissue itself or the interactive emotional response system retains an imprint of the trauma. Psychotherapy provides a place where words, pictures, and somatic experiences can be creatively generated and elaborated for the purpose of expressing in vivid metaphor crucial aspects of early and otherwise unrememberable trauma.

The most powerful and useful form of memory in bringing to light those primordial experiences is reexperiencing, in the context of an intimate and emotionally significant relationship with the psychotherapist, the patterns of the early abuse experience.

I call this earliest level of transference experiencing with the psychotherapist the *organizing transference* because the traumas to be brought into focus in the relationship occurred during the period of life when an infant is actively engaged in organizing or establishing physical and psychological channels and connections to his or her human environment. Other psychoanalytic researchers speak of the "psychotic transference" or the "transference psychosis."

I round out my arguments by considering in detail the nature of the organizing transference as it appears in psychotherapy and illustrate its definition and the working-through process with clinical case material. These illustrations make clear how easy it would be for a therapist to become derailed with the client into externalizing onto the past and onto supposed perpetrators the intensity of early transference anxieties. The case illustrations also make clear how easy it would be for the client to establish transference feelings toward the therapist and then to turn the accusatory process, based on early neglect and abuse, against the therapist.

Given the intensity of the early or primitive transference that is being brought to the psychotherapy situation for analysis and the actual dangers to the therapist that this kind of work entails, it is not difficult to understand (1) why many counselors and therapists without training in transference and resistance analysis are eager to direct the intense blame away from themselves and onto others from the client's past, (2) why so many therapeutic processes end abortively when transference rage and disillusionment emerge and psychotic anxieties are mobilized, and (3) how therapists can so easily become targets for transferentially based accusations of neglect and abuse. If personal responsibility for ongoing internal processes cannot be assumed by the client and worked through, then the blame becomes externalized onto figures of the past or onto the therapist of the present. Continuing externalization of responsibility for feeling victimized and/or not adequately cared for is the hallmark of therapeutic failure.

I conclude with some remarks based upon my study of therapists who have mistakenly stepped over a boundary. I show how personally and professionally vulnerable therapists become when they attempt to empathize with early or primitive traumatic experiences. I specify how it is that a parent, a teacher, a priest, a scout leader, or a therapist, when correctly and empathically in tune with a person's primitive anxieties, can so easily and unwittingly momentarily lose his or her boundaries and create a violation when none was intended.

We are far more vulnerable to our own psychotic anxieties than we may wish to think. When we choose to open our lives to people in deep emotional distress, we willingly make ourselves the transference target of organizing level or psychotic anxieties. We are then in a position to be falsely accused of abuse we never committed. Further, the empathy we extend necessarily opens up our own delusional vulnerability. When we empathically connect to trauma arising from the deepest levels of the human psyche, our own most primitive selves become activated without our immediate awareness and against our best intentions and interests. What kinds of safeguards can we institute to protect ourselves from these kinds of vulnerabilities?

In the course of therapeutically remembering and working through deep abuse, the helping partner, in an effort to reach out and offer some helping connection, becomes empathically ensnared in a strong and powerful web of interpersonal and familial insanity that extends backward in time through generations of neglect and abuse.

It is my hope that readers with many different interests will find the issues and concerns I am raising in this book interesting and useful. But my book is finally addressed to the extreme danger faced by, and the ultimate personal vulnerability of, the helping professional, especially the psychotherapist.

PART I

TAKING RECOVERED MEMORIES SERIOUSLY

1

Varieties of Remembering and Forgetting

THE EMERGING SCANDAL AROUND RECOVERED MEMORIES

Psychotherapy as we know it today began when Sigmund Freud first had occasion to doubt the veracity of certain molest memories recovered through hypnosis and free association. He was thus forced to reconsider his hypothesis that psychological disturbance was inevitably and directly related to traumatic seduction experiences that were repressed in childhood. Freud's abandonment of the seduction hypothesis has been widely misunderstood to mean either that he denied childhood seductions had actually occurred or that recovered memories are not to be believed. Neither is true. Hedda Bolgar, a psychoanalyst and native of early twentieth-century Vienna, has assured us that there was at least as much incest in Vienna at that time as there is in any American city today (personal communication), and that Freud was no fool—he certainly knew about it. Rather, Freud's critical discovery that has fueled psychoanalysis and psychotherapy up to the present is that, *from a treatment standpoint*, understanding the nature of internalized personal experience and its effects on a person's present life takes precedence over understanding the details of actual past experiences as remembered or related.

A century later, grassroots therapists and the public-at-large are encountering the same set of issues. How are we to consider recovered memories of past lives, birth trauma, multiple selves, dissociated experiences, childhood violence and seduction, satanic ritual abuse, and abductions by aliens? A whole population has watched *Sybil* and witnessed impressive pictures of otherwise respectable and ordinary citizens recounting various atrocities that they have been victim of. Our cinema takes us aboard alien spacecraft where we see aliens at work; we know they are watching us. Our courts are filled with suits against an array of alleged perpetrators of shocking and violent crimes. Our media is filled with moving reports of victims whose emotionally laden claims can hardly be denied. But our collective credulity is being taxed and we now hear of a large-scale backlash movement decrying the injustices being brought about by accusers with a "false-memory syndrome." We read of therapists being sued for hypnotically leading their clients into false beliefs and accusations that have resulted in considerable damage to family relations. Newspapers and magazines now carry stories about "recovered memories"—of vengeful accusations and hateful counteraccusations. In short, we have a scandal of major proportions whose stakes are high and whose social outcome is unclear.

Fascinating as the current state of affairs is, I must defer these broader issues for study by sociologists, cultural anthropologists, and legal scholars. But as a psychoanalyst I can offer some thoughts about issues that have evolved over the course of a century to help analysts think through the complex issues involved in (1) considering the general nature of memory, (2) screen and telescoped memories, (3) the search for narrative truth, (4) the varieties of remembering and "forgetting," (5) recovered memories as relationship dependent, (6) the freezing of environmental failure, (7) the devious and delayed effects of "cumulative strain trauma," and (8) some ways in which therapists may misunderstand memories and collude with psychic resistance.

Chapter 3 considers four developmentally determined forms of memory as they present themselves in the four broadly defined varieties of personality organization, and then moves to the central puzzle of recovered memories. Chapter 4 considers the issue of "to believe or not to believe," the problem of recovery through being believed, the alarming liability of the treating therapist, the earliest forms of transference and resistance memories, the clinical fears of emptiness, breakdown, and death, and the nature of delayed "cumulative trauma."

My formulations regarding recovered memories pose challenges to (1) oversimplified views taken by the recovery movement, (2) the limited scope of the false-memory syndrome approach, (3) the misinformed layman's "video camera theory of memory," (4) the widespread belief in a nonsensical view of repression, (5) the ethics involved in "validating" experience and "supporting" redresses, (6) therapists' collusion with resistance to transference analysis through encouraging memory recovery, and (7) therapists doing recovered memory work with the specter of psychotic acting out and malpractice suits looming down the road.

CONSIDERING THE NATURE OF MEMORY

Popular imagination holds a video camera theory of memory. We tend to be committed to the belief that our memories impartially and accurately store pictures of daily events as though we were walking camcorders. But it takes no more than simple reflection on our everyday domestic disagreements to conclude quickly that even if our memories do function more or less like sophisticated video cameras, there are widespread discrepancies between stories and pictures recorded by cohabiting cameras! That most homicides involve immediate family members points to the passion with which we hold our own view of things to be correct. Further, we have recently witnessed some dramatic and devastating civil violence in this country. The cause? Simply how different people "saw" what happened on a piece of videotape that was less than one minute long. It appears that how one sees the magnetically recorded memory varies radically depending on such variables as color of skin, socioeconomic and employment status, political and religious affiliations, and so forth. So our video camera theory of memory miserably fails us—because not only do we not see or remember facts as well as we think we do, but even when recorded facts are plainly before us, our subjective biases determine our interpretation of them. In short, we see what we want to see and we remember things the way we intend to remember them.

Scientific evidence regarding observer agreement in psychological, sociological, and legal studies is remarkably consistent with these anecdotal observations in demonstrating that we see and remember things quite unreliably (Loftus 1993). Considering the overwhelming lack of anecdotal and scientific evidence to support the video camera theory of human memory, whence comes the passionate plea that our perceptions and memories record unbiased truth? We do, of course, subjectively maintain a certain sense of continuity in our lives. And, regardless of how aware we are of gaps in the human ability to perceive and remember accurately, we often do have the sense that if we just dwell on some past event for a few moments we can likely conjure up a reasonably accurate recollection. And for most practical, everyday purposes our powers of memory do get us by.

But recalling early childhood memories poses a different set of issues. Diverse and wide-ranging studies confirm that childhood amnesia for most events before the age of 4 or 5 is universal, although the exact nature and causes of childhood amnesia are little understood by most people. True, most of us possess a set of internal pictures of those early times. But these pictures seem to fall into several classes: (1) memories stimulated or created by photos or family lore, which may or may not be our memories; (2) frightening or otherwise intense or traumatic experiences that seem to be recallable due to the sheer impact certain events had on our lives; and (3) so-called screen and telescoped memories. It seems that these latter kinds of early childhood memories are the most common. Screen memories warrant our focused attention because they are memories subjectively attributable to childhood experiences, which we know do not function like camcorders but rather as complex mental abstractions.

SCREEN AND TELESCOPED MEMORIES

Freud formulated that screen memories from early childhood function to gather many emotional details into a single picture or narration. Many emotional events or a whole emotional atmosphere becomes projected onto a screen, as it were, so that a certain picture or story remains as an emotionally compelling "memory." The picture an individual recalls may be vivid and perhaps be clung to tenaciously as absolute truth, even in the face of reliable contradictory evidence. A screen memory may also be a reasonably accurate rendition of what actually happened. But it is recalled, says Freud, because of its power to condense a whole emotional complex. *Freud believed that what is essential to remember from early childhood has been retained in screen memories and that the analyst's task is one of knowing how to extract it.* But regardless of whatever objective accuracy a given screen memory may or may not possess, its true value, like that of dreams is primarily subjective and its images are subject to the primary processes of condensation, displacement, symbolization, and the requirements of visual representability so that the memory can never be understood concretely or literally.

At one point Freud felt that screen memories represent the forgotten years of childhood "as adequately as the manifest content of a dream represents the dream-thoughts" (1914, p. 148). But Freud came to designate first transference, and subsequently resistance to the transference, as the most fundamental repositories of critical relatedness memories from childhood, which are even more important than screen memories. Screen memories freeze in dream time images of the lived past, while the critical memories that live on in our daily lives are manifest in transference and resistance. Transference and resistance as the most critical forms of early childhood memory are understood by psychoanalysts to be unconscious and also considered governed by the same kind of primary process thought seen in dreams.

Heinz Kohut (1971, 1977) notes a special type of screen memory, the telescoped memory, which serves to collapse over various time periods of one's life a certain category or class of emotional events into a single vivid and compelling picture or narrative. For example, one recalls a convincing memory of a certain event in a relationship that can clearly be placed in one's adolescence. But that picture may serve to summarize, collapse, and represent the subjective truth of a series of emotionally similar experiences, dating perhaps from earliest infancy.

Freud notes that the emotional themes of the analysis that lead to an understanding of transference and resistance are regularly foreshadowed in dreams, slips of the tongue, sexual fantasies, and childhood memories. Freud observes that phantasmagoric pictures and stories presented to the analyst as early childhood memories contain embedded in them crucial thematic elements required for an analysis of the developing transferential relationship with the analyst. Recovered memories and dreams spontaneously emerge as analyst and analysand struggle to define hidden aspects of the here-and-now analytic relationship—both real and transferential. The importance of this type of childhood memory lies in the way lifelong emotional themes are condensed and displaced in much the same way as primary process material in dreams. Memories thus recovered are most profoundly appreciated if they can be considered less as representations of actual events and more as creative dreamwork that represents the transference and resistance themes as they emerge in the analytic relationship.

Psychoanalytic case studies are filled with examples of such screen memories. Analysts for years have been engaged in studying how the person in analysis tends to reexperience (i.e., to remember by repeating) his or her emotional past in the context of current relationships, especially the one with the analyst. Perhaps the most interesting and widely reported aspect of memories recovered during psychoanalysis occurs when some heretofore unnoticed aspect of the emotional past can be interpretively pointed to as operating in the here-and-now present of the analytic relationship. Suddenly, long forgotten memories flood into consciousness and are reported to the analyst. It has not been uncommon for analysts to judge the degree of correctness of the transference interpretation according to the kinds and qualities of early memories that spontaneously erupt into consciousness to "confirm" the interpretation. To what extent such memories are actual memories, screen memories, or complex psychological constructions that serve to represent current relational realities remains a topic for discussion. But no seasoned psychoanalyst ever assumes any memory, no matter how vivid or seemingly true it must be, is an indisputable historical fact. Memories are understood as mental functions that serve present purposes—in analysis, the purpose of reviewing and restructuring our identities and the way we live our lives.

Following Freud's abandonment of the seduction hypothesis, and the considerations set forth above regarding the special nature of screen as well as transference and resistance memories, psychoanalysts have tended not to take childhood memories recovered in analysis at face value. It is widely recognized that the moment a person addresses an analyst, powerful unconscious transference and resistance (memories) come immediately into play—although it may be some time before the nature of those memories can be understood. Historically, many psychoanalysts became interested in reconstructing the emotional influences of early childhood based not on a literal understanding of the memories but on detailed studies of memories projected onto the analyst and into the analysis in the form of current and active manifestations of transference and resistance.

THE SEARCH FOR NARRATIVE TRUTH

Psychoanalysis erroneously gained a reputation for being interested in the distant childhood past. But in fact, no form of psychotherapy has been more vehemently focused on the here-and-now transference situation than psychoanalysis. Even the psychoanalytic enthusiasm for reconstructing childhood emotional life based upon current experience in the analytic relationship had dwindled considerably by the late 1970s. Roy Schafer (1976), Donald Spence (1982), and a host of others definitively shifted psychoanalytic concerns away from the search for "historical truth" in favor of establishing "narrative truth." A century of psychoanalytic practice had succeeded in demonstrating how unreliable and pale in importance are recovered memories of historical fact in comparison to the vivid and compelling forms of memory that are alive, active, and manifest in narratives, narrational pictures, and narrational interactions of current relationships, especially the analytic relationship.

Since the beginning of time, human truth has been recorded in myth, image, story, and archetype as Freud, Jung, and others have pointed out. Individual records of experience may similarly emerge in an analytic dialogue in which two create pictures and narrations that capture, at least for the moment, the essence of some feature of their shared emotional life. Dreams, childhood memories, and sexual fantasies contribute in a major way to the joint construction of narratives that have an "emotional fit" to the here-and-now relationship.

The psychoanalytic enterprise may be studied scientifically like any other human activity. But the psychoanalytic process itself forever remains an encounter between two subjective worlds that lends itself to the same kinds of systematic study as other interpretive disciplines. That is, a sharp distinction is to be made between the objectivity involved in studying psychoanalytic work *across* cases, and the dual subjectivity that necessarily governs the process of any single analysis and the stories and images that emerge to characterize it. Joseph Natterson (1991) clarifies what has been known for some time—that narrative statements emerging from any psychoanalytic dialogue are subject to a host of creative distorting influences and power manipulations operating in the transference/countertransference and resistance/counterresistance dimensions. In short, it is sheer folly to attribute the status of historical or legal fact to any conclusion arising from a psychoanalytic or psychotherapeutic process. Participation in a psychotherapeutic process has a validity of an entirely different order.

FOUR KINDS OF REMEMBERING AND "FORGETTING"

Psychoanalysts and psychologists have no viable theory of forgetting, only a set of theories about how different classes of emotional events are remembered or barred from active memory. "Forgetting impressions, scenes, or experiences nearly always reduces itself to shutting them off. When the patient talks about these 'forgotten' things he seldom fails to add: 'As a matter of fact I've always known it; only I've never thought of it.'" (Freud 1914, p. 148). (The only exception Freud makes is the way links from feelings to memories are dissolved in obsessive-compulsive neurosis.) There are many things around us that we do not notice and therefore do not recall. Further, much of our life's experience is known but has never been thought about. Much of this "unthought known" (Bollas 1987) can be represented in the analytic dialogue and understood by two. Even if sometimes "a cigar is just a cigar," psychoanalytic study has never portrayed human psyche as anything so passive as to be subject to simple forgetting. How then do analysts account for what appears to be forgotten experience? We have four viable ways to consider different classes of memories recovered in analysis and the ways in which remembering some things necessarily bars other things from recall.

At the lower end of the developmental spectrum of memory, which begins in infancy, forgetting is accounted for by Freud's doctrine of *primary repression*, which first appears in notes he wrote on the train returning from Berlin to Vienna (1895a) after visiting his close friend and colleague Wilhelm Fliess. In this quasi-neurological model of the mind, Freud speaks of a neuronal extension meeting with pain and, as a result, erecting a counter-cathexis so as to avoid future encounters with the same pain. *The memory of the encounter with the painful stimulus exists in the form of a barrier to ever extending or experiencing in that way again.* No memory of the experience per se is involved; the memory exists in the automatic avoidance of broad classes of stimulus cues. An anecdotal example might be a curious infant putting her finger in kitty's mouth. While her capacity for ordinary cause–effect thinking may be limited, we do note that she tends not to risk her finger there again! Freud's theory of primary repression is essentially a conditioning theory based upon experiences of pleasurable and painful reinforcement at the neurological level. What is stored as memory is an aversion – as if a sign had been posted in the neuronal system saying "never reach there again."

At the advanced end of the developmental spectrum of remembering and forgetting is Freud's doctrine of *secondary repression* or repression proper, as a psychological defense against internal somatic or instinctual stimulation. Freud's notion of repression does not apply to externally generated impingements, but repression is seen as the only way the psyche has to place limits on overstimulation arising from *within* the body. By the age of 5 a child is actively representing his or her bodily experiences in verbal-symbolic logic and controlling physical and social behavior by auto instruction. As the social undesirability of somatic experiences such as rubbing up against Mother's breast, playing with one's genitals, biting or hitting people, or jumping up and down on Daddy's lap becomes clear, the child adopts a policy decision against engaging further in such activities and thoughts.

Fingarette (1969) makes clear that the psychoanalytic doctrine of repression never includes the notion that undesirable activities or thoughts are simply forgotten, or that they somehow disappear or vanish into a black hole. Repression entails a volitional activity of adopting a personal policy never to spell out in consciousness again the exciting but taboo thought or activity. That we may claim not to remember ever consciously adopting such policies can be put in the same category as not remembering all of the trials and errors of learning any other complex and coordinated activity such as reading, riding a bicycle, playing tennis, or typing. After somewhat protracted and painful practice we simply know the right way to behave and what pitfalls to avoid. We may speak of the painful memories as though they were forgotten, but the flawless retention of complex and coordinated activities attests to the living presence of painful memories in our lives. Freud's theory of neurotic symptom formation assumes that repression resulting from conscious policy decisions against powerful biological forces remains perennially precarious and only partially effective so that the forbidden life forces continue to manifest as mysterious "symptoms."

Midway on the developmental spectrum of remembering and forgetting, between the early primary (neurologically conditioned) repression of physically painful experience and the much later secondary (policy decision) repression of socially undesirable, instinctually driven thoughts and behavior, psychoanalysts speak of splitting and dissociation. In *The Three Faces of Eve* (Thigpen and Cleckley 1957) Eve White sits prim and proper in her reputable secretarial position all week. But on Saturday night Eve Black puts on her red dress and dancing shoes to go out on the town. During the week Eve White might well notice any of a number of pieces of evidence around her apartment that would confirm the existence of her split-off or dissociated self, but she does not. Eve Black thinks what an uptight prude Eve White is as her lusty self-assertiveness comes to life. In relation to her psychotherapist a third self, Jane, slowly emerges who is able to tolerate, appreciate, and integrate both her need for adult responsibility and her love of adolescent play.

Clinicians and theoreticians employ the terms *splitting* and *dissociation* in a variety of different contexts and often employ the terms interchangeably. For present purposes it is useful to distinguish between two quite different psychoanalytic concepts of remembering and forgetting. "Splitting" is used here to designate the developmentally earlier form, which more closely resembles primary repression. "Dissociation" designates a developmentally later form, which more closely resembles the ego defense of secondary repression. There is a great deal of confusion and misinformation in the field of psychotherapy about all of these remembering and forgetting processes so that even these terms often become confused by being reversed. A discussion of each follows.

Kernberg (1976) is perhaps the clearest and most persuasive writer on the subject of affect and ego splitting. His formulations, which involve the splitting (or keeping separate) of "good" and "bad" affects or ego states, echo the experiences of pleasure and pain from Freud's doctrine of primary repression. But Kernberg's terms designate subjective psychological experiences that are a step removed from neurological processes. In studying the positive and negative affective building blocks of early personality development, Kernberg observes that people may exhibit specific areas of "impulse disturbance." According to Kernberg, variations in impulsiveness represent

> an alternating expression of complementary sides of a conflict, such as acting out of the impulse at some times and specific defensive character formation or counterphobic reactions against that impulse at other times. The patients were conscious of the severe contradiction in their behavior; yet they would alternate between opposite strivings with a bland denial of the implications of this contradiction and showed what appeared to be a striking lack of concern over this "compartmentalizing" of their mind. [1976, p. 2]

Kernberg thus postulates an active force of *mutual denial* of independent contradictory sectors of psychic life. These sectors or independent ego states are repetitive, temporarily ego syntonic, and compartmentalized affectively colored psychic manifestations. But more importantly Kernberg notes, "each of these mutually unacceptable 'split' ego states represented a specific transference paradigm, a highly developed regressive transference reaction in which a specific internalized object relationship was activated in the transference" (p. 20). Kernberg thus understands "contradictory and chaotic transference manifestations"

as oscillatory activation of mutually unacceptable ego states—
representations of "nonmetabolized internalized object relations" (p. 20).

The implication of Kernberg's thinking is that in early
childhood development the personality has failed to develop in
certain delineated areas a high-enough level of psychic integration in which ambivalence toward significant others in the
child's environment can be tolerated. Rather, certain ego-affect
states prevail during different preselected interpersonal conditions, and contradictory ego-affect states become activated
when the interpersonal situation shifts. His explanation is that
certain aspects of early internalized affective relationships with
significant others were not fully integrated ("metabolized") into a
smoothly flowing fabric of personality, and that they show up
later as emotional contradictions that appear in analysis as
"split" positive and negative transference and resistance memories. A whole continuum of affect states (moods) can be seen in
this way to form an array of (multiple) ego-affect or self states.
The presence of each in consciousness is dependent upon the
experience of the interpersonal situation prevailing at the moment.

In Kernberg's formulations there is no mention of forgetting. Rather, various ego-affect possibilities are present or absent
depending upon how the person perceives or experiences the
current relationship situation. Kernberg's accent is on the early
development of positive and negative affect states and how these
mutually exclusive or "split" affect or ego states determine the
specific kinds of transference and resistance (memories) likely to
become activated in the analytic relationship at a given moment
in time. Various affectively colored memories will be present in
or absent from consciousness depending on how one is experiencing the current emotional relationship. Contradictory parts
of the self are split off and not permitted direct access to
consciousness in the moment. They are not repressed. Nor have
they vanished, been forgotten, or gotten lost in some sort of

black hole. In fact, they may reappear at any moment depending on how the interpersonal emotional interaction goes. In Kernberg's formulations of affect and ego splitting, contradictory experiences of self and other are or are not activated depending on how the person experiences the current relational context. Such a theory has major implications for what is and is not to be remembered when one is experiencing split-off states. When one's black (evil) motives are in play, black and evil narrations of the past will be activated. When one's good, angelic self is operating, the sun is shining on good and idealized loved ones and the current relationship with the therapist is idealized. The precariousness of these kinds of splitting experiences is that what state of mind and affect memory one lives in is dependent upon which direction the wind is blowing in transference relationships. Good people suddenly turn evil when one's mood changes; revenge is sought toward the one once idealized for the humiliation one felt at being the one who envied or adored.

The developmentally more advanced form of personality splitting that, for purposes of discussion, I am calling *dissociation*, bears a close resemblance to Freud's doctrine of secondary repression in that it has more of a defensive quality in contrast to the earlier splitting process, which has more of an unintegrated (pleasure versus pain) quality. In describing the operation of dissociation, Cameron (1963) contrasts the so-called horizontal split between conscious and unconscious processes with what has been called a vertical split in personality, which functions to separate or wall off whole (conscious and unconscious) sectors of personality. Cameron speaks of the "span" of the overall ego and what kinds of experiences it is prepared to encompass within that span. When psychic stimulation occurs that cannot be smoothly integrated into the operative span of the existing ego, the experience is set aside in a dissociated ego state rather than integrated within the overall personality. Sleepwalking, sleeptalking, amnesias, fugues, and limited splits in the personality are examples of dissociation. The fictional Dr. Jekyll and Mr.

Hyde and the earliest simplified report on Eve in *The Three Faces of Eve* (Thigpen and Cleckley 1957) provide examples of dissociated sectors of the personality that at times may assert their claims over the main personality. It is important to note that Kohut (1971) invokes the notion of the vertical split similarly when he speaks of the narcissistic sector of the personality as dissociated from the main (more object related) personality.

Summarizing, four distinctly different processes have been postulated in the history of psychoanalysis to account for the various conditions of memory. In developmental order they are:

1. primary (neurologically conditioned) repression, which acts to foreclose the possibility of reengaging in activities formerly experienced as physically painful;

2. ego-affect splitting, in which mutually contradictory affect states give rise to contrasting and contradictory self and other transference and resistance memories;

3. dissociation, in which certain whole sectors of internal psychic experience are (defensively) walled off from the main personality because they cannot be integrated into the overall span of the main personality; and

4. Secondary (policy decision) repression brought about by self-instruction against socially undesirable, internal, instinctually driven thought and activity.

The layman's notion (which judges, jurors, and survivors' groups are most likely to hold) that presupposes *massive forgetting of an intense social impingement and the later possibility of perfect video camera recall*, is not a part of any existing psychoanalytic theory of memory. A century of psychoanalytic observation has shown that the commonsense notion of forgetting, derived as it is from the everyday experience of lapses in memory with sudden flashes of recall, simply does not hold up when emotionally charged interpersonal experiences from early childhood are involved. What appears to the layman as forgetting is considered by psychoanalytic theory to be the result of the operation of selective forms of recall that are dependent upon the nature of the relationship context in which the memories are being recalled. Nor do psychoanalytic theories regarding how emotionally charged memories operate support the common prejudice that human beings are accurate recorders of the historical facts out of which their personal psychic existences are forged! Human memory is simply not an objective camcorder affair, but rather a calling forth or creation of subjective narrational representations within a specified and highly influential relational context.

RECOVERED MEMORIES AS
RELATIONSHIP DEPENDENT

Transformation of personal experience through making sense of recovered memories has always been at the heart of psychoanalytic theory and practice. The psychoanalytic concepts of primary repression, splitting, dissociation, and secondary or defensive repression have evolved within the context of accruing knowledge about the relational conditions required for the emergence of limiting forms of early childhood emotional memory. The psychoanalytic situation, characterized as it is by nonjudgmental empathic concern for all aspects of a person's psyche, was created by Freud to replicate the safe holding environment of the early mother–child transformational situation (Bollas 1987). As such, psychoanalytic theories of memory must be understood as inextricably tied to the relationship setup of the psychoanalytic situation.

The error of isolating concepts evolved in one field of study and uncritically generalizing them to other fields has been repeatedly and regrettably demonstrated in all sciences. It is clearly an error to generalize to other settings (e.g., family confrontations, social settings, and courtrooms) psychoanalytic notions of recall, developed as they have been within the circumscribed context of the analytic relationship for purposes of personal transformation within a safe, well-defined, confidential, and limited interpersonal environment. The most devious kind of dual relationship that a therapist can engage in is authorizing the acting out in the client's real life of impulses and motivations condensed and displaced in the form of dreams and recovered memories produced in the context of the therapeutic relationship for analysis as transference and resistance. This unethical procedure is apparently running rampant at present. I will shortly give an explication of the four kinds of interpersonal listening situations in which each of these theories of remembering is best suited along with the transference, resistance, and countertransference dimensions. But first a few words regarding how psychoanalysts have considered the problem of "massive forgetting" and sudden "total recall" as it is reported by many individuals.

Conceptually, the two upper developmental level forms of remembering, secondary repression and defensive dissociation, are the result of the person attempting to solve *internal* problems. In the case of repression it is the sense of driveness of the somatic instincts themselves that have become a problem to the 5- to 7-year-old child, so that he or she must develop policies not to spell the impulses out in consciousness in order to live harmoniously in a world that does not care to have sexuality and aggression freely expressed. In the case of dissociation, whole (conscious and unconscious) sectors of the (3- to 4-year-old) personality, such as narcissism, are set aside, because they cannot be encompassed within the overall span of the existing personality structure. The psychic problem involved in these two forms of memory is one of *internal economics* of what parts of the self can and cannot be smoothly integrated. The world may have a negative view of unbridled narcissism, lust, or aggression; but the move to isolate or not to think about parts of the self is an internal move, motivated by solving internally generated problems. Because these psychoanalytic doctrines were devised to describe how the personality may attempt to solve internal dilemmas, it is totally inappropriate to use these notions to account for massive forgetting due to externally generated trauma.

However, in the developmentally earlier forms of memory, primary repression, and ego-affect splitting, the occasion for remembering appears to be more external in nature. Primary repression has already been discussed as a somatic experience based on pleasurable and painful experiences. McDougall (1989) points out, "Since babies cannot use words with which to think, they respond to emotional pain only psychosomatically. . . . The infant's earliest psychic structures are built around non-verbal 'signifiers' in the body's functions and the erogenous zones play a predominant role" (pp. 9–10). Her extensive psychoanalytic work with psychosomatic conditions shows how through careful analysis of manifestations in transference and resistance the early learned somatic signifiers can be brought from soma and represented in psyche through words, pictures, and stories. McDougall illustrates how body memories can be expressed in the interpersonal language of transference and resistance. Bioenergetic analysis (Lowen 1971, 1975, 1988) repeatedly demonstrates the process of bringing somatically stored memories into the here and now of transference and resistance in the therapeutic relationship. In bringing somatically stored memories out of the body and into psychic expression and/or representation, whether through psychoanalytic or bioenergetic technique, considerable physical pain is necessarily experienced. The intense physical pain encountered is usually thought of as resulting from therapeutically "forcing through" or "breaking through" long established aversive barriers to various kinds of physical experiencing that have been previously forsaken. That is, the threshold to more flexible somatic experience is guarded by painful sensations (parallel with Freud's [1926] theory of "signal anxiety") erected to prevent future venturing into places once experienced as painful by the infant or developing toddler. Similarly, the split-affect model of early memory postulates the presence in personality of mutually denied contradictory ego states that represent specific transference paradigms based on internalized object relations. Whether a split ego state is or is not present in consciousness is dependent upon the way the person experiences the current interpersonal relationship situation. This means that what is remembered and the way it is recalled is highly dependent upon specific facilitating aspects of the relationship in which the memory is being expressed or represented. Neither of these developmentally lower forms of memory can, therefore, be seen as supporting the layman's notion of massive amnesia for trauma with the possibility of a later lifting of the repressive veil to permit perfect recall. The concept of primary repression fails in this regard because it does not record any memory per se, but rather builds a barrier to certain broad classes of somatic experience that are very painful to approach. And splitting as a concept fails because nothing is forgotten or made unconscious, but rather recall is seen as dependent upon the current relationship context. Thus it can be seen that no existing theory of memory derived from a century of intense psychoanalytic observation supports the layman's naive view of massive repression followed by full and reliable recall.

THE FREEZING OF ENVIRONMENTAL FAILURE

Winnicott, a British pediatrician trained as a psychoanalyst, is renowned for his understanding of early psychic development. It is his view that there is a possible maturational or unfolding process for each child in which environmental provision is a necessary facilitator. An environment with limited provision or unempathic intrusiveness may leave the child with a painful sense of personal failure.

> One has to include in one's theory of the development of a human being the idea that it is normal and healthy for the individual to be able to defend the self against specific environmental failure by a *freezing of the failure situation*. Along with this goes an unconscious assumption (which can become a conscious hope) that opportunity will occur at a later date for a renewed experience in which the failure situation will be able to be unfrozen and re-experienced with the individual in a regressed state, in an environment which is making adequate adaptation. [1954, p. 281]

Winnicott's use of the metaphor "unfreezing of the failure situation" makes clear that he has a specific psychoanalytic situation in mind that fosters emotional regression to the dependent infantile state in an environment in which, it is hoped, more understanding and empathic adaptation to the infantile need can be made the second time around. Note that what he speaks of as frozen until it can later be reprocessed in some relationship is a *specific environmental failure*. There is no mention of forgetting and recall but rather that a failed situation is set aside (frozen) until a relationship comes along that permits a reliving of infantile dependency in which there is believed to be the possibility that the failure can be made good. The purpose of Winnicott's formulation is to define a kind of memory that the psychoanalytic relationship calls forth so that an earlier failure of the environment can be worked on in the current relationship.

Winnicott's formulation does point to how traumatically experienced environmental failures may be set aside until an analyst or therapist comes along with whom the person can relive the failure. The popular notion of recovery being the recall of early memories, having them validated by others, and then confronting those responsible for the long ago failure misunderstands the psychotherapeutic process of reviving in the present the environmental failure situation so that it can be worked through in transference and resistance with the person of the analyst as therapist, not acted out in the person's contemporary world. It would seem that many therapists today collude with the acting-out process so as to avoid the difficult and sometimes dangerous transference working-through process.

Winnicott's formulation clearly points to a treatment situation in which the split-off internalized object relation has an opportunity to become manifest in the analytic relationship as transference and resistance to transference. Psychoanalytic technique as practiced by analysts and psychoanalytically informed therapists is designed to bring early childhood experience into the here-and-now relationship so that transference and resistance memories have an opportunity to emerge. Such recovered memories, like screen memories, are never to be taken at face value because the very way in which they are secured for analytic study necessarily imbues them with extensive primary process thinking (condensation, displacement, symbolization, and visual representability).

Thus, even the psychoanalytic concept that held out the most hope for accounting for massive forgetting, which is later subject to accurate recall, fails completely, for three reasons. First, it is a theory about how certain conditions provided by the psychoanalytic situation foster emotional recall, not how a traumatic event is forgotten. Second, the nature of the recall is dreamlike in its basic nature and only emerges in the form of privately experienced versions of the here-and-now relating of the analytic session. Third, the formulation highlights how that damage can be internally repaired, not how memory works. Even the memories that often follow transference interpretation are not assumed to be veridical by psychoanalysts, but rather psychological constructions validating transference and resistance themes.

In short, there are no psychoanalytic theories that support

the widespread claims of massive forgetting of traumatic child-hood experiences, which are then subject to accurate video camera recall. If such experience exists, a century of worldwide psychoanalytic observation—through two World Wars, the Holocaust, Korea, and Vietnam—has certainly failed to discover it. To the contrary, psychoanalytic research supports an understanding of various types of memory that are characteristic of different levels of human psychic development, the emergence of which is situation dependent, and the nature of which is subjectively determined narrational truth. All memories recovered in the course of the psychoanalytic encounter are to be taken seriously as representations of relatedness experience emerging in the here-and-now analytic relationship. For an analyst to consider memories recovered under these conditions as literally and objectively true colludes with the resistance to transference analysis and runs the risk of (unethically) encouraging an acting out of material that is emerging in response to the analytic relationship. The proper target of the abusive transference is the analyst and how he or she relates or fails to relate to the needs of the client. If the therapist deflects the rage, helplessness, impotence, or revenge from its proper transferential locus in the here-and-now therapeutic relationship toward figures or events from the past or toward the outside present, the possibility of psychotherapeutic transformation is completely foreclosed in favor of family confrontations, lawsuits, and the continued operation of the internalized environmental failure in the person's psychic life. In short, any simplified version of the recovery approach is anti-psychotherapeutic. Practicing a simplified recovery approach under the name of psychotherapy clearly creates a serious liability for the therapist. The next chapter takes up these issues from several other vantage points.

2

Transference and Resistance Memories

FOUR DEVELOPMENTALLY DETERMINED FORMS OF MEMORY

Childhood memories recovered in the psychoanalytic situation fall into four general classes: (1) *recollections* of wishes and fears of oedipal triangular (4- to 7-year-olds) relating; (2) *realizations* of self-to-selfother (3-year-olds) resonances; (3) *representations* of self and other (4- to 24-month-olds) scenarios—in both passive and active interpersonal replications; and (4) *expressions* of the search for and the rupture of potential channels or links to others (four months before and after birth).

These four types of transference each have their own particular forms of resistance memory and are directly related to the four theories of memory that have evolved in psychoanalysis—(1) primary repression, (2) affect splitting, (3) ego dissociation, and (4) secondary repression—only I have reversed their order for the discussion that follows because our understanding of the nature of early childhood memories has historically evolved developmentally downward.

Triangular (Oedipal) Recollections and Secondary Repression

Freud points out the way humans feel seen, reflected, and inhibited by observing third parties. The loves and hatreds of our 5-year-old selves toward significant others in our childhood environments are depicted in the cultural myth of Oedipus and powerfully echoed in the character of Hamlet. The tragedy of human life, Freud holds, is that the intense lustful and aggressive strivings of early childhood too often cannot be adequately contained or encompassed within family relationships. The result is that the child feels forced to blind him or herself (as did Oedipus) or to kill off the self (as did Hamlet) to experiences of lustful passion and aggressive self-assertiveness rather than to risk (castrating) punishment for experiencing the intense and natural longings that are forbidden by the incestual and parricidal taboos implicit in the family structure.

Psychoanalysts have been fond of reviewing our cultural lore and fairy tales for the endless ways in which the hero or heroine is rendered personally impotent by a wicked parental imago. The witches in "Hansel and Gretel," "Snow White," and "The Little Mermaid," the wicked stepmother in "Cinderella," the caged monster in "Iron Man," the phantom of the opera, and countless other folk images operate as unconscious symbolized recollections of internalized oedipal parents who deprive the tragic child of the fullness of lived instinctual life.

Our impotence in face of many of life's challenging circumstances is by now known to us as neurotic self-inhibition stemming from our failure or refusal to assume a full measure of sexuality, aggression, masculinity, femininity, adulthood, and/ or separateness. By now, the lessons of the Freudians have become an integral part of our culture itself. In a thousand litanies we tell ourselves to grow up, to be independent, not to seek a mother or father to marry, not to be codependent, to stop being a victim, a wimp, or a castrating bitch, and to get out of the Cinderella or Peter Pan role! Lately we have been starting to tell ourselves to "come out of the closet," or at least we have begun wrestling with the problem of what closets we have been hiding in! We have all learned what it means to accept something intellectually. And we know how intellectualizing differs radically from when we let something really hit us in the gut where we live. Our experiences in therapy, our interactions in groups, and indeed even our literature and media—in short, all of contemporary relatedness culture—bears the mark of Freud's insight into how each person's Oedipus complex crops up to sour our loving relationships and to spoil our joy and assertiveness in daily living.

Therapists are well taught how to look for the sexual and aggressive in feelings and attitudes that are transferred to the therapist. They know well how to interpret the barriers of fear and inhibition that comprise the resistance memories to feeling anger and attraction toward the therapist. So no more need be said about how these forms of memory appear in the psychotherapeutic situation or the importance of the therapist's being able to encourage them being brought into light of conscious day.

Narcissistic Realizations and Dissociation

While it has become fashionable to own sexual and aggressive strivings in our relationships, we still tend to squirm when someone mentions our narcissism. Kohut (1971, 1977) has pointed out that hypocrisy in Freud's day centered around

Victorian censorship of sex and aggression. And that hypocrisy today revolves around our reluctance to honor authentic and wholesome self-centeredness, our natural sense of self-love, our narcissism.

Those familiar with Kohut's work know that he specified three types of transference memories derived from the legitimate needs of our 3-year-old selves that he viewed as defensively dissociated from our main personalities: the need to be affirmed as a grandiose self through mirroring, the need to be confirmed as a worthy person through twinning, and the need to feel inspired by others whom we can idealize. The others we turn to for self-affirmation, confirmation, and inspiration we know (intellectually) to be separate from ourselves. But in these regards they are used more as parts of ourselves like an arm or a leg—thus Kohut's concept of the *selfother*.[1] Kohut reminds us that we all need selfothers—people who affirm, confirm, and inspire us from birth to death. But at age 3 the developmental focus is on establishing for the first time a true sense of self that is independent in certain definite ways of how mother needs us to be.

Kohut's clinical theory postulates that many of the ways we continue as adults to seek affirmation, confirmation, and inspiration in our everyday relationships are retained, defensively dissociated memories of the ways we first sought selfother resonance from our parents and other family members as toddlers. That is, the self we daily realize in relationships frequently uses archaic means in an attempt to gain mature goals. Kohut demonstrates how the reflecting effect of the psychoanalytic encounter can be used to bring these archaic memories—dissociated modes of realizing the self through self-to-selfother resonance—under scrutiny.

The chief resistance to realizing the dissociated archaic

---

1. Kohut's term is *selfobject*—as in a love object who is experienced as an extension of the self.

memories in the analytic relationship takes the form of shame that we so want to be the center of the world, that we so want everything to go exactly our way. But once the resistance to the *realization* in the analytic transference relationship of the archaic grandiose, narcissistic self is analyzed, once empathy with the legitimate needs of the self can be restored, Kohut demonstrates how we can achieve more vibrant and fulfilling self-realization.

So the second general class of memories is defensively disavowed or dissociated in early childhood and recoverable as transference and resistance in psychoanalysis or psychotherapy. These memories relate to the natural strivings of a 3-year-old to have his or her self be lustily and aggressively realized in relationship to significant others. The archaic (historically developed) ways of searching for self-affirmation, confirmation, and inspiration are living relatedness memories that appear in selfother or narcissistic transferences. Self state dreams and fragmented hypersexuality and aggressiveness may give the therapist information about the ways in which self realization and confirmation is failing. Shame over desires for narcissistic self-aggrandizement marks the resistance (memory) to allowing one's self the freedom to take center stage and to be properly applauded.

Many therapists have come to understand narcissistic transferences and how resistances to narcissism can be interpretively worked with. However, many other therapists and most workers at the level of institutional or self-help groups become uncomfortable when strong self-realization needs begin to be expressed. Legitimate self-aggrandizement and seeking for self-approval are often met with narrow and naive moralizing attitudes about "learning to get along with others." Or they may be met with a reaction formation that supports the general attitude, "I'm going to take care of myself—fuck everybody else." Either approach, of course, misses completely the possibility of studying selfobject needs as forms of recovered memory. Either approach misses the opportunity to relive the vital transference resistance memories about how one was shamed for legitimate self love.[2]

Split Representations of Replicated Self and Other Scenarios

Transference memories from the 4- to 24-month olds' "symbiotic" era (Mahler 1968) are without words, pictures, and verbalizable feelings because thought and memory during this essentially preverbal period are organized around affective interactions, not words, symbols, or pictures. That is, the salient features of internalized symbiotic memory are the workable patterns of affective relatedness experience that serve *to articulate in actions and emotional interactions* oneself to important others for the purpose of making the world operate in an acceptable or at least tolerable manner. The toddler learns a series of rules about what does and does not work in his or her world of people, under varying sets of circumstances. The toddler actively teaches significant others ways of providing for his or her needs that are more or less satisfying and/or satisfactory. The most important and earliest mapping is of the mother's unconscious emotional life, which governs almost everything that is of critical importance to the child.

When we present our toddler selves to our therapist there are no words or pictures to express what the crucial relatedness memories are. We can only do it to the other, live out or emotionally replicate the split-off affectively laden relatedness scenarios directly with the person of our therapist. Or conversely, we can make ourselves available for interactions to happen to us, for emotional interactions of which we were once the passive victim to be emotionally replicated within the ther-

---

2. I have elaborated Kohut's theory and provided extensive case illustrations of this approach (Hedges 1983b).

apeutic transference relationship. The overlearned idiom of (m)other–child interaction is an emotional, characterological, physically charged, *interactive internalization* that is retained in body and psychic memory, which Bollas (1987) has called *the unthought known*. There are many different scenarios that occur between mother and infant or toddler, each with its own rules and expectable sets of outcomes. And there are other scenarios learned with each significant other in the child's life at that time, including the family pets.

Though scenarios as memories, by virtue of their preverbal, presymbolic internalized interactive nature, cannot be retrieved in picture or word or spoken to the analyst, they can become known through the way various affective interactions are *represented* in the living out of or in the replication of the symbiotic transference and resistance in the analytic relationship.

Recapping, repressed memories from the oedipal level of development are *recallable* through dreams, symbols, jokes, sexual fantasies, slips of the tongue, and triangular transferences and resistances. Dissociated memories from the narcissistic period of relatedness development are *realizable* through the way the archaic dissociated self seeks affirmation, confirmation, and inspiration from the selfother and through the ways self-realization is resisted through shame. But at the symbiotic, character, or "borderline" level of development, the internalized split-off memories of the ways in which self and other interact that are experienced as "all good" or "all bad" take on a "knee jerk" or automatic quality, thereby becoming *represented* in the transference relationship that the analyst is expected to be able to reverberate with. Represented interactions that are experienced as good are actively sought out, developed, and affectively rewarded, while those represented interactions experienced as bad are avoided, shunned, shut off, and/or affectively punished.

When the therapist shows signs of mistaking or missing the implicit relatedness rules, there may be an intense negative reaction of coldness, collapse, or unmitigated rage – according to whatever style or mode of relatedness punishment the person experienced as a toddler for his or her transgressions. When the therapist is performing properly there will be a regalia of positive experience. That is, the passive victim role is turned to active victor. Memories implicit in the person's ego-affective splits of toddlerhood demand certain kinds of relatedness and foreclose other possible modes of relatedness. I have hoped here to make clear that critical splits of memories from the symbiotic period can be effectively *represented* in the affective interactions or character scenarios of the replicated transference, resistance, and countertransference – in both passive and active versions.

Most therapists are familiar with having to assume the role of "all bad" or "all good" parent imago in the borderline or symbiotic transference interaction. Therapists are painfully aware that the power of the split-off (remembered) transference role does not diminish with verbal interpretation, but only gradually subsides through long and laborious relating in which the symbiotic interaction that is represented in the transference/countertransference dimension is gradually and relationally confronted by the therapist so that the need for such rigid roles is slowly relinquished. The resistance is to giving up a way of being in the world that memorializes primordial love for one's (m)other, no matter what the quality of that early interactional attachment may have been. Depression manifest in suicidal ideation and fears for the health and safety of the real mother mark the relinquishment of symbiotic scenarios.

However, few therapists have systematically learned the psychoanalytic skill of "interpreting the countertransference." The idea behind the technique is simple. In the earliest symbiotic relationship with the (m)other, the modes of relating are two-way because the earliest way of knowing the (m)other is through primary identification or imitation, physical mimicry – monkey see, monkey do; I smile at you, you smile at me; I gurgle at you, you gurgle back. That is, the roles of the earliest mother–infant idiom are interchangeable and we internalize both parts of the scenario. As we simply interact with our analyst, the way we put ourselves out and the kinds of responses we anticipate or elicit in return serve to project our infantile position in the symbiotic exchange into the analyst! Since the interaction to be represented (remembered) is preverbal, presymbolic, and affectively interactive, it is only when the analyst begins to verbalize countertransference responsiveness to being held in such a tight emotional spot with such rigid expectations that the split-off infant role (memory) will at last be given verbal and emotional representation. That is, speaking the countertransference, when done carefully and thoughtfully, serves to bring the split-off "unthought known" into the realm of replicated representation in the scenarios that serve as memories of the earliest symbiotic interactions (Hedges 1992).

To review, transference and resistance memories from the oedipal period relate to the driveness of the instinctive life of the 4- to 7-year-old child and to his or her internalized means of inhibiting by psychic repression various aspects of somatic life that are not acceptable within the family structure. Critical relatedness memories from the 3-year-old period relate to the way that disavowed or dissociated aspects of the developing self can be realized in relation to the therapist as selfother. At the 4- to 24-month level relatedness memories are manifest in the knee jerk, character scenarios that are played out in all relationships. The transference and resistance associated with living out these preverbal, presymbolic symbiotic relatedness modes are met with affective countertransference and counterresistance on the part of the analyst who alternately experiences split and projected symbiotic relatedness memories of good and bad, parent and toddler, self and other imagos at an affective, interactive level. Finding ways to refuse the scenarios, using the countertransference as the "royal road" to comprehending the way that the borderline scenarios are represented in the replicated affective exchange, points to ways of relinquishing the tight emotional hold that preverbal, prepictorial relatedness memories (transference) from the symbiotic era have on the person in analysis.

Expressions of the Search for and the Rupture (Primary Repression) of Channels or Links to the Other

The earliest transference and resistance memories that are presented for analysis are those from the "organizing" period of relatedness development (Hedges 1983b, 1994c). *In utero* and in the earliest months of life, the fetus and neonate have the task of organizing channels to the maternal body and mind for nurturance, evacuation, soothing, comfort, and stimulation. Infant research (Tronick and Cohn 1988) suggests that only about thirty percent of the time are the efforts made by an infant and mother successful in establishing that *rhythm of safety* (Tustin 1986) required for two to feel satisfactorily connected. The many ways in which an infant fails in securing the needed contact from its (m)other *become internalized as transference to the failing mother*. Because the biological being of the baby knows (just as every mammal knows) that if it cannot find the maternal body it will die, any serious impingement on the infant's sense of continuity of life, of *going on being* (Winnicott 1965) will be experienced as traumatic. An internalized terror response marks that failed possible channel of connection with a sign that reads, "never reach this way again." Such traumatic organizing level transference memories are not only presymbolic, but preverbal and somatic. Resistance to ever again reexperiencing such a traumatic, life-threatening breakdown of linking possibilities is expressed in somatic terror and pain that mark "where mother once was."

Green (1986) speaks of "the dead mother" internalization as the earliest psychic structure (memory) that is laid down by the early sensual, pleasurable links to mother that are bound sooner or later to be experienced as maternal failure. (Note that the real mother may be working hard to stay attuned to the organizing needs of the infant, but for any of a variety of reasons the pleasurable connection cannot be maintained.) We are left forever searching for this internalized mother of pleasure who "died," trying in every way to revive her through searching the world for love and stimulation according to the pleasure mode we once experienced with her in a primordial and primeval Eden—the paradise we knew before we tasted of the fruit of the tree of knowledge of good and evil (splitting). Of course the search fails because the paradise of life as pleasure is not to be found in the outside world but inside our own bodies. But the human search for the dead mother of primordial pleasure, along with her failures and our incessant futile efforts to bring her back to life by finding her outside of ourselves, outside of our bodies— expresses the earliest transference and resistance memories we bring to the analytic relationship.

Winnicott (1965) points out that early impingements on the infant's sense of continuity with life oblige the infant to react to environmental failure before the infant is fully prepared to begin reacting and thinking. The result of premature impingement is the formation of a primary persecutory mode of thought that forms the foundation from which all subsequent thought pro-cesses of that person arise. That is, traumatic impingement on the infantile (omnipotent) sense of "going on being," insures that the first memory that is destined to color all later memories is "the world persecutes me by intruding into my mental space and overstimulating (traumatizing) me. I will forever be on guard for things coming at me that threaten to destroy my sense of being in control of what happens to me (my omnipotence)." As a lasting imprint this earliest memory is psychotic because the world at large offers many kinds of impingement. And searching the environment tirelessly for the kind of primary intrusion that once forced the infant to respond in a certain way not only creates perennial paranoid hazards where there may be (in reality) none, but causes the person to miss other realistic dangers that are not being scanned for because of this prior preoccupation of the sensorium.

The literary works of Franz Kafka, *The Castle* (1926), *The Trial* (1937), (also see Kafka 1979), portray an organizing stance toward the world—always searching, always striving—and then when something good is within tasting distance, always "something happens so it is lost." Jerzy Kosinski's *Being There* (1970), Patrick Suskind's *Perfume* (1986), and David Hare's play *Plenty* (1983) all vividly portray the primitive and primary organizing search that never finds satisfactory or sustaining connections. In the later living out of the organizing experience whether it exists as pervasive to the personality or only in well defined "pockets," the vital *transference memories are set up to prevent connection to the human world*. We hear in our consulting rooms, "I'm weird or strange somehow, not quite human like other people. I do the right things, go through the right motions, but I don't feel the same emotions as everybody else, I don't quite tune in the way others do. It's as though I live behind a wall of glass, somehow not participating fully in the human world, feeling somehow not fully human" (Hedges 1994d).

RECOVERED MEMORIES AND FOUR VARIETIES OF PERSONALITY ORGANIZATION

In the previous chapter I reviewed the four basic mechanisms of memory that a century of psychoanalytic research has produced. What emerged was essentially a psychoanalytic theory that inextricably links memory to significant relationships. In *repression*, the 5-year-old volitionally decides not to experience or spell out in consciousness his or her incestual and parricidal urges that have proven undesirable within the family structure. In *dissociation*, a whole line of personality development, or a whole sector of the personality such as narcissism, is disavowed or dissociated—walled off from being realized as an active part of the central personality as it relates to others. In *splitting*, various whole sequences of emotional interaction, symbiotic character scenarios, are valued as good and sought out, or devalued as bad and shunned, based upon the person's original experience with the mothering partner. In expressions of searching for and breaking off (*primary repression of*) the possibility of contact with others, the early traumatic ways the nurturing other ruptured or failed to sustain contact live on as transference and resistance memories in subsequent attempts to make human contact that might lead toward human bonding. Organizing (or psychotic) transference memory involves the search for connection versus a compulsion toward discontinuity, disjunction, and rupture of connections. The resistance memory exists as the person's automatic or inadvertent reluctance to establish and/or sustain consistent and reliable connection to the other (which might serve to make interpersonal bonding of these somatic experiences a realistic possibility).

It is to this organizing experience and the reluctance to permitting or to sustaining deep, here-and-now connectedness experience that we will later return in order to show how "recovered memories" operate in the therapeutic relationship. A brief example will suffice at this point to be suggestive. A therapist working with a multiple personality presents her work to a consultant. After an overview and general considerations, the consultant asks the therapist to bring "process notes" (event by event) of the next session for review. The therapist begins reading the process notes, telling how her client, Victor, began the hour and how the client gradually zeroed in on a particular emotional issue. The therapist hears the concerns and very skillfully empathizes with the client's thoughts and feelings. Suddenly "little Victoria, age 4" appears in the room. The "switch" is significant in all regards and the therapist now listens to what the alter, Victoria, has to say. The consultant asks how the therapist understands what has just happened. The answer is that Victor felt very understood in the prior transaction, and in the safety of the presence of the understanding therapist a more regressed alter (Victoria) can now appear.

This kind of event is ubiquitous in the treatment of organizing experiences—an empathic connection is achieved by the therapist and there is a smooth, seemingly comfortable shift to another topic, to a flashback memory, or to an alter personality. The therapist had to work hard to achieve this connection and feels gratified that his or her interpretive work has been successful. The therapist feels a warm glow of narcissistic pleasure that is immediately reinforced by the client's ability to move on to the next concern. Wrong! When organizing or psychotic issues are brought for analysis, what is most feared on the basis of transference and resistance is an empathic interpersonal connection. This is because in the infantile situation the contact with the (m)other was terrifying in some regard.

A more viable way of seeing the interaction just cited is to realize that *the successful empathic connection was immediately, smoothly, and without notice ruptured with the shift!* The therapist fails to note what happened for perhaps several reasons: (1) the therapist is a well-bonded person and assumes unwittingly that empathic connection is always experienced as good by everyone; (2) the therapist doesn't understand how organizing transference and resistance operate and so is narcissistically pleased by the apparent connection he or she has achieved; (3) the client is a lifetime master at smoothly and efficiently dodging interpersonal connections—across the board or only at certain times when organizing issues are in focus; (4) a subtle mutual seduction is operating in the name of "recovery," in which resistance and counterresistance are winning the day with both parties afraid of personal and intimate connectedness, presumably because of its intense emotional demands; (5) the personality switch, sudden flashback, or change of subject focuses both on the historical causes of the dissociation or other red herrings; or (6) the search for memories and validation forecloses the possibility of here-and-now transference experiencing of the emotional horror and how connection with the therapist is causing it to arise. Thus the very real possibility of bringing to life and putting to rest traumatic memory is lost by the therapeutic technique being employed!

In this chapter I have reviewed the four major categories of transference and resistance memories that have emerged from a century of study of the kinds of memories that appear in the psychoanalytic and psychotherapeutic situation. In *neurotic personality organization*, the subjective sense of a 5-year-old child's instinctual driveness is remembered in transference along with intense fears of experiencing sexual and aggressive impulses toward anyone so intimate as the analyst because such intensity was forbidden in the family, triangular structure. In *narcissistic personality organization* a 3-year-old's intense needs for admiration, confirmation, and inspiration in relation to his or her selfothers are central to transference memories. The natural narcissistic needs are enshrouded in shame (resistance memory) surrounding the desire to be at the center of the universe. In *borderline personality organization* transference remembering is rooted in the replication of a set of emotional scenarios. Resistance memories mitigate against living out the positively and negatively charged emotional interactions in the analytic relationship so that they can achieve representation and be relinquished. In *personalities living out the earliest organizing processes*, what is structured in transference memory is the continuous rupturing or breaking of each and every attempt to form sustained organizing channels to the other. Resistance takes the form of terror and physical pain whenever sustained contact with a significant other threatens.

THE CENTRAL PUZZLE OF RECOVERED MEMORIES

What is manifestly evident from this review of a century of psychoanalytic exploration of early childhood memory is that no known memory mechanisms and no known forms of relatedness memory can conceivably support the widespread popular belief that traumatic experiences occurring before the age of 3 or 4 can be subject to massive repression, which can later be lifted in such a way as to allow perfect and accurate video camera recall of facts and events.

The view that has captured the popular imagination is contrary to available knowledge. Memories that do occur as a part of a therapeutic process and have been studied widely are memories that link past emotional relatedness experience to the present relationship realities of the psychoanalytic setting through various forms of transference and resistance. According to the ways in which personalities may be said to organize themselves, there is simply no place in which massive interpersonal trauma resulting in total amnesia that can later be lifted like a veil can possibly occur.

The only possibly explanations for the existing reports of recovered memories of all of the considerations thus far made are the following:

1. Memories that are based upon later hearsay, which has produced pictures believed to be memories but are not.

2. Memories of traumatically intense events that endure by sheer force of their emotional impact. But such memories, like the death of a parent or physical or sexual abuse that is known and confirmed at the time are not "forgotten," but always accessible to memory—though perhaps not thought about for long periods of time because recall is painful and one does not

wish to recall unless there is hope of making things better. That is, memories of known and real trauma may be set aside as painful to remember and not thought about for long periods of time, but they have not been totally lost and later accurately recovered through hypnosis or the free association of psychotherapy. This choosing to remember is different than (policy) secondary repression.

3. Screen or telescoped memories that are, by definition, like dreams, products of primary process condensation, displacement, symbolization, and visual representability. But such memories, because of their nature and function as abstracting processes, cannot be considered fully and objectively real no matter how vivid or how corroborated by external evidence they may be, or how accurately they portray subjective emotional truths.

4. Memories of environmental failure that have been "frozen" (Winnicott 1954) until a relationship situation presents itself in which the failure can be emotionally lived in a present regressed relational state, so that the environmental failures of empathy can be made good in the present relationship. This last prospect is the most promising for our purposes. But the emergence of "frozen failure" memory is situation dependent and relationship dependent – and can hardly be considered objective, unmotivated, or undistorted. Further, if the emotional events to be recalled are before the age of 3, there will be no capacity for verbal, symbolic, or pictorial recall per se that could possibly be operating; so that whatever is recalled must be a construction, a narration artfully created to fit the current relationship situation (or an intervening one) so that the emotional sense of environmental failure from the past can be relived in regressed form in the relational present.

In conclusion, there is no conceivable way that recovered memories as they are being currently touted in the marketplace, public media, and courtroom can possibly be remembering anything that we can reliably count as objectively real or totally factual.

But the people who claim absolute and literal truth for their recovered memories are, at least for the greatest part, credible people without discernible motive for deliberately perpetrating a hoax. Serious intention can be read in the many and wide-ranging reports of recovered memories. Furthermore, the desperation, the urgency, and the compelling arguments these people offer make clear that their efforts and motives in some essential way must be trusted, must somehow be taken seriously. But if all evidence regarding the nature of memory goes against their claims and no conceivable understanding we can muster supports their purported ability to remember the complex stories and events in the way they say they remember them, how then do we find a way to take memories recovered in psycho-therapy seriously?

3

The Fear
of Breakdown,
Emptiness, and Death

TO BELIEVE OR NOT TO BELIEVE

I have pondered considerably how to take memories recovered in psychotherapy seriously, not from a theoretical armchair by any means, but as a witness to twenty-five years of listening to various kinds of recovered memories and as consultant to numerous other therapists who have witnessed amazing experiences with recovered memories of all conceivable types.

As I have considered the problem, one striking feature began to emerge with clarity that was common to or implicit in all circumstances—the demand, insistence, yea the desperate almost life-or-death plea that the person's memories be believed. Suddenly it struck me that there is more to this single impelling feature than meets the eye. The dramatic and at times almost desperate insistence *demands* full and literal belief—with the additional claim or veiled threat that, "if you don't believe me I won't feel validated in my experience, and I will never be able to feel that I am a real and worthwhile person. These things really happened to me, they must be believed, and if you won't believe me this ends our relationship and I will find someone who will." But this (blackmail quality) demand being issued as a desperate plea or a relationship ultimatum doesn't stop here. "These atrocities happened. You believe me. Now you must support me in my redress of my grievances, my efforts to gain restitution for those crimes committed against me. My 'recovery' of my sanity depends upon my being believed, validated, and aided in my attempts to gain redress. 'They' must be made to confess and to pay for the wrongs they have done to me." In the case of alien abduction memories the final part of the plea is not so clear cut, but reads something like, "People must be made to believe that these things are happening, that lives are being ruined, that my life is ruined by the fears I live with. Until the truth is known and believed we will have no collective way of banding together to protect ourselves from these invading aliens and stopping this use of us like common animals in a zoo or research laboratory."

There is, of course, a certain impelling logic in these various claims and demands. And it would seem that this logic, taken along with the passionate persuasion of its absolute truth value, has led numerous therapists to lose their ordinary therapeutic stance.

As therapists we were all taught while in training to become dynamic psychotherapists never to "believe" anything told to us in psychotherapy, but to take everything told to us seriously. To believe is to step out of the professional therapist role and gets into a dual relationship with the client, which destroys the therapeutic stance and with it the possibility of ever being able to interpret the illusory and delusional aspects of transference and resistance. Ever entering the client's life in a realistic way colludes with unconscious resistance. So we are taught to remain neutral, equidistant between the personality agencies of id, ego, and superego and the client's external reality.

Someone arrives in our consulting room and tells us he has a headache because of too much stress. The internist says it's "nerves." We would be out of business quickly if we believed either conclusion. Instead, we learn to receive the complaint along with the proffered interpretations. Then we ask the person to continue telling us about himself. A woman comes to tell us that she feels pain during intercourse and it is because her husband is so insistent on having sex with her all the time. We hear that the child who is brought for therapy is lying and stealing despite all of the parent's best efforts to raise him correctly. In couple or family work we always hear conflicting "realities." We take each reality seriously as we work, but we refrain from losing our neutrality, our therapeutic stance, and therefore our ability to be of value, by not becoming swept away with the question of whose version of reality is correct or true. And the list goes on. We never take at face value what we are told, but we always receive it seriously and ask for more.

Then I began to realize that some of my colleagues are not plagued by this demand to believe the recovered memories told them. Surprise! I suddenly realize that they are the most seasoned therapists, those with the greatest experience and competence in analyzing transference and resistance, regardless of what school of therapy they have been trained in. They take what is told to them seriously and ask for more. Now the trail is getting hotter! Seasoned therapists who understand transference and resistance work, no matter how they label it, feel no need to believe the childhood abuse or abduction memories, but take everyone's concerns and beliefs very seriously and go to work. Oh, if pressed, they might be more or less inclined to believe that a given person's experience actually did or did not happen, but that is not their concern. They are aware of the existence of massive abuse and denial in our society (Hilton 1993). And without overwhelming objective evidence of specific facts, they have no need to believe or doubt – they are acutely aware that believing simply isn't their job as psychotherapists.

One colleague asked, "Whoever gave it to us to be the arbitrators of objective truth? Where but the psychotherapy consulting room are we less likely to be indulged with objective fact?!"

THE PROBLEM OF RECOVERY THROUGH BEING BELIEVED

Now the insistence (1) on "being believed," (2) on "having to have one's experiences validated," and (3) on "only being able to achieve recovery by being supported in actually seeking realistic redress" began to look more like symptoms of something else. But if so, I asked myself, "What is the common root to these many symptomatic demands?"

Almost as if by divine intervention, a deeply distressed and horrified therapist appeared in my next consultation group. Her horror? "Tomorrow a client I have worked with for two-and-a-half years has arranged, with the aid of members of her survivors' support group, a full family confrontation of her childhood molests."

Consultant: Survivors' groups encourage this kind of thing all the time, what's the problem—surely you're not involved in all that?

"No, of course not. But after six months of therapy when all of these abusive memories began coming out during sessions she became quite fragmented and was having a hard time functioning. I sent her to a psychiatrist who put her on Prozac, which helped. She is on a managed health care plan so her psychotherapy benefits ran out rapidly. I continued to see her once a week for a low fee but she clearly needed more. I suggested she check out the Community Women's Center for a support group. At the Center she was referred to an incest survivors' group. I thought, 'Oh, well, she is working on those issues so maybe they can help her.' Over the last two years numerous memories have emerged of absolutely terrible things that happened with her father and brothers. She insisted on my believing all of the memories that came up in group and in session."

Consultant: And were the things believable?

"Well, that's hard to say. She is clearly very damaged, borderline at best with organizing pockets around all of this abuse. I don't question whether she has been somehow badly abused. But I have no idea about the actual memories – there are so many of them and they are so grotesque."

Consultant: But she insisted on your believing all of them?

"Yes, she did."

Consultant: And how did you handle that?

"Well, I did my best to get out of it. You know, to tell her that I know some horrible things must have happened to her, that we would do our best to figure things out and find ways for her to face whatever happened and to find new ways to live – I said it all. But she had to *know* that I believed her. Then the memories began to be more explicit, things an infant can't possibly imagine unless they had actually happened to her."

Consultant: And so you believed her?

"Well, in a way yes. I mean, I don't know about all of the memories but clearly something awful happened to her. I let her know I believed that. But I'm sure she thinks I believe it all, just like her survivors' group does. But what I'm worried about now is she has all of this energy and support gathered for the grand confrontation tomorrow. She wants them all to confess, to say that they did all of these horrible things to her, to say they are sorry, that they are horrible people to have ever done such things, that they can never forgive themselves, and that there is no way they can ever make it up to her."

Consultant: Is that what she wants, some form of recompense?

"I don't really know what she wants. Her father and her brothers do have money, maybe she wants some kind of payment. And there is a lot of insurance money. Her survivors' group has educated her to that. But that's not the main thing. Or at least I don't think so. It's like her sanity is somehow at stake. She now has amassed all of the believers she needs to validate her experiences and her memories. She now feels absolutely certain that these many things happened. If they don't confess, if they don't grovel, if they don't agree that she is right and they are wrong I'm afraid she'll have a psychotic break! But what's got me scared is that I have somehow colluded in all of this without really meaning to. She is going to confront the family about all of these things, things that I have no way of knowing ever happened. And she's going to say that she remembered all of this in therapy and that her group helped her get the courage to finally speak the truth. You see, it's awful. I don't know how I got into this jam. And just yesterday I read about a group that's helping families fight back. They are encouraging families to sue the therapist for encouraging people to believe false memories. And, of course, therapists have lots of money to sue for. I have three million dollars in insurance this family could come after. And do you know what's scariest? I have all of those memories written down in my notes. Sure enough, with her shaking, sobbing, writhing as she remembered it all — event by event. Her family — at least on the surface — appears ordinary and normal. I don't think they're going to take well to being told they're criminals, and to being threatened with lawsuits for crimes they supposedly committed twenty-five years ago. It's all one horrible mess and I have no protection in all of this. If the family contacts me for information, I am bound by confidentiality. I can't tell them anything or help mediate in any way. The bottom line is, I'm fucked!"

Consultant: Follow me for a minute as I throw out some possibilities. When I hear your dilemma from the perspective of borderline or symbiotic personality organization, I hear the bottom line is that your client has succeeded in molesting you, violating your personal and professional boundaries in much the same intrusive or forceful way she may once have experienced herself as a very young child. According to this way of considering your dilemma, you are telling me that your life is now in as much danger as she may have felt in as an infant or toddler when all of whatever happened took place. The flashback dream memories are vivid and intensely sexual. What she experienced may have objectively looked very different. But the grotesque sexualized memories metaphorically express a certain true sense of how she felt then, or at least how she feels now when attempting to express intense body sensations that do contain a memory. By this view, you are saying that all this time you have been held emotional hostage in a similar helpless and vulnerable position to the one she felt she was in as a child—without having the slightest idea of how to protect yourself from this violence.

"Oh, God, I'm sick in the pit of my stomach just realizing how true what you are saying is. I'm feeling all of the abuse in the symbiotic role reversal of the countertransference."

Similar versions of this story are being lived in therapist's offices wherever psychotherapy is practiced. Talk shows are filled with the same human tragedy. Television audiences are being forced into the same position as this therapist of somehow judging the fate of those who are producing recovered memories. Judges and juries are being asked to decide the fate of family members who stand accused by the emergence of recovered memories from many years ago. The therapist I described is bright, well trained, sincere, and well intentioned. Her course was carefully thought out and managed but nevertheless has proven dangerous. Her training, like that of the vast majority of therapists practicing today, did not include how to work with primitive transference and resistance states so as to forestall massive acting out. By the therapist's own report her client was in danger of a mental breakdown.

The source of the powerful energy that fuels the recovery movement is primordial fear, which leads therapists to search for memories that aim the helplessness and rage toward an external source in the past and thereby to shift the focus of this terrifying energy out of the present transference situation. If the client were allowed her breakdown, terrifying and primitive body states would emerge in the consulting room and involve her therapist. She would, for that time period, lose completely her ability to observe her own experience, to test reality, and she would experience the therapist as the abuser, the molester. The accusation and demand for confession and empathic under-standing would be ideally aimed at the therapist in such a way that the primitive transference and resistance memories could at last be worked through rather than externalized and acted out. Freud discovered before the turn of the century (1895b) that hypnotic "remembering" and cathartic abreacting may indeed be intense emotional experiences that are momentarily compel-ling and tension relieving; but that without the activation of ego and body-ego memories in transference and resistance and without an intense and extensive working-through process there is no transformative cure.

When we believe people, are we perpetuating a fraud? When we fail to believe people, are we refusing to help them with their recovery? And what will ethics committees, licensing boards, and malpractice judges and juries be saying about how we conducted ourselves a decade from now when the psychotic transference finally slips into place and it is we who finally, but now publicly, stand helplessly accused of abusing this person in any of a variety of ways—by believing, by not believing, by molesting, by seducing . . . ? "It looks like we're all fucked!," was the response of the consultation group.

THE FEAR OF BREAKDOWN

This therapist's horrifying vignette brought abruptly to my attention a second feature of the recovered memory flap going on all around us. She feared that if her client did not get her way in the family confrontation she would have a psychotic break-down. The therapist herself was afraid of a malpractice suit or disabling ethical complaint. Suddenly I realized that everyone touched in any way by the phenomenon of these popularized recovered memories is somehow afraid that something uncertain but catastrophic is going to happen to them in the vague but foreseeable future. Hmmm . . . something catastrophic is *going to happen* in the future that is somehow related to the distant, unknown, and unrememberable past?

At that point the key to taking recovered memories seriously suddenly leapt out in a conversation with Bob and Virginia Hilton.[1] Virginia was preparing a paper on the topic for delivery to a bioenergetic conference the following week and we were brainstorming trying to get to the bottom of the recovered memory mystery (V. Hilton 1993). Bob had just finished a paper to be delivered at the same conference on a related topic (R. Hilton 1993) and Winnicott's last paper, which was published posthumously, "Fear of Breakdown" (1974), was fresh on his mind.

Donald Winnicott was the first pediatrician to become a psychoanalyst. His understandings of the early mother–child interaction have made a significant contribution to British psychoanalysis and his powerful influence is now rapidly spreading worldwide. As a result of Dr. Margaret Little's (1990) publication of her own analysis with Winnicott, *Psychotic Anxieties and Containment*, we now realize that Winnicott was the first psychoanalyst to learn how to fully and systematically foster a "regression to dependence" in which the most primitive of human psychotic anxieties could be subjected to analysis — even in people who are otherwise well developed.[2]

---

1. Dr. Robert Hilton is Senior Trainer in the Southern California Institute for Bioenergetic Analysis where Dr. Virginia Wink Hilton is Director of Training.

2. A full review of the psychoanalytic dialogue over the last century on the nature of therapeutic "regressions to dependence" has recently been undertaken by Robert Van Sweden (1994).

In "Fear of Breakdown" Winnicott shows that when people in analysis speak of a fear of a psychotic break, a fear of dying, or a fear of emptiness, they are projecting into the future what has already happened in the infantile past. One can only truly fear what one has experienced. Terrifying and often disabling fears of breakdown, death, and emptiness are distinct ways of remembering terrifying processes that actually happened in a person's infancy. This nugget of an idea and all that has followed in its wake has changed the face of psychoanalytic thinking. What is dreaded and seen as a potentially calamitous future event is the necessity of experiencing in the memory of the psychoanalytic transference the horrible, regressive, (once death threatening) dependent breakdown of functioning that one in fact experienced in some form in infancy.

The fear of breakdown manifests itself in many forms as resistance to reexperiencing in transference and resistance (memories) the terror, helplessness, rage, and loss of control once known in infancy. Therapists and clients alike dread disorganizing breakdowns and there are many ways in resistance and counterresistance that two can collude to forestall the curative experience of remembering by reliving the breakdown experience with the therapist. One way of colluding with resistance to therapeutic progress would be to focus on external perpetrators or long-ago traumas to prevent having to live through deeply distressing and frightening breakdown recreations together.

Bob read us the passage from Winnicott that relates the original breakdown to precipitous loss of the infant's sense of omnipotence, however that may have occurred — before or after birth. When the environmental provision fails to support the infant's need to control life-giving necessities of his or her world, a massive breakdown of somatopsychic functioning occurs. The break constitutes a loss of whatever body-ego functions the infant may have attained at the time. Rudimentary or developing ego functions are not fully independent of the interpersonal situation in which they are being learned. So when the environment fails at critical moments, the infant experiences a loss of his or her own mind, a loss of any attained sense of control, and a loss of whatever rudimentary sense of self as agency may have been operating. From the point of view of the infant, the loss of psychic control over his or her environment is equivalent to the loss of the necessary life support systems so that fear of death (as an instinctual given) is experienced as terrifyingly imminent, complete with the frantic flailings we see in any mammal whose contact with the warmth and nurturing maternal body is interrupted. The environment is empty, the environment that is not experienced as separate from the infant's rudimentary consciousness. When the necessary environmental support for ego skills and consciousness is lacking, the infant psyche collapses. In Green's (1986) terms, the mother of primary desire and pleasure dies.[3]

At the level of the infant's primary organizing attempts there is a functional equivalence between disruption or failure of environmental provision and a sense of emptiness, loss of control, loss of omnipotence, total panic-stricken and painful psychic breakdown, and the terrifying prospect of death. Memories of primordial breakdowns are embedded in somatic symptoms and terror. Some such memories appear universal since, regardless of how good the parenting processes are, there are unavoidable moments of breakdown that occur in every person's infancy. However, the subjective experience of intensity, duration, and frequency of breakdowns is markedly traumatic in some people and not possible to be adequately soothed or recovered from. This level of memory is guarded with intense physical pain attributable to the process of (quasi-neurological) primary repression. No one wants to go through the excruciating gross bodily pain and terror necessarily entailed in physi-

---

3. See Chapter 2 for Green's formulations regarding the internalized "dead mother" formed out of a loss of infantile experiences of satisfaction.

cally remembering the process of early psychic breakdown. A simplified recovery approach may foster repeated intense abreactions that bring the body to the pain threshold in an acting out that is then endlessly repeated in the name of recovery. But a century of psychoanalytic research has repeatedly and unequivocally demonstrated the futility of this abreaction approach—whether it be acted out in the form of screaming, kicking, accusing, confronting, switching personalities, generating yet more flashbacks, or whatever.

Acting outside or acting inside the therapeutic situation is *never* seen by psychoanalysts as therapeutic though at times it may be unavoidable or uncontrollable. Analysts and all responsible therapists—whether they work with psychoanalytic transferential concepts or with transference concepts such as parent–child tapes, birth memories, or wounded inner child—seek to frame within the therapeutic relationship the relatedness memories from the past that remain active in the personality. Transference and resistance memories can be secured for analysis and found to be illusory and delusory in contrast to the realistic possibilities offered in the present by real relationships that the person has the capacity to enjoy.

Winnicott (1974) holds that in more normal development the environment is able to manage infantile frustration and disillusionment through small and tolerable doses, so that the terrifying fear of death and an empty world (and therefore an empty self) may be averted and the breakdown of omnipotence gently helped along rather than traumatically forced and abusively intruded into the child's body and mind. It is now possible to make sense of the strange and compelling nature of recovered memories. Environmental failure in infancy has led to a breakdown of early psychic processes with accompanying terror and the active threat of death (as the infant experiences it). The breakdown experience is blocked by primary repression that says "never go there again." The breakdown fear lives on as the somatic underpinning of all subsequent emotional relatedness but cannot be recalled because (1) no memory of the experience per se is recorded—only a nameless dread of dependence; (2) the memory of the breakdown experience itself is guarded with intense pain, somatic terror, and physical symptoms of all types; and (3) the trauma occurred before it was possible to record pictures, words, or stories so it cannot be recalled in ordinary ways, but only as bodily terrors of approaching death.

THE MYTHIC THEMES OF RECOVERED MEMORIES

The mythic themes of recovered memories (incest, violence, multiple selves, cult abuse, birth, kidnapping, and alien abduction) have been present in all cultures since the beginning of recorded time and can be called upon by the creative human unconscious to allow for a creative narration to be built in psychotherapy that conveys the emotional essence of the infant's traumatic experience. The demand to be believed represents in some way the sense of urgency of the violation of infantile boundaries. The primordial boundary violation that is registered can be interpreted in the countertransference as the therapist feeling violated by the demand to "believe me." The working through of the repeated ruptures of interpersonal contact by flashbacks, sudden physical symptoms, bizarre thoughts, panic attacks, personality switches, and boundary violations can be accomplished through securing the organizing transference and resistance for analysis.

THE CONCEPT OF CUMULATIVE TRAUMA

A final consideration regarding the problem of recovered memories relates to the frequent claim by parents, family members, and accused therapists that the adult child now making accusations based on false memories has, until stressful problems in living were encountered, always been basically normal and well adjusted. And that family life has always been characterized by basically sound group life and parenting. Masud Khan's (1963) concept of "cumulative trauma" adds a new set of possibilities to those already discussed.

Beginning with Freud's early studies of childhood trauma (1895a, b), psychoanalysis has studied a series of possibilities regarding how the human organism handles overstimulation arising from the environment as well as from within the body. As early as 1920, Freud envisioned the organism turning its receptors toward the environment and gradually developing a "protective shield."

> *Protection against* stimuli is an almost more important function for the living organism that *reception* of stimuli. The protective shield is supplied with its own store of energy and must above all endeavor to preserve the special modes of transformation of energy operating in it against the effects threatened by the enormous energies at work in the external world. [Freud 1920, p. 27]

This protective shield later develops into consciousness, but even so remains somewhat ineffective in protecting from stimuli arising from within the body. One way the organism may attempt to protect itself from overwhelming internal stimuli is to project them into the outer environment and treat them as "though they were acting, not from the inside, but from the outside, so that it may be possible to bring the shield against stimuli into operation as a means of defence against them" (p. 29). The false memory syndrome appears to originate in earliest infancy (pre- or postnatal) when environmental stimuli cannot be effectively screened out, or when strong internal stimuli are projected to the exterior in an effort to screen them out. In either case, due to the operation of primitive mental processes, the environment may be "blamed" by the infant for causing stimulation that cannot be comfortably processed – though blame may be objectively inappropriate to the circumstances. For example, one accuser's early problems were traced back to placenta abruptio, a detachment of the placenta from the uterine wall giving rise to at least several prenatal days without nourishment. Often accusations are traceable to shortages of oxygen *in utero*, to early feeding problems, to infant allergies, to surgeries and medical procedures early in life, to incubators, to severely depressed mothers, to marital distress of the parents, or to an endless array of stressful and unusual early life events that were not deliberately cruel or abusive.

Anna Freud (1951, 1952, 1958) and Winnicott (1952) emphasize the role of maternal care in augmenting the protective shield during the period of early infantile dependency. Khan (1963) has introduced the concept of cumulative trauma to take into consideration early psychophysical events that happen between the infant and its mothering partners. The concept of cumulative trauma correlates the effects of early infant caretaking with disturbing personality features that only appear much later in life. Cumulative trauma is the result of the effects of numerous kinds of small breaches in the early stimulus barrier or protective shield that are not experienced as traumatic at the time but create a certain strain that, over time, produces an effect on the personality that can only be appreciated retrospectively when it is experienced as traumatic.

Research on infantile trauma and memory (Greenacre 1958, 1960; Kris 1951, 1956a,b; Milner 1952) demonstrates the specific effects on somatic and psychic structure of cumulative strain trauma. Khan holds that " 'the strain trauma' and the screen memories or precocious early memories that the patients recount are derivatives of the partial breakdown of the protective shield function of the mother and an attempt to symbolize its effects (cf. Anna Freud, 1958)" (p. 52). Khan further comments:

> Cumulative trauma has its beginnings in the period of development when the infant needs and uses the mother as his protective shield. The inevitable temporary failures of the mother as protective shield are corrected and recovered from the evolving complexity and rhythm of the maturational processes. Where these failures of the mother in her role as protective shield are significantly frequent and lead to impingement on the infant's psyche-soma, impingements which he has no means of eliminating, they set up a nucleus of pathogenic reaction. *These in turn start a process of interplay with the mother which is distinct from her adaptation to the infant's needs.* [p. 53, emphasis added]

According to Khan, the faulty interplay between infant and caretakers that arises in consequence of strain reactions may lead to (1) premature and selective ego distortion and development, (2) special responsiveness to certain features of the mother's personality such as her moods, (3) dissociation of archaic dependency from precocious and fiercely acted out independency, (4) an attitude of excessive concern for the mother and excessive craving for concern from the mother (co-dependency), (5) a precocious adaptation to internal and external realities, and (6) specific body-ego organizations that heavily influence later personality organization.

Khan points out that the developing child can and does recover from breaches in the protective shield and can make creative use of them so as to arrive at a fairly healthy and effective normal functioning personality. But the person with vulnerabilities left over from infantile cumulative strain trauma "nevertheless can in later life break down as a result of acute stress and crisis" (p. 56). When there is a later breakdown and earlier cumulative strain trauma can be inferred, Khan is clear that the earlier disturbances of maternal care were neither gross nor acute at the time they occurred. He cites infant research in which careful and detailed notes, recorded by well-trained researchers, failed to observe traumas that only retrospectively could be seen as producing this type of cumulative strain trauma. Anna Freud has similarly described instances in which, "subtle harm is being inflicted on this child, and . . . the consequences of it will become manifest at some future date" (A. Freud 1958, p. 57).

There are several implications of this research for the problem of recovered memory. There are many kinds of trauma that an infant can silently and invisibly be reacting to that are not the result of gross negligence or poor parenting. In such instances only retrospectively, in light of later disturbance or breakdown of personality functioning, can the effect of cumulative strain trauma be inferred. The origin of the difficulty can be traced to the environmental function of the protective shield, to the (m)other's role in providing an effective barrier that protects the child from intense, frequent, and/or prolonged stimuli that produce strain, though there may be no visible signs of trauma at the time.

Early or recovered childhood memories representing cumulative trauma are seen by psychoanalysts as screen memories that abstract, condense, displace, symbolize, and represent visually the strain effect. The unconscious of the client creates a compelling picture or narrative that describes in metaphor what the strain trauma looked like in the mind and body of the infant.

Many symptoms and/or breakdowns in later life, occasioned by conditions of acute living stress, have their origins in infancy. The adult experience of vague and undefinable earlier trauma is attributable to the cumulative effects of strain in infancy caused by environmental failure to provide an effective stimulus barrier during the period of infantile dependency. There may have been no way at the time of knowing what kinds of stimuli were causing undue strain on the infant because they were not gross and they were operating silently and invisibly. Or the circumstance may have been beyond the parent's capacity to shield, as in the case of medical problems, constitutional problems, or uncontrollable environmental problems, for example, war, food shortages, concentration camps, family discord, and so on. But the key consideration for our present topic is that when a person in later years, under conditions of living stress, produces memories of the effects of the cumulative strain trauma, what is remembered is abstracted, condensed, displaced, symbolized, and represented visually in screen memories that operate like dreams so that an accurate picture of objective facts is, in principle, forever impossible to obtain from recovered memories.

BEYOND THE UNTHOUGHT KNOWN

Bollas (1987), following Winnicott, speaks extensively of psychoanalysis of "the unthought known." His focus is on preverbal patterns, emotions, and moods that characterize the early interactions the child establishes with its caretakers. As these patterns become established in the here-and-now emotional interaction of psychoanalytic relating, what has heretofore been "unthought known" can now be thought in the developing relatedness context. Memories of the unthought known from the first three or four years of life do not arrive in pictures or narrations. Rather they are relatedness memories embedded deeply in our characters and in our characteristic modes of interacting with significant others (Hedges 1983b). Memories recovered from this period in the form of pictures and stories are bound to be unreliable as such. When the memories emerge within the context of detailed analysis of resistance and transference that directly involve the analyst and the analytic process, then two can participate in the creation of words, pictures, and stories that serve as metaphors of what the early experiences that are being nonverbally and somatically revived in the present might have looked like. The objective facts of early emotional life are simply not accurately retrievable in the form of pictorial and narrational memories, no matter how vivid and emotionally compelling mental pictures and somatic sensations relating to the past may be.

Hedges (1994c) researches the developmentally earlier (plus or minus four months from birth) organizing level transference that sets up a block to experiencing others before interactions can begin. He cites Fraiberg's (1982) observations of infants in which "predefenses"—the tendency to fight, flight, or freeze—serve as behavioral modes that characterize the resistance to experiencing the terrifying response sequences that produced in infancy the tendency toward compulsive blocking or rupturing of interpersonal contact.

Early impingements of omission or commission into the infantile sense of continuity force the infant to respond and to problem solve before it is equipped to do so or would ordinarily be inclined to create a response pattern. Such early impingements may be subtle and operate invisibly but do form a person's basic foundations of thought. By definition they are persecutory in nature, in that these fundamental experiencing templates have been formed based on response to intrusive impingements. Thus faulty primary and primordial learning of thought patterns results, which serves (1) to keep the person focused on certain classes of danger cues when no danger exists, (2) to preoccupy the person with certain classes of danger cues so that he or she misses completely other dangers that "common sense" would otherwise inform the person of, and (3) to freeze for the person certain aspects of sensorimotor responsiveness at the level of infantile dependency—global or amodal perception and motor responsiveness—which forecloses further elaboration by more mature differentiated modes of perception in situations of greater independence. Memories of such primordial persecutory responsiveness that are recalled at later points of life will necessarily be subject to early distorting influences as well as influences of the recall situation. It becomes patently clear that memories recovered from infancy are complex constructions that include many unreliable sources of variance. As such they must be understood to be mentally operating in the same way as dreams—the products of abstraction, condensation, displacement, symbolization, and considerations of visual representability.

CONCLUSIONS

Memories recovered in the course of psychotherapy can be taken seriously if one has clearly in mind what kinds of early life events are subject to what forms of later recall and how the recall can be accomplished through transference and resistance analysis. A review of a century of psychoanalytic observation has demonstrated that the kinds of recovered memories arising to public attention currently cannot possibly be veridical memories in the ways and forms that they are being touted. We have long understood the constructed effect of screen and telescoped memories that operate like dreams, as abstracting processes that help to weave together in plausible images and sequences psychic events that might not otherwise belong together, in order to make them seem sane and sensible.

We have studied the way human truth gets projected into creative and expressive narrations and narrative interactions that capture the essence of psychic experience. We know that plausible narration demands such features as a beginning, middle, and end. Characters must have motives and act in believable ways with purposes and effects. In a plausible narrative various gaps or inconsistencies in the story, the character structure, or the cause and effect of purpose are glossed over, filled in, or seamlessly woven together in ways that are vivid, flow naturally, and are emotionally compelling and logically believable.

We are taken in by Dr. Jekyll and Mr. Hyde because we all know what it means to experience ourselves in various convincing and contradictory parts. Every time *Sybil* is on national television or a talk show airs live appearances of satanic ritual abuse, our clinics are flooded with self-referrals. After the atomic bomb we looked to the skies for danger and sure enough our efforts quickly brought us flying saucers. We begin affirming more rights for women and children and our culture begins noticing actual abusive incidents as well as many other violent and molest stories that seemed to have other sources. When our culture could no longer believe in conversion hysteria, we saw peptic ulcers, then stress, now viral contagion. When we could no longer believe in Bridie Murphy's past lives, we turned to multiple selves, alien abductions, and satanic ritual abuse. The list of possibilities goes on and will keep expanding as our collective imagination continues to generate believable images that can be used in our screen, telescoped, and narrative constructions to clarify what our infancies were like and what the structure of our deepest emotional life looks like.

"My parents in raising me were more concerned with creeds and ritual than they were with my needs to love and to be loved by them. The reverence they kept was like a cult. My father was the high priest, my mother a priestess who looked on emotionless while I was led to the altar and forced to kill a baby (me?) and to drink its blood. Then I was placed on the altar as a sacrifice to the carnal wishes of all of their friends, the other participants that supported their belief system. The most unbearable part of all is that I was forced do the same things they did, to become like them, to sacrifice human life in the same manner they did, in the same cult, at the same altar. As a result, I am a damaged wreck."

"There is a higher intelligence that comes into my sphere,

that picks me up, puts me down, and exchanges fluids with me through my umbilicus. They want my soul, my fertility, and they want to impregnate me with their superior mental structure. I have no control over the coming and going of the higher intelligence that governs my life but I am frightened by it and suddenly swept away. It's like being lost in an endless nightmare that I can't make go away. Like losing yourself in a horrible science fiction movie you just can't shake off. I have no control over these higher intelligences that watch me."

"My father loved me too much, I remember when he used to come into my room. I remember my mother was somewhere in the background. My childhood longings were misread by him and he took advantage of me. If she had done her job in keeping him happy like a wife should I would not have been given to him."

"My mother ruled my every thought, we were always close, we shared everything. My father was an irrational, alcoholic brute, no one whom I could learn masculinity from. He gave me to her because he didn't want to deal with her dependency and so I had to be parent to her, husband to her—no wonder I am what I am."

In all of these familiar stories and more, we can suppose that what must eventually be expressed or represented in the interactional exchange of the psychoanalytic transference and resistance is the loss of power, the loss of control over oneself, and a personal destiny to continue experiencing emptiness, breakdown, and death as a result of internalized environmental failures. The kinds of stories that must be told and the kinds of painful somatic memories that must be relived will vary according to the nature of the infantile breakdown experience.

Someone will arise now to ask, "But isn't this all speculation? How do we know that all these things didn't really happen exactly as they are remembered?" The answer lies in our understanding of the hope that the psychotherapeutic situation holds out for people to be helped in reliving a dependent state past trauma. And then, of transforming themselves through better relating in the present. The effects of infantile breakdown resulting from misfortune, misunderstanding, neglect, or abuse can only be transformed in our daily lives through reliving in the transference present the traumas of the infantile past. Acting out or displacing the accusation onto the past never helps us transform our inner lives.

A well-meaning accused parent who has been searching his memory for some evidence that he has, in fact, trespassed in the way his adult daughter alleges, now arises to ask, "But doctor, isn't it possible that if I were so horrified by the deed I had done that I would have repressed it totally?" The answer is unequivocally "no."

Repression as conceptualized in psychoanalysis simply doesn't work this way. When we have been traumatized the problem is that we can't forget it. We set it aside, we manage not to think about it for long periods of time, but a sudden noise instantly shuttles us back to the concentration camp, to the trench where our buddy lies bleeding and dead, to the bedroom with the yellow flowered wallpaper and musty smell where from our perch on the ceiling we look down watching Father take his pleasure with our unfeeling bodies.

Psychological repression happens to a 5-year-old child whose sexual and aggressive impulses press for forbidden expression. Repression as we have studied it for a century only works against stimulation arising from *within* the neuropsychic system, not merely in harmony with abstract moral convictions. Such a notion of repression belongs to Hollywood.

"But doctor, isn't it possible I might begin having flashbacks of my having actually committed the acts my daughter says I did?" Of course, anyone can have flashbacks about anything. But flashbacks operate like dreams, not like memories. Flashbacks are unconscious constructions and, as such, have many determinants. If you were working on my couch and started having flashbacks I would encourage careful and systematic attention to them. I would assume they contained the history of *your* infantile past that was now being re-created in dream mode in order for us to study how your relationship with me was pointing toward what had happened in your otherwise unrememberable infancy. If the flashbacks seemed also tied to your daughter and other family members, I would be listening for how the infantile past being revived for us to study in our relationship has also been activated at various moments in transference experiences toward them as well. I would never assume we were looking at facts or memories.

Therapists who, in the course of working with primitive transferences, have lost their professional boundaries momentarily are regularly able to report vivid memories of experiences of dissociation. There is never any question of what they did or did not do—no matter how heinous or how ego dystonic it was. In a given moment they felt the pull of a desperate (asexual, infantile) woman who needed their touch to keep from falling into blackness and death. As they reached out to her they slipped into the place in themselves where long ago they mobilized total reaching, total yearning, and went for the (asexual) breast so powerfully desired and so potently alluring. Retrospectively, they know beyond the shadow of a doubt that they experienced a psychotic moment in themselves while trying to rescue this woman. And while they are duly horrified at what they did, there is no possibility of its ever being truly forgotten. Perpetrators know exactly what they did and did not do, despite however much they squirm to deny, defend, and blame the other. The only exceptions are people who chronically live in psychotic experiences and have never been able to keep very good track of reality. Ordinary people are simply not able to accomplish such repressions no matter how much they may wish to.

A century of accumulated psychoanalytic knowledge says that relatedness memory simply does not work the way so many people claim it does, but rather that relatedness memories are manifest in people's daily lives and in transference and resistance memories in psychotherapy. People who have experienced infantile breakdowns attempt to turn passive trauma into active mastery by molesting us with their memories, the demand to be believed, and the insistence on being supported by us in their redress. As human beings who have been subjected to infantile trauma they deserve so much more from us than simply being believed!

Believing the traumas, and therapists encouraging people to do things in the real world about the horrible memories they recover in psychotherapy, can only be colluding with the forces of resistance as we know them to arise to prevent painful transference reexperiencing. What is being avoided is clearly the breakdown of primitive mental functions that can only be done in the safety and intimacy of a private transference relationship. Not only clients but therapists also dread the intensity and the intimacy of such primitive transference reliving. We have a whole population of people who have suffered humiliating and traumatizing childhoods and infancies who are yearning for regressive psychotherapy experiences in which disorienting experiences can be subjected to transference, resistance, and countertransference analysis.

There is no shortage of customers. But there is a great shortage of therapists who have been prepared by their professional training to delve deeply into the meanings of recovered memories within the context of the therapeutic relationship. And there is great risk to the therapist working with deep personality trauma. There is not only the risk of litigation arising from the wild acting-out damage that clients are inflicting on their families as a result of recovered memories. There is the greater risk that the therapist will be successful in mobilizing the early organizing or psychotic transference, will be interpretively successful in not having it deflected toward revenge on the family, but will be caught with the accusations aimed squarely at him or her while the client is in a frame of mind with little reality testing. No wonder so many therapists are eager to deflect these psychotic anxieties onto personages in the past rather than to attempt to contain them!

As professionals we have not yet begun to assess the grave danger each of us is in as a result of recovered memories emerging in the therapeutic transference relationship. Escalating law suits, increasing disciplinary action by ethics committees and licensing boards, and skyrocketing costs of malpractice insurance make clear that the problem is real and that it is serious. For these and other reasons I advocate the inclusion of a third party "case monitor" whenever organizing or psychotic transferences are being worked on so that all parties are aware of the work and all parties are protected from accidental derailing of the psychotic process (see Hedges 1994c). We know there are abuses and that they must be limited. But the national wild accusatory atmosphere surrounding recovered memories is only the tip of the iceberg of universal psychotic transference feelings.

It is not abusive or neglectful parents and families that are the proper therapeutic target of primitive abusive transference feelings. It is ourselves and the work we do. How are we individually and collectively to protect ourselves from an abusive psychotic monster that an enlightened society with concern for the emotional well being of everyone has unleashed on us?

IMPLICATIONS FOR SOCIAL AND LEGAL ISSUES

1. *Clinical, theoretical, and experimental research fails to support the popularized video camera theory of memory.* The widely held view that externally generated psychic trauma can produce total amnesia for many years and then be subject to perfect total recall of fact is a Hollywood invention that is completely fallacious. As a dramatic device for generating horror and suspense,

the specter of capricious memory loss in response to unwanted experiences has indeed been successful in convincing millions that such things can and do happen—as attested to by an utterly spellbound population at present.

2. *Recovered memories cannot be counted as fact.* Consideration from a psychoanalytic point of view shows there to be too many sources of variance in recovered memories for them to ever be considered reliable sources of factual truth. Memories produced in hypnosis, chemically induced interviews, or psychotherapy are setting, technique, and relationship dependent. The most important recovered memories that attest to a history of trauma originate in the earliest months and years of life. Our knowledge of the way the human mind records experiences during this period makes it impossible for pictorial, verbal, narrational, or even screen images to provide facts that are reliable.

3. *Nor can memories recovered in psychotherapy be counted as merely false confabulations.* We have a series of viable ways to consider the potential truth value of memories recovered within the context of psychotherapy. Much has been said concerning screen memories, telescoped memories, and narrational truth. Little attention has been given in the recovered memory literature to the kinds of transference and resistance memories that can be expected to characterize each developmental epoch of early childhood. The terror that many people experienced in the first months of life due to misfortune, misunderstanding, neglect, and/or abuse is recorded in painful aversions to dependent states that might leave them at risk for psychic breakdown. The effects of cumulative strain trauma in infancy can be devastating in a person's later life, though no trauma was visible and no abuse present at the time. People resist at almost all cost having to reexperience in transference (i.e., to remember) the terrifying and physically painful memories of environmental failure in earliest infancy. But externalizing responsibility for

one's unhappiness in life onto people and events of childhood goes fundamentally against the grain of responsible psychotherapy.

4. *A simplified recovery approach tends to collude with resistance to the establishment of early transference remembering and, to the degree that it does, it is anti-psychotherapeutic.* In acceding to the client's demand to be believed, to have their experiences validated, and to receive support for redress of wrongs, recovery workers foreclose the possibility of securing for analysis the transference and resistance memories mobilized by the psychotherapeutic relationship. Encouraging the acting out of multidetermined recovered memories in the name of psychotherapy is clearly creating malpractice liabilities for these therapists.

5. *Studies of recovered memories cannot draw responsible conclusions when collapsing over diverse categories of memory, developmental levels, and modes of personality organization. Nor can conclusions uncritically be generalized from the psychotherapy setting, which is situation and relationship dependent, to other social and legal settings.* Human memory is complex, elusive, and multidimensional so that all attempts to arrive at simplified or dogmatic conclusions are bound to be faulty. This includes attempts to consider the physiological aspects of memory as well.

6. *Taking recovered memories seriously involves establishing a private and confidential relationship in which all screen, narrational, transference, and resistance memory possibilities can be carefully considered over time and within the ongoing context of the psychotherapeutic relationship.* Therapeutic transformation of internal structures left by childhood oversight, neglect, and abuse necessarily involves mobilizing in the therapeutic relationship a duality in which the real relationship with the therapist can be known in contrast to the remembered relationships from childhood that are being projected from within the client onto the person of the analyst and into the process of the analysis as transference and resistance.

Responsible psychotherapeutic work with memories recovered from infancy and early childhood requires much time and a well-developed interpersonal relationship between the client and his or her therapist. The temptation for a therapist to take recovered memories at face value and to encourage restitutive action against presumed perpetrators is great. The current limited managed care approach guarantees that help for the several million who suffer from infantile trauma will not be provided. How many billions of dollars will we spend on litigational activities and criminal prosecutions before prevention and treatment are realistically considered? How many lives will be ruined and families destroyed before we attend to the truly horrible problem of infantile trauma and its effects in later adulthood? How long before we invest in ourselves, in our children, and in our lives as a free people?

PART II

MULTIPLE
PERSONALITY
RECONSIDERED

4

Background and History of Multiplicity*

THE HISTORY AND THEMES OF MULTIPLE PERSONALITY

Throughout recorded time and across all cultures, altered states of consciousness have continued to claim a special place in human existence—a place often shrouded in mystery, mysticism, and religious zeal. At times altered states have been exalted to heights of cultural wisdom and prestige as in prophets, oracles, seers, and religious glossolalia. At other times altered states have been associated with evil, witchcraft, devil worship, and madness. In the twentieth century, hypnosis, drugs, and meditation have been among the more common ways of producing and perhaps of benefiting from the effects of altered states. Such techniques have largely replaced ritual incantations and other

*Presented at the Second International Congress on Multiple Personality/Dissociative States in Chicago, October 1985.

rhythmical and social forms of ecstasy production and enjoyment known for centuries. The recent emergence into visibility
in the psychotherapeutic setting of a large group of persons said
to be possessing or to be possessed by multiple personalities
represents one growing form of altered-state phenomena war-
ranting special study. One psychiatric observer (Schafer 1984)
estimates a rapidly increasing incidence of persons experiencing
multiple personalities, currently numbering more than fifty per
million in Southern California, which makes multiple personalities hardly rare.

As an observer who is neither an enthusiast of mysticism
nor a skilled practitioner of hypnosis, I would like to examine a
few aspects of altered states as they appear repeatedly in the
psychotherapeutic consulting room. I will begin with a historical
survey of how altered states have been considered in the past
several decades in American psychiatric nomenclature. I will
review some of the salient themes appearing in recent research
and clinical lore having to do with multiple personalities. I will
then explain the context out of which my own interest in
multiple personalities has grown and summarize my own *listening perspective* approach, which promises a fresh vantage
point from which to consider some altered-state phenomena.
The style of this chapter will be informal rather than scholarly,
perhaps capturing the spirit of the current state of knowledge
and understanding in an area much in need of more systematic
research.

BRIEF HISTORICAL SURVEY AND
RESEARCH QUESTIONS

The first *Diagnostic and Statistical Manual* of the American
Psychiatric Association (*DSM-I* 1952) reflected the general view
that dissociative neuroses are relatively rare, if not somewhat
esoteric forms of psychological disorder. Fugues, amnesias, sleep-

walking, sleep talking, multiple personality, and other altered-state phenomena were thought to be among the manifestations of persons who employed dissociation as a *repressive* defense. The general notion was that a few persons, well enough developed to merit the general diagnosis of neurotic, employed dissociative mechanisms in the service of fending off unwanted or unacceptable ideas and impulses. Dissociation was formulated as a "vertical" splitting of the personality, that is, a temporal or contextual separation or walling off of one or several aspects or constellations of personality from other aspects. Vertical splitting was thought to contrast with the more widespread concept of repressive "horizontal" splitting, that is, a separation of so-called conscious from unconscious personality manifestations or constellations.

It was thought that *The Three Faces of Eve* (Thigpen and Cleckley 1957) and similar rare cases could be understood as basically neurotic phenomena in a personality prone to employ repressive vertical splitting. Since more or less intact ego structure was assumed to be present in neurosis, the expectation was that such splits would be restricted in number to one or possibly another. That is, the assumption of good ego development in neurosis would be considered contradicted if extensive vertical splitting occurred so that a character diagnosis more in the direction of psychosis would be in order if many splits were in evidence. For example, the later reported and widely publicized case of *Sybil* (Schreiber 1973) could hardly be considered an instance of repressive neurosis.

The fate of the dissociative neuroses of the 1950s appears to have paralleled in American psychiatric history the fate of all the neuroses—a radically diminished reported incidence over time. Since the dissociative pictures were already the rarest, they were the first to go. In *DSM-II* (1968) dissociation was collapsed as a category into a subspecies of the broader class of hysterical neuroses. Whether the number of diagnosed neuroses have diminished in proportion to the character disorders, narcissistic constellations, and borderline states due to cultural changes, conceptual advances, refinements in diagnosis, alterations in therapeutic practices, or fluctuations in psychiatric fads is an issue still up for debate.

Elsewhere I have detailed the powerful arguments for continuing to consider certain styles and levels of personality organization as oedipal-neurotic even if contemporary understanding of preoedipal development modifies the way neurotic constellations are considered (Hedges 1983b, 1992). A spatial metaphor for considering dissociation as repressive activity was involved in conceptualizing the "span" of the ego. The reasoning was that certain (potentially traumatic) impulses, ideas, and experiences that belonged to conscious awareness could not be "contained" or "integrated into" the existing ego span (Cameron 1963). But because these selected psychological contents or experiences were so powerful they could not be relegated easily to unconsciousness, they were thought to become "dissociated," with their manifestations appearing only in altered states of consciousness.

This way of thinking about dissociated experiences has a certain clinical appeal. For example, I recently consulted on the psychotherapy of a bright, lovely, shy, and markedly "feminine" little girl aged 7½ whose presenting complaint was nightly sleepwalking and sleep talking. The child was also requiring special education procedures for problems in learning. By day, this sweet, extremely pleasant, delicate little girl charmed everyone. At night she stalked angrily to her mother's bedside to scream obscenities, accusations, and dreadful names. It seemed no mystery that such feelings and words could not be easily integrated into her kind and gentle waking personality. The approach taken by her play therapist was to verbalize even the most subtle nuance of negative affect that conceivably could be a part of the various play situations the child created. The results, as anticipated, were that the shy, quiet little girl gradually became more certain of herself and assertive in her general approach to life. Verbalization of her disagreeable affects first appeared in the mouths of little boy dolls before fathers, mothers, and little girls were able to express such intense, aggressive feelings, or forbidden thoughts. Needless to say, her learning problems cleared as she was able to be more aggressive in her approach to learning materials and in her challenge to her mother and her (woman) teacher. She was extremely bright and quite bored with the simple tasks she had been presented to learn at home and at school. Soon her reading and mathematics soared above her classmates and her parent, teacher, and peer relationships became drastically improved.

Similar dissociations are by no means uncommon in clinical practice and a wide variety of expressive techniques have been employed by therapists of all persuasions with similar favorable results. The general formulation would be that expressions of assertiveness and negative affect had become unacceptable to this little girl, perhaps because of her associations to the meanings of masculinity or her wish not to be a nuisance like her little brother. These expressions might be thought of as having become repressed through dissociation into her nocturnal activities. An expressive, interpretive technique shed light on her impulses and inhibitions, thereby unraveling (analyzing) the need to repress her assertiveness with its accompanying consequences for learning activities and important relationships in school. This sort of clinical formulation is common enough in practice and regularly yields sufficient enough clinical gain that there is seldom cause to question it.

Formulations of neurotic dissociation styled after *DSM-I* and *DSM-II* specified the criterion of amnesia for all or parts of the split-off material, confirming the basic assumption that the dissociation mechanism was successful as a neurotic defense in preventing (at least temporally or partially) certain ideas from crystallizing in full consciousness. A large conceptual shift occurred in *DSM-III* (1980), which portrayed neuroses in general as a vanishing species and relegated advanced level repressive activities to relative unimportance in psychiatry. The shift was partly based on the diminishing reported statistical incidence of neurosis, but many observers felt it was also based upon various political biases within the psychiatric community that have placed increasing emphasis on neurophysiological formulations in deference to psychological or psychoanalytic formulations.

DSM-III-styled thinking virtually obliterated the notion of dissociation as a neurotic level activity with the omission of amnesia as a necessary diagnostic criterion. Multiple personality disorder received its own classification under dissociative disorders in DSM-III. Braun and Braun (1979) have provided a brief diagnostic description that incorporates the shift in psychiatric conceptualization.

> [O]ne human being demonstrating two or more personalities with identifiable distinctive and consequently ongoing characteristics each of which has a relatively separate memory of its life history. . . . [T]here must also be a demonstration of the transfer of executive control of the body from one personality to another (switching). However, the total individual is never out of touch with reality. The host personality (the one who has executive control of the body the greatest percentage of the time during a time) often experiences periods of amnesia, time loss or blackouts. Other personalities may or may not experience this.

Does this shift in diagnostic thinking mean that dissociation cannot be nor perhaps ever was a form of repressive activity and that multiple personality involves more primitive splitting processes that are predominantly preneurotic? How are we to consider the radical increases in reported incidence in recent years? In what ways have the repeated showings of *Sybil* and other altered-state adventures on network television and widely publicized court defenses affected the emergence of altered states in the therapeutic situation? Do multiple personalities represent (as some observers suggest) an iatrogenic effect of a therapeutic technique (such as hypnosis), which tends to encourage or at least permit the therapeutic experiencing of altered states?

SALIENT THEMES FROM CLINICAL
RESEARCH AND LORE

Psychiatric Annals devoted its January 1984 issue to a series of updated reports from prominent researchers and clinicians in this area. Donald Schafer in June 1984 had reported on his impressions from a long-term multiple personality study group that he heads. Since that time a mushrooming literature suggests a marked increase in frequency of multiple personality diagnosis. Most authors in one way or another attribute this increased frequency to increased sensitivity on the part of members of the therapeutic community. The effects of media information on the clinical population seem to be, "It is okay to be a multiple, there are others like me." But some observers question even if multiple personalities exist or if the idea represents some sort of ruse people use to "get off the hook" for things they do. Legal implications regarding personal responsibility for activities sometimes cloud clinical issues.

The vast majority of reported cases are women (nine out of ten or at least four out of five). The chief etiological hypothesis is exposure to overwhelming experiences in early childhood, usually of a violent, intrusive sexual nature. The supposed early traumas are often reported as some form of incest perpetrated by an older or adult male, although mothers or other women are frequently named as co- or passive collaborators. More recently multiples present memories of satanic ritual abuse or abductions by aliens. Frequent homosexual themes are said to appear in male multiple personalities and are presumed etiologically related to the maleness of the molester. It is interesting to note that no other significant etiological hypotheses tend to be cited in the literature, although direct trauma or abuse cannot be confirmed and evidence of satanic cults and alien abduction is lacking in many cases. The possibility continues to arise that since the therapist expects to hear of early abuse, the person produces it —

certainly a possibility that has been noted often enough in other kinds of therapeutic research. In the earlier literature persons with multiple personalities are generally spoken of as being exceptionally intelligent with IQs often estimated to exceed 130, though that factor is not emphasized so much recently. High intelligence has sometimes been postulated as a key factor that kept the person from becoming seriously psychotic (Schafer 1984).

The central dynamic universally cited is based on the supposition that at the moment of severe stress part of the personality "defensively splits off." That is, altered states are said to emerge for the purpose of avoiding traumatic (sexual or violent) overstimulation. The effect of the split in terms of pervasiveness is said to range on a continuum from most of the person's conscious life to only occasional dissociations under conditions of severe stress in an otherwise intact personality. Schafer (1984) puts it, "a personality comes into existence when the personality already in existence can no longer tolerate the world. That new personality may then be brought back in parallel emotional situations." Researchers are not altogether clear on the nature of subsequent additional splits—whether later traumas that are different in character tend to produce altered personality states compatible with the type or source of the new trauma or whether splitting simply becomes adopted as a style with later splits representing attempts to cope with other aspects of one's personality. In using the concept of *defense* as a cause for splitting, researchers neglect to differentiate between "defense" meaning fending off real intrusions and "defense" as used in the more traditional sense of fending off unconscious wish/fear contents or psychic conflicts of various types. The diagnostic and therapeutic approach most often described is generally based upon the assumption that there was (in fact) traumatic abuse or seduction and that therapeutic benefit is best obtained through encouraging repeated abreactions related to the supposed realistic traumas. Since traumatic etiology and cathartic therapy approaches have repeatedly been found to be oversimplified in other areas of psychological research, they certainly must be questioned as the exclusive or effective explanatory hypotheses or as treatment approaches in multiple personality as well.

Much to their credit, hypnotherapists as a group seem to have been the earliest to sense this emerging and apparently highly hypnotizable clinical population. This is no doubt partly because hypnotists are trained to be sensitive and responsive to alternating states of consciousness. Perhaps they also tend by virtue of training to be more comfortable or at least less upset than the average therapist when strange or contradictory mental states begin emerging in psychotherapy. Perhaps hypnotherapists have less of a need to observe monistic, consistent personality functioning than other groups of psychotherapists. Responsible hypnotherapists are sensitive to the limits of hypnosis as a technique and are judicious in its application within an overall psychotherapeutic context. Braun (1984) states,

> I withhold the use of hypnosis until I have exhausted other means. One consideration is to avoid difficulties and criticism (including artifacts). A more substantial reason is that since these patients have been abused, I do not want to do something abruptly or early on that might be perceived as another assault. Spending extra time in observation and building rapport is generally worthwhile. [p. 35]

There also seems to be a general awareness in the hypnotherapy community that, especially with the multiple personality population, the hypnotic trance experience itself can be used as a way of evading social or unconscious issues. Conversely, Braun (1984) has pointed out that "heterohypnosis may facilitate rapport via its association with autohypnosis which has rescued them so many times before from overwhelming circumstances" (p. 36). There is limited recognition in the literature so far that hypnosis itself might well serve to constitute a replication of whatever early traumatic invasion the person might have experienced in the past. That is, the hypnotist may be unwittingly repeating the intrusion. To the extent that replication might be involved, the therapeutic approach that I will offer later has something to say.

The current prevalent assumption of an abusive etiology in early childhood suggests to most authorities a definite therapeutic direction—remembering and abreacting to the early trauma(s). In attempting such an approach, therapists speak of the importance of early establishment of rapport and trust. Further, it is generally deemed important to establish various indirect ways of obtaining data about the alter personalities since the main or host personality cannot be expected to be consistent and reliable.

Kluft (1984a, b) has elaborated a number of ways of inquiring indirectly about the alternate personalities. Kluft suggests that an inquiry might include questions about problems with memory, overwhelming experiences in one's lifetime, or as a child being called a liar or blamed for things one could not remember doing. The clinician may inquire about inner voices, imaginary companions, and autohypnotic experiences. Kluft indicates that most multiples had school problems and it is interesting to note what kind. For example, did the rest of the class seem to have been taught something that the person had missed? Has one ever found something in their possession that he/she cannot account for, such as personal articles, artwork, or handwriting? The therapist might inquire about perplexing incidents in relationships such as people behaving as if the relationship had been affected by factors they could not understand or explain. Perhaps people they don't know appear to know them on occasion and even to greet them by another name. Are there experiences of passive influence such as thoughts being put into one's head or being withheld from consciousness or sudden impositions of thoughts, feelings, or acts? Kluft suggests that the person maintain a journal in which for thirty minutes a day the person writes whatever thoughts seem to be present in his/her mind. Other personalities may announce themselves in the journal.

Most earlier authors report an extended therapeutic interval of perhaps a year or more as not unusual before a confirmed diagnosis of multiple personality is established. Putnam and colleagues (1983) reported a median of 6.8 years from time of initial therapeutic contact to diagnosis. That time has been shortened drastically in more recent years. Most of these people apparently do believe that something is wrong but they frequently cannot say quite what (Schafer 1984). Once a diagnosis is made and/or the alter personalities begin to appear in the therapeutic setting, therapists typically attempt to gather as much information as possible on the attributes and habits of the alters and eventually to establish names, ages, life histories, and times of emergence of each personality. Keeping careful notes and even a family tree of the various personalities has been suggested since the therapist can easily become confused. This material is then used by different therapists in various styles of working. Perhaps they inform the main personality of information provided by alters or encourage conversations among the various personalities. To the extent that the trauma theory is correct, the importance of remembering, restoring, and abreacting in some way to the traumatic scene is assumed to be central to the course of therapy. Interestingly, both patients and therapists often question the actuality of traumatic events reported or relived in the therapeutic setting (with or without hypnosis).

In addition to the "main," "host," or "birth" personality, another or a variety of "alter" personalities may be constellated. Sometimes these have names or telling nicknames and may have even been thought to have participated in an inner dialogue for years. They may have begun as imaginary companions. Some alter personalities emerge only slowly as therapy proceeds. They may take on designations such as "the bitch," "the rapist," "the competent one," "momma's little angel," "the anesthetic personality," "the memory trace personality," and so forth. There may be an opposite sex personality and perhaps even one or more homosexual or otherwise perverse personalities.

Allison (1974) has suggested the term *internal self-helper* (ISH) to designate the core of the personality that desires to be healthy. Schafer (1984) has commented that "the killer" personality often possesses considerable strength that the therapist can ally with. Suicidal and homicidally prone personalities often exhibit no understanding that all of the other personalities in the same body will be punished or die if the offending personality murders, commits suicide, or is killed.

Therapists working with multiple personalities have become accustomed to entering a subjective world in which sometimes characters switch rapidly, each in turn giving its special messages to the therapist. A therapist has more than once been used as a switchboard for intercommunication of the various characters until the time they can comfortably "talk to each other."

Most cases reported in the past have had relatively few personalities. For example, Taylor and Martin (1944) reported that forty-eight of the seventy-six cases they reviewed had only two personalities while twelve had three and only one had more than eight. Among modern cases "Sybil" had sixteen, "Eve" had twenty-two, and "Billy Milligan" had twenty-four. Kluft (1979) reported in one study a modal range of eight to thirteen personalities in a series of seventy. In a later study (1982) he reported 55.7 percent had between two and ten personalities while 44.2 percent reported eleven or more. The historical change in the number of personalities suggests either an emergent phenomenon or increased clinical sensitivity.

A certain *tone* often found in reports of multiple personalities may demonstrate how difficult it is even for therapists and researchers to completely free themselves from the amazing, awesome, otherworldly, unreal, or near-mystical qualities frequently associated with altered states of consciousness. For example, otherwise bright and objective researchers tend to report with a tone of awe or amazement (as if to challenge the reader's disbelief) that evoked EEG potentials, Rorschach protocols, or EKG tracings are markedly different when different personalities dominate. That cardiac arrhythmia or petit mal seizures can be prevented by the person's recognizing the physiological or prodromal signs and switching personalities may be presented in the literature as evidence for the existence of multiple personalities. Perhaps this tone derives its justification from the numerous attacks that have been made on practitioners involved in this area of work or some of the challenges posed in courts of law. The existence and influence of altered states apparently is still puzzling, troublesome, or even unbelievable to many.

Diagnostically, reports indicate that it is not unusual for multiples to have been previously diagnosed as hysteric or phobic or to have received any one of a variety of major (psychotic or character disorder) psychiatric diagnoses. A wide range of somatic or psychosomatic disorders frequently accompanies the multiple personality picture that require medical attention. Psychotropic drugs are considered at times to benefit one personality but simultaneously they may put other personalities out of commission, so drugs have tended to be used conservatively. Hospitalization tends to be advisable when a controlled environment for the expression of rage may be required or other disruptive psychotic manifestations occur.

Kluft (1984b) proposes a multidimensional treatment approach in which he sees the therapist's empathic capacities as often being greatly taxed. In speaking of hospital treatment he has a series of suggestions to make to therapists.

1. A private room should be provided so that the person will have a refuge for diminishing crisis situations.

2. The personalities should be met "as they are," calling the person by whatever name he or she desires at the moment and treating all alters with respect.

3. The therapist should not assume the responsibility for promptly being able to recognize each alter as it emerges nor try to play dumb.

4. Likely crises should be discussed with the staff in advance. They should be encouraged to phone the therapist rather than pressing extreme measures without consultation.

5. The ward rules should be personally explained by the therapist instructing all alters to listen. When amnesia or inner wars lead to infractions, the rules should be reexplained to the offending alter in firm but nonpunitive terms.

6. The therapist should consider excusing multiples from verbal group therapy (at least at first) since confusions often result for the patient and for other group members. Participation in art, music, and occupational therapy groups should be encouraged.

7. The staff should be warned that disagreements often arise in planning for and working with a multiple personality. The staff should be prepared to work through their disagreements gradually.

8. Issues of greatest priority should be focused on with the multiple rather than permitting minor mishaps to take center stage. Side issues frequently preoccupy the multiple patient.

9. The therapist should make clear that no other person should be expected to relate to the various personalities in the same manner as the therapist.[1]

Group therapy is often reported to be useful for increasing the time of therapeutic contact (though not necessarily with the same therapist) as well as producing the ameliorating effect of

---

1. A more recent but similarly conceived psychoanalytically informed institutional treatment approach has been put forth by Ganaway (1991).

knowing that there are others with similar difficulties. Caul (1984) has developed an interesting "internal group therapy" technique to be used judiciously. Joint patient and therapist videotape viewings of sessions in which the alter personalities have appeared can provide a valuable form of feedback to the patient if done in a collaborative and nonthreatening manner.

The age of confirmed diagnosis of multiple personality disorder tends to be between 18 and 30, with children seldom receiving this diagnosis. Early reports of treatment were characterized by extensive involvement with the therapist over a protracted period of time. Now it is generally believed (after Beahrs 1982) that the therapeutic relationship can usually be constructed and maintained on as little as an hour or two a week, perhaps with additional group time. Countertransference is regularly viewed in the literature as a potential danger since this clinical population can be experienced by a therapist as extremely demanding of time and energy if reliable boundaries are not set and maintained. Schafer (1984) sees five to seven years of several times a week psychotherapy as not unusual therapeutic contact for functional integration to occur with multiple personalities.

In attempting to make a differential diagnosis, most authors agree that multiple personalities are not overtly psychotic in the traditional sense of presenting delusions and hallucinations or their affects being radically out of control. Like schizophrenics, multiple personalities report "head voices" but the nature and content of these voices tends to be quite different (Schafer 1984). Schizophrenic auditory hallucinations tend to feature voices that are not always identifiable or are perhaps identified as mother or vaguely as a man or a woman who is castigating them harshly or telling them to do something. In contrast, the head voices of multiple personalities are more likely to have whole conversations with one another, often carrying on complex discussions and disagreements between the characters who frequently have names and assume various roles.

Schafer (1984) emphasizes distinguishing the true multiple from the "pseudo" multiple. The pseudo generally has a life history of social isolation through puberty, often having one or several imaginary companions that at that time are thought to become "introjected as internal characters." In contrast to the true multiple, when the therapist "calls out" one of the personalities, the pseudo may close his or her eyes and go through a variety of "getting into character" rituals or fantasies. The true multiple simply opens his or her eyes and "switches." At that moment he or she *is* the other personality. Schafer speculates that the pseudos are likely to show little real differences on EEG evoked potential or on psychological tests when in different characters whereas pronounced differences are reported in true multiples. Sociopaths in trouble with the law may indeed attempt to appear multiple but Schafer maintains these can be easily unmasked through common diagnostic procedures. On the other hand, most psychiatrists agree that occasionally multiples can and do have run-ins with the law when in alter personalities and since this is a psychiatric difficulty they do have a legal right to an opportunity for therapy.

Discussion of psychotherapy with multiple personalities tends to center around the notion of establishing trust so that traumatic situations that produced the original splitting can be remembered and abreacted to. The process is spoken of as making possible gradual "fusion" or "amalgamation" of personalities, which finally permits a "resolution of the conflict" and "integration of the personalities." Some quasi-religious techniques are based upon mystical or ritual exorcisms, but whatever beneficial effects may be appreciated by these techniques are not fully explainable at this time. Schafer (1984) makes it clear that each personality must be valued and respected if it is to be fully understood and finally traced to its origins, abreacted, and integrated.

Beahrs's (1982) approach in *Unity and Multiplicity* stresses that complete unity is not always necessary if all of the personalities remaining are fully aware of all of the others. His therapeutic aim is not so much for unity as for a person who does not need to split defensively, for a person who has developed new ways of handling stressful situations. Schafer (1984) holds that every important trauma must eventually be worked through. All reports in the literature portray successful treatment of multiple personalities as a long and arduous task, requiring continuous therapist availability. Availability is especially important during the working through phases of the psychotherapy since various personalities tend to emerge spontaneously, giving rise to confusions of all sorts.

Wilbur (1984) formulates that,

the ultimate goal is to fuse the alternates with one another and the original personality. . . . Fusion begins with the coming together of alternates who are close to one another and deal with the same or similar conflicts and affects. . . . As the affects are abreacted and the conflicts resolved, fusion often takes place automatically. Fusion, of course, can be encouraged or facilitated by suggestion, but in my experience fusions which occur through suggestions will come apart more readily than those that take place spontaneously. . . . Final resolution is the result of the total integration of all personalities into the birth personality. [pp. 28–31]

Marmer (1980) has published a quite interesting and detailed case study of a multiple personality treated with fairly standard psychoanalytic technique. His discussion revolves around Freud's concept of "split in the ego" and the use of self as a transitional object. In time his patient came to use her analyst in a transitional way, which made personality integration possible.

One can see from this brief review of the salient themes in the multiple personality literature that many questions remain unanswered and many paradoxes remain unresolved. It is my purpose to present a way of considering multiple personalities that is compatible with but basically different from the approaches discussed so far. But before going to the specifics of theory and technique that I wish to propose, I must outline briefly the listening perspective approach that I have spelled out in detail in *Listening Perspectives in Psychotherapy* (1983b).

THE LISTENING PERSPECTIVE APPROACH

The psychotherapeutic enterprise has been considered in a variety of ways over the past century. Central to any discussion of the nature of personal psychological dilemmas is the language and conceptual system in which the issues are framed. Ekstein (1984) has pointed out that implicit in each of the languages of psychotherapy and psychoanalysis is always a working technique. That is, we formulate issues in terms that reveal the way we tend or intend to work in the clinical setting. Far from being an objective or neutral way of considering issues in human lives, theories of psychotherapy and psychoanalysis have always turned out to be laden with various assumptions, values, and implied technical approaches. For example, Kohut (1984) has pointed out the hidden moralities in the Freudian and Kleinian criteria for cure (i.e., adult genital heterosexuality and post-ambivalent object relations). Kohut further acknowledges a strong value system implicit in his own self psychology approach (i.e., mature self to selfobject resonance.)

Post-Einsteinian science no longer assumes that there are observer-free, value-free, context-free, theory-free facts, but rather that we have defined a series of specified approaches for noting and interacting with the realities of the universe. In translating these notions to psychoanalysis, I have borrowed from the work of the philosophers Gilbert Ryle (1949), Ludwig Wittgenstein (1953), Jean-Paul Sartre (1956), and J. Michael

Russell (1978a,b; 1980) to demonstrate how four distinct listening perspectives have evolved in psychoanalytic and psychotherapeutic thought over the last 100 years (Hedges 1983). I have also reviewed the scientific paradigms used by quantum physicists and chaos theorists, which further point toward the importance of a listening perspective approach in psychotherapy and psychoanalysis (Hedges 1992).

In considering four vantage points for listening to people who address a therapist for the purpose of personal exploration, I have chosen a line of consideration known as "self and object representations" (following Jacobson 1954, 1964, and Sandler and Rosenblatt 1962). This approach finds it interesting and useful to consider the expanding psychoanalytic narrative in terms of how at any given moment in time the person experiences sensations or "representations" of self (ego, I) as distinguishable or indistinguishable from various sensations or "representations" of others. The criterion for making such inferences is not the verbal content or linguistic form of the narration (such as using "I," "you," or "they"), but rather *the manner or mode of relatedness actually being lived at the moment*. A very brief statement of each listening perspective should serve to clarify my general approach.

1. *The listening perspective of the constant self and the constant other* is a way of listening in which the speaker appears to be making a clear and reliable distinction between his or her needs, motivations, and activities, and those of others. Other people are considered and related to as separate (parallel, contrasting, or conflicting) centers of initiative. The activities and motivations of other people may be experienced as gratifying to, harmonious with, or frightening and dangerous to the needs and activities of a reliable unitary, consistent, and constantly experienced sense of self. It is within this listening context that "normal/neurotic" modes of relating that persist from the oedipal period of development have been defined. The specific

ways in which an oedipal child (aged 4 to 7) experiences loved ones tends to persist so that various expectations based on those separate but intimate relationships tend to be transferred to new people in subsequent life experiences. Until the last two decades all psychotherapies have been characterized by an implicit assumption of experienced separateness and constancies between selves and others. Most writers and clinicians still speak as though all people fully experience themselves as separate and constant centers of initiative.

2. *The listening perspective of the selfother* is a way of listening when the speaker's mode of address or activities indicates that the other person is *thought of* as separate but in fact *is being related to or used* as a part of or an augmentation of a fragile or nascent sense of self. Heinz Kohut (1971, 1977) has specified an era prior to the oedipal (i.e., Mahler's "rapprochement," [1968]) in which the growing child's sense of self relies upon various mirroring, twinning, and inspirational experiences in connection with important others (so-called selfothers or selfobjects). Kohut has shown the ways in which these grandiose, twinned and idealized aspects of self are transferred to others and has developed therapeutic techniques for analyzing what he has called narcissistic or selfobject transferences.

3. *The listening perspective of the symbiotic or merger object* is a way of listening to a speaker who may appear (linguistically or cognitively) to be making a distinction between self and other but who, in fact, fuses, entangles, or confuses the distinction in any of a variety of ways. Metaphorically, the merger experience is thought to date from the eras between 4 and 24 months of life that Mahler (1968) has called "symbiosis" and "separating." A young child is thought to engage with various close or important others in mutual cuing, which establishes more or less permanent modes or character styles of relating to other people. What mothers have come to call "the terrible two's" is thought to mark the (separating) opposition that a child may develop to relinquish the established symbiotic bonds. Individuation to the

later selfother era is facilitated by parental acceptance and containment of the separation-individuation activity. To the extent certain entrenched modes of fusing with, entangling with, or opposing the relatedness demands of early others are retained, the ongoing personality displays what have been called "borderline features." For listening purposes the concept of "scenario" captures and defines the interpersonal relatedness dimension or *interaction* that persists from the symbiotic or separating era and that tends to be replicated in subsequent relationships, especially the therapeutic one. That young toddlers internalize both active and passive roles of the scenario means that skills in "interpreting the countertransference" (Hedges 1992) are important.

4. *The listening perspective of the part-self and part-other* is a way of listening to a person whose basic modes of living and relating are of a "personality in organization." My work on "The Organizing Personality" (Hedges 1983a,b; 1992; 1994c) takes the position that infants organize basic sensorimotor and cognitive-affective systems in accordance with the way they *experience* various types of consistency or inconsistency in relationships with early others. Exposure to and assimilation of a consistent patterning of caretaking leads to a highly stylized, idiosyncratic symbiotic mutual cuing process with others. However, if for any reason (genetic, physiological, or environmental) the infant cannot experience and learn a consistent address for reliably available others, various incomplete or faulty organizational patterns are established that create a wide variety of limitations in cognitive controls and/or affective regulation. The early limitations of personality functioning may produce later psychotic indicators or simply give rise to a loosely or idiosyncratically organized individual. The "organizing personality" is thought to be in continuous search for connections with people but is generally not able reliably or consistently to sustain connections once they have been established. The patterns or styles of relatedness of the personality caught in continuous

organizing activities are in some sense so unchanneled, un-
formed, or unreliable that even connections that may become
established have no secure permanence.

The work of Franz Kafka illustrates the unending, confusing, and generally unrewarding or frustrating search that organizing personalities conduct in pursuit of organized modes of
establishing and maintaining reliable connections with the environment. Jerzy Kosinski's hero in *Being There* (1970) provides
another such example of a character in search of identity and
personhood who is only able to obtain limited, confusing,
changing, or ungratifying relationships. Hedges (1983a) has
developed the concept of "mimical self" to capture the qualities
of highly sophisticated mimicry or imitation of others that
characterizes personalities suspended in various forms of per-
petual organizing activity. A "mimical self" would be a formation
that precedes developmentally Winnicott's "false self" (1952),
which arises out of conforming to environmental demands in
deference to more authentic demands of the infant's nature. A
highly sophisticated mimical self is portrayed in David Hare's
1983 play *Plenty*.

THE LISTENING PERSPECTIVE APPROACH
WITH MULTIPLE PERSONALITIES

As mentioned earlier, the vast majority of persons in the
group now being defined as multiple personality are not readily
classifiable as neurotic (i.e., regularly suitable for the listening
perspective of self and other constancy). This is so by virtue of
the multitude of ego splits and the general failure of repression.
The multiples now emerging in clinical practice seldom address
the therapist narcissistically either, that is, the listening perspective of the selfobject is also largely inapplicable. In merger or
borderline states (the listening perspective of the symbiotic or

merger object), as puzzling as many of the symbiotic and separating scenarios can be to the clinician, the expectable feature stemming from early mutual cuing experiences is a reliable mode or set of modes for experiencing and engaging others. It may take the therapist several years to find ways of emotionally interacting with (joining, replicating and ultimately standing against) the highly idiosyncratic but stylized relatedness modes established during the symbiotic period. Understood in this way, "bad self" experiences might be split off from "good self" experiences and experiences of "bad" others might be split off from experiences of "good" others (Kernberg 1975, 1976). But a host of identifiable alter selves with various affective potentials would *not* be expected in the good–bad split. That is, borderline features are essentially definable as vestigial or retained modes of interaction based on extensive early symbiotic and separating mutual cuing experiences featuring more or less consistent but alternating affects.

As strange as many varieties of parent–child bonding may appear to an outside observer, in time the modes can be shown to be entrenched, reliable, and once understood, to make a certain special kind of sense within a given parent–child rearing context. Ultimately in the therapeutic study of borderline level personality features, the clinician begins to discern a "method in the madness." Certain relational demands and expectations that early on seemed puzzling, self-destructive, chaotic, fragmented, abusive, and so forth, slowly begin to form a pattern that is understandable or comprehensible in light of the developing creative narrative and narrational transference interaction reflecting the parental personalities and early life experiences. Analysis of the replicated transference in contrast to analysis of the transference neurosis, or the selfother transferences (at higher developmental levels) gives rise to a series of individuating boundary issues between the personality needs, activities, or personal space of the person and his/her therapist's activities, understandings, and personal space. These interactional modes and conceptual tools used with borderlines are likely to be minimally helpful in responding to the variety of (presymbiotic) organizational aspects presented by multiple personalities. The split-off selves portrayed by the multiple are born in isolation and disaffection rather than in interaction.

Despite what I have just said about multiples not being treatable in the same fashion as borderlines, it is important to notice that almost all of these lower-level personality features are indistinguishable from one another upon initial clinical presentation. Typically, a personality style or styles are presented to the clinician that represent the person's favorable and unfavorable capacities for adjusting to and conforming with important demands of the world. Winnicott (1952) has described the "false self" capacities that a person mobilizes in order to conform to early parental and later environmental demands. As an avenue for interacting the false self maneuvers arise in response to symbiotic or borderline developmental demands.

My central thesis is that multiple personalities represent the emergence and creative elaboration in the psychotherapeutic or psychoanalytic setting of a variety of early affect-ego states, and that they may be considered unintegrated "ego nuclei" (Glover 1932) or early centers of organizing experiencing. "False self," "mimical self," or "social self" adaptations may take many forms so that the person's life adjustment may be highly effective. The person may be a basically well coordinated, intelligent, pleasant, capable, and quite likable individual. The overall style and effectiveness of the social self may or may not have permitted awareness of various types of ego, self, or altered states that emerge at various times for various purposes. If we grant that in some sense all people have multiple selves or various frames of mind, moods, or affect-ego states, it is not difficult to understand how under various circumstances the usual, expectable, or hoped for integrating effect in personality formation might not have been completely achieved. Kohut's (1979) notion is that a unitary cohesive self develops because from the first day the mother addresses her child as if he or she had a self. The many affect-ego states of the first months of life are thought to come under the conditioning influence of what Mahler (1968) has called the symbiosis (4 to 24 months). Gradually in later individuation (Mahler's "rapprochement"), emerging individual self states may become admired, confirmed, and inspired under the influence of selfothers, thus bringing all of the early affect-ego states into what Kohut calls the cohesive self. The constant self and constant others of the oedipal period inherit this development. But the roots of the experience of multiple selves hark back to the earliest organizing affect-ego centers or ego nuclei before they have been brought into reliable unification through symbiotic bonding.

On the basis of recent clinical experience with narcissistic, borderline, and organizing states, we can now surmise that several difficulties might arise in the self consolidation process. These possibilities stand as clinical hypotheses regarding how we might view the experience of multiple selves in different individuals.

1. Integration of various self states may be *limited* due to faulty, inadequate, or insufficient age-appropriate consolidating experiences. Symbiotic bonding experience has been partial or incomplete so that only some affect-ego states are excluded.

2. Self consolidation may be warped or *deformed* through systematic conditioning experiences. The demands of bonding or later selfother experiences may continue to exclude or warp affect-ego states as they develop and leave some self states unintegrated.

3. The process of evolving a cohesive self may at any developmental era be *disrupted* by overstimulating experiences that interrupt or destroy the effectiveness or cohesion of tentative ego or self experiences causing a (perhaps even chronic)

*functional regression to previous unintegrated levels of affect-ego
states.*

4. Problems in the self consolidation sequence *may frequently undergo later repetitions or replications* fostered by persons
in the child's environment and/or invited by the child (usually
inadvertently) as a part of a chaotic or ineffective search for
connections with people. These later encounters are often so
intense that they produce regression and fragmentation to
earlier unintegrated states.

Current literature on multiple personalities places etiological emphasis on actual traumatic disruptions (item 3, above)
that were perpetrated by intrusive and/or abusive older persons
in the child's environment. But similar disintegrating effects can
be achieved in at least these three other ways. Access to multiple
early affect-ego states is retained to the extent that later opportunities are insufficient to coalesce early merged symbiotic selves
and a subsequent personal cohesive self. Certain types of symbiotic molding can promote a socialized or false self that fails to
integrate many early affect-ego nuclei. When the social self is
traumatized or has an opportunity to relax (as in psychotherapy), the more basic states or personality constellations may
become accessible.

The replication possibility (item 4, above) is difficult to
explain succinctly. In wandering, searching, organizing states or
certain established symbiotic ways of connecting with others, a
person may reach out to people in the environment in ways that
regularly serve to invite, induce, or seduce others to invade,
abuse, or molest him or her. This is *not* to say as we might in an
individual with more advanced symbiotic, narcissistic, or neurotic structures that the person "sets himself up" for abuse or that
a clear motivating repetition compulsion is engaged. Rather it
would appear that, lacking certain nuances of self consolidation
or social skill that ordinarily develop through satisfactory relations with people, the personality in organization moves about

the world almost as a ready or available target ("sitting duck") for those whose need is to intrude or abuse.

We have seen this kind of phenomena with brain defective and retarded children who are frequently abused and molested because they seek human contact and yet do not know how to prevent being taken advantage of. In a given instance some repetition compulsion or motivated phenomenon might or might not be detectable. But I suspect that most of the time these people as children, and often in many circumstances of adolescence and adulthood, simply miss (receptively and/or expressively) subtle social cues and fail to understand fully the implications of how abusive others approach them. And in their approach to others they may fail to understand exactly or fully what they are (inadvertently) making themselves available for. This point is sensitive and important since many clinicians have tended to think of the repetition compulsion as a way of holding the person responsible for social consequences of their activities. Or conversely, in not blaming the person who has received abuse, clinicians may miss an opportunity to understand what personality needs and features may have contributed to the person's availability as a target for various forms of abuse.

I wish to stress the importance of considering multiple etiological possibilities because a therapist committed to the position that a person with multiple personalities was invariably molested may become enmeshed in a serious and naive listening error. For the therapist to believe that each personality was necessarily created by another traumatic intrusion or that all early traumas must invariably be tracked down and catharted may also lead to grave listening errors. The content, memories, and affects produced in organizing states cannot be trusted in the same way that we tend to trust similar events and activities emanating from more integrated states. We have now studied enough about screen memories (Freud 1914), telescoped memories (Kohut 1971), and the workings of projective identification (Klein 1952) to know that anyone can produce memories and affects (with or without hypnosis) that are not veridical but contain significant emotional or phenomenological truths. A therapist would do well to keep to the task of encouraging the subtle growth of the therapeutic relationship and its analysis and to suspend judgment (permanently) on such matters.

My impression is that for every molest or abuse scene that can be narrated in psychotherapy or psychoanalysis, many more emotional experiences of a like genre have occurred that will not and probably cannot be narrated but are contained in moods, self-management styles, and longings for transformation (Bollas 1987). These statements bring us face to face with some of the many problems of therapeutic technique. I oppose considering the appearance of any memory, affect, or affect-ego state per se as evidence of anything. Therapeutic narrations stem from an ageless human tradition of myth making, storytelling, and cultural legends (Schafer 1976, Spence 1982). As such, the narrative truth of psychotherapy must be considered profoundly allegorical. Truth contained in narrations and allegories need not be confused with historical truths nor need its truth value in any way be discounted. But a naive listener believing the simple story at face value is in a poor position to consider the broader picture or to know how to call for an effective creative elaboration of various key elements of the narration. A naive therapeutic approach is bound to slow things down. An exclusive insistence on ascertaining and catharting to the effects of events remembered or perceived to be real runs the risk of failing to broaden the catharsis to include all similar events and then to move the concerns onto the plane of transference and countertransference. That is, the therapeutic value of straightforward historical truth pales by comparison to the rich possibilities of narrative truths that reach into all recesses of the mind and leave no emotional effect untouched.

Surely here someone will say, "But it is often so important for some of these people to be believed since many times they have tried to tell their stories and have been discounted." I say,

"Believe them for sure; but don't for one minute assume that the narration and its accompanying affect anywhere near tells the entire story—becoming too literal or too concrete means one only gets exposed to the tip of the iceberg. *Psychoanalytic empathy means keeping many possibilities of meanings simultaneously before us.*" By analogy, as therapists we must be able to take a conversion paralysis seriously, but an eventual therapeutic effect depends upon our also taking the person seriously in many other ways as well. In couples work we hear two versions of reality but seldom feel a need to side with one or the other as more true. So what can be our therapeutic approach to the multiple personality?

5

Understanding and Working with Multiples

PSYCHOTHERAPY AND PSYCHOANALYSIS WITH MULTIPLE PERSONALITIES

Ekstein (1984) maintains that the psychotherapeutic and psychoanalytical languages we use always contain hidden technique. I will begin by briefly surveying the treatment dimensions implicit in the listening perspective approach before specifying further treatment ideas related to multiple personalities. The four listening perspectives follow a developmental format for reasons of logic, consistency, and coherence. That is, one's listening interests might be specified in many different ways. The implicit value system of the listening perspective approach is not developmental, but rather one that places a premium on noticing the nature of each uniquely interacting analytic couple. It does not promote a value system that promotes mature development, or holds separation-individuation as an ideal, or promotes self cohesion, self and object constancy, or unity in personality as necessarily positive achievements. While these may all be worthwhile values, aims, and goals, they are misleading in analysis and sidestep what I take to be most important in our work — *developing the capacity to listen in the most comprehensive and flexible ways possible* to the person who has come to tell a story.

We can and often do define the development of human possibilities with an unfolding or growth metaphor that has a strong attraction because we know that living things grow and that complex functions can and do expand in surprising ways. To conceptualize psychoanalysis as a process to promote unfolding or growth is therefore tempting. One unfortunate consequence of succumbing to the temptation of the growth or developmental metaphor is that we then consider the therapist as some sort of a parent, teacher, guru, or gardener. Again, not a bad set of models to put before ourselves, but surely by now we are able to do better.

The listening perspective approach is organized around the chief task that faces the therapist or analyst — listening, not with our ears only, but with our entire being to what people have to tell us, to show us, to do to us, and have us do to them. Arranging one's listening perspectives along a developmental axis emphasizes the wide range of human activity to be communicated and considered in psychoanalysis and the various ways in which communication can be achieved. It further suggests that activities and engagements of most humans span the entire developmental continuum. Some of our most delightful moments are clearly infantile and some of our greatest sufferings spring from the most mature parts of ourselves. Further, conceptualizing psychoanalysis exclusively along either oedipal-neurotic, self psychological, or self and object representation lines necessarily limits which of the many features of an analytic hour we are likely to consider and narrows considerably what we believe our analytic function to be.[1]

---

1. I have considered the issues involved in values and empathy exten-

I find that even the most efficaciously conceived theories and therapeutic guidelines are in some sense utterly useless when I sit trying to contemplate and to appreciate the person before me. Who is this person? What does he or she want or expect from me and from our time together? What on earth will we come to do with one another? How will I manage to stay abreast of what is being shown to me? These are the questions with which I face each clinical hour – as much as possible, it is hoped, in the way Bion (1962) has suggested, without memory or desire, without undue preoccupation with the past or the future. A rich armamentarium of theories and techniques may indeed serve to reduce my fear of the unknown, but I can't imagine how they will help me – except as they sharpen my listening habits and open my mind to a wider range of listening possibilities each hour. The listening perspective approach thus promotes a value of individualized listening but specifies four broad categories of types of human activities and interpersonal engagements that we may expect to experience or hear about during analytic hours. In *not* considering these categories as developmental levels but rather as four distinctly different but simultaneously useful perspectives, vantage points, or positions from which to hear what is told to me, I realize that I am always adrift, never certain, and always appealing to the person before me for help in understanding how it is or was for him or her. I will now summarize a few of the implications that the listening perspective approach provides for the psychoanalytic hour.

The Constancy Perspective (For Neurotic Personality Organization)

In states of self and object constancy verbalizations and gestures can be assumed to be symbolically integrated and

---

sively under the heading, The Paradigm Shift in Psychoanalysis (Hedges 1992).

expressive of often disparate or conflicting feelings or thoughts. Because the constancy mode is predominantly an individuated way of reacting and interacting, both members in the analytic couple can generally rely on some degree of mutual restraint and rapport within a contractual atmosphere containing a certain degree of emotional distance or separateness (i.e., "the therapeutic frame"). All that Freud taught about wishes, conflicts, dreams, symbols, impulses, defenses, compromise formations, and so forth can be assumed to be operating as neurotic transference configurations. What one experiences as inner life is basically, or will through analytic narrations ultimately be, connected to or accessible through verbalization and verbal-symbolic interpretations. In constancy states a person seeks out and perpetuates complex cognitive-affective states and interactions. These complexes can be expected to appear in therapy as neurotic transferences and eventually to be largely resolved through a creative narrational process involving verbal-symbolic interpretation, insight, and working through.

The Selfother Perspective (For Narcissistic Personality Organization)

Selfobject states are communicated partly by verbalization but usually are most evident in the orienting or approach of the person to the analyst. Although the analyst is known to be separate, emotional affirmations, confirmations, and inspirations are actively sought from the selfother analyst. Kohut has formulated these trends as having the purpose of completing or coalescing the sense of self. Transference repetitions usually take the form of disappointments with the functioning of the analyst (so-called selfother failures), which result in various forms of stressed, tense, and/or disturbed behavior. If the therapist can acknowledge the failure and correct his/her understanding with empathic words or gestures, the self gradually develops the capacity to maintain constancy and cohesiveness without such frequent, intense, or archaic selfobject supports.

The Merger Perspective (For Borderline Personality Organization)

Merged or borderline states take on as many forms as there are parent–child dyads in the world. When the original mode or patterning of relatedness can be achieved in the therapeutic relationship, a sense of wholeness ensues, even if that pattern may seem grim, depriving, or somehow abusive to an outside observer. Preverbal idiosyncratic patterns are always difficult to grasp. Verbalization by the client only rarely or partly provides the therapist access to the scenarios that the person must actively live out or replicate in the emotional interchange of therapeutic relationship. Countertransference responsiveness often serves as the "royal road" to understanding borderline scenarios (Hedges 1983b, 1992). Countertransference responses serve as informers providing rough approximations of the (passive or active) merged states being sought after and lived out. *Interpreting the Countertransference* (Hedges 1992) involves the therapist being able to speak the countertransference experience in such a way as to show a recognition of the infant side of the mother–child interaction. Only after emotional togetherness is in some way achieved is the therapist's knowledge of the scenario or scenarios sufficient to be able to engage in activities that promote separating and individuating modes. The false or socialized self constellation that may seem cooperative with the treatment must ultimately be confronted as *not* operating in the person's best expressive interests.

The Organizing Perspective (For Use with Various Psychotic States and the Personality in Organization)

Every infant's perceptual-motor and cognitive-affective systems organize around various available features in the immediate caretaking environment. The wide range of affective responses in the early months of life is subtle and may appear limited because the infant has so few ways of communicating. The unobservant or untrained adult may only perceive pleasure-pain potentialities since these match the best available communication modes. In therapy, quests for connection to the person of the therapist or for experiences with various part-aspects of the therapist or the early self-other milieu are bound to take many forms that may seem as puzzling to the therapist as the seemingly odd things that infants seem to request from their parents. Affective states vacillate widely and rapidly. The phenomenology of experience is unpredictable and psychic content often seems controlled by forces other than human volition. Delight in and study of various sensorimotor and cognitive-affective experiences with available others predominate. Many infants learn to flee from traumatic or overstimulating human contact in various ways or to organize their cognitive-affective systems in idiosyncratic ways that may change rapidly and vary widely (Tustin 1981). Such fluctuations may make it difficult for a therapist or observer who is functioning in a more stable organized state to empathize. Transference expresses the internalized modes of disconnecting used by the earliest (m)other. Rupturing of interpersonal contact and continuity is the hallmark of personality functioning at the organizing level. This is vividly manifest in the multiple "switching." In a therapeutic milieu that permits the emergence of organizing states, largely freed of the burden of false self conformity but not the effects of mimicry, the personalities of the multiples have maximal opportunity for creative elaboration and expression. The search for contact and the many (transferential) ruptures become the focus for study in this listening perspective.

RECOMMENDED THERAPEUTIC APPROACHES TO MULTIPLE PERSONALITIES

Every experienced psychotherapist or psychoanalyst has developed his or her own individual working style and has explicitly or implicitly adopted a set of theoretical constructs that provides a consistent backdrop and justification for that style. In my view, what the analyst says he or she is doing is invariably embodied in an impersonal theoretical framework and is not nearly so important as the personal availability and consistent listening attitude that he or she is able to establish and maintain during the analytic hour. I believe that actual working techniques are primarily a matter of personality and choice and that the analytic work goes forward so long as the person in analysis continues to sense that he or she is being heard or responded to according to his or her individual expressive and interactional needs. While this is not the place to spell out my epistemological views of psychotherapy and psychoanalysis, the foregoing comments will perhaps serve to orient the reader to my general preference for elaborating *perspectives* from which to listen, rather than defining psychiatric features to be identified and manipulated.

What has traditionally distinguished psychoanalysis from the other therapies has been close systematic attention to the developing transference neurosis, that is, the emergence in the analytic relationship of features that characterized the child's oedipal relationships. As psychoanalytic inquiry has broadened its scope to include pre-neurotic personality constellations, the distinguishing feature of an emerging transference neurosis per se is no longer expectable in analytic work with preoedipal states. However, the history of the study of oedipal transference neurosis provides a relevant context for contrasting the expectable clinical effects now being spoken of as "selfobject transferences," "borderline replications," and "organizing connections." Each of these four sets of relational phenomena can be expected to characterize certain developmental configurations and to become available to analytical attention through each of the four listening perspectives. Each set of experiences or attitudes may be thought of as built upon or growing out of the successes and failures of previous layering(s) of experience.

Thus, when considering the listening context for higher

organizational aspects, features from each of the lower constellations may well make an appearance at various points in the analysis. Conversely, when considering a listening context for lower level organizational aspects, one does not necessarily expect that aspect to be meaningfully integrated with or connected to other (similar or parallel) aspects or to be fully integrated with higher order organizational achievements. According to this use of the developmental metaphor, we would expect at more differentiated levels to hear strivings for a more integrated, cohesive, monistic and separate sense of "I," while at less differentiated levels various disparate, unintegrated, confusional, partial, or pluralistic "I's" will be more apparent.

It is my belief that during the last decade hypnotherapists and developmental psychoanalysts have been more prepared than ever to hear and to experience in the clinical setting these unintegrated and often contradictory aspects of early self development and that this preparedness has contributed to a general atmosphere in which the configurations found in multiple personality pictures can now emerge with greater frequency and clarity. To say this, however, does not in any way imply iatrogenesis in the usual sense that the treatment causes the illness. It would be more accurate to say that since Freud first opened his ears to hear the hidden features of hysteria, the history of our field has been one of creating a body of knowledge of how to create an empathic listening atmosphere in which elusive aspects of personality have an opportunity to be interpersonally experienced, expressed, and transformed. Basic organizational aspects of personality are not thought to be readily accessible for therapeutic study via the usual verbal-symbolic, introspective modes of investigation that have characterized the analysis of neurotic and narcissistic configurations. Nor are they available to interactive modes of investigation or systematic countertransference studies commonly used in understanding the symbiotic and post-symbiotic relatedness encountered in borderline personality organization. The investigative mode for listening to aspects of personality arrested at the organizing level necessarily becomes that of interception (Hedges 1983b). Organizing personalities must be met (intercepted, contacted) during moments of sensorimotor extension in order for the organizational impetus to be understood by the observer and in order for the impact of the inconstant contrasting configurations of the (part) other to be experienced and registered in the emerging personality formation along with various experiences of (part) selves. The crucial implication of this line of thinking is that therapeutic connection with early organizational aspects of personality usually will *not* be possible through extensive analysis of symbolic or body-symbolic representations (the so-called symptom constellation) since these manifestations are secondary or reactionary to faulty early object relations. That is, psychotic phenomena represent abortive attempts at self stabilization or self nurturing and soothing that only seldom include representations favorable for realistic relatedness to others. Grave therapeutic limitations have been repeatedly demonstrated through exclusive reliance on (1) extensive analysis of the symbolic content of the psychotic life, (2) therapeutic immersion in the subjective psychotic world, and (3) systematic utilization of countertransference reactions to (the fragmenting/withdrawing aspects of) psychosis.

The infant, child, or adult whose personality is arrested at or regressed to early organizing attempts is usually seen as living in a world of his/her own. The nurturing, soothing, pacifying other must patiently wait until the infant or person is momentarily oriented for contact with the other. The child Celeste reported by Ekstein (1979) played quietly every day in her therapist's room until at last representations began to emerge in the form of small Kleenex figures that begin to relate silently to one another until the magic day when one special Kleenex figure approached and came to rest on the therapist's shoe! Had the therapist intruded on her play before she was ready to acknowledge his presence he would no doubt have been repeating the intrusive trauma of her infancy. The therapist's work consists of creating an atmosphere in which sensorimotor extensions can be met or intercepted when they occur. In Bollas's (1987) language, the task of the mother/other is to be available to assist in the transformation of various self states as they occur. Stimulating experiences produced by internal states as well as experiences produced by impinging external stimuli are intercepted with affective containment and pacification, thus teaching (almost by classical conditioning) the possibility of altered or transformed states. Adequate interceptive pacification experience leads to mutual cuing, which characterizes the "protective shield" (Khan 1963) of the symbiotic envelope or canopy. Subsequently overwhelming states are only experienced during the absence of the symbiotic partnering experience (Hedges 1983a).

In taking this general approach to the early organizational aspects of personality formation I have specified several critical listening dimensions, discussed in the following subsections.[2]

Reflexive Mental States

Freud (1900, Chapter VII) first described elemental mental processes as "reflexive." While many writers speak of early mental states as unintegrated, segmented, disintegrated, or fragmented, such terms reveal an observer bias or describe confused or pluralistic states, but fail to describe fundamental organizing processes. Images in earliest mental states, according to Freud, can be thought of as passing reflexively forward and backward along a reflex arc, whereas a later buildup of memory traces causes the arc to become unidirectional. Freud's conceptual model prepares clinicians to listen for often confusing and

---

2. These and other dimensions for listening to organizing personality structures are discussed in detail with case illustrations in Hedges, 1994c.

fragmented reflexive sensorimotor and cognitive-affective experiences passing into and out of awareness with hallucinatory vividness. Observation of reflexive mental processes is frequently obscured by regressive phenomena such as those seen in psychotic symptoms and in multiple personalities the rapid switching from personality to personality.

Nonhuman Imagery

Victor Tausk's (1919) classic paper on "The Influencing Machine" was the first of a long series of psychoanalytic formulations that have highlighted the dominance of nonhuman imagery in early personality organization. Searles's (1960) focus on *The Nonhuman Environment* has clarified the kinds of relatedness that tend to characterize organizing processes. His careful delineation of mechanical, impersonal, and supernatural forces that govern the nonhuman world prepares the analytic listener for a special nuance of observation and interpretation that operates in attempts to organize sensorimotor and cognitive-affective experience. Searles's attention to the mystical, mythical, totemistic, and animalistic sheds light on a wide range of possible interpretations of sensorimotor and cognitive-affective phenomena that are likely to figure in one way or another in any given person's effort to organize and relate to perceived dimensions of the world. The mechanical or nonhuman features of organizing experiences are frequently found in multiple personalities in a particular "robot" personality or can be seen to operate in the way that the personalities interact with one another or in which certain personalities interact with the world. Content involving demons and devil worship, as well as mystical, otherworldly, or past life experiences and vivid "memories" of uncontrollable beatifications and atrocities all feature the nonhuman aspects that can be expected to constitute as "real" in organizing states.

The Centrality of Bodily Sensations

The early organizational strivings that form the core of what is to become known as the self begin with cognitive-affective sensations and sensorimotor operations. Mahler (1968) and Tustin (1981) in their studies of disturbed children have regularly observed preoccupations with and exaggerations of various sensory experiences. Sensations or hypersensitivities often represent more than simply symptoms, but rather must be listened to in the context of developing potentialities for personality integration and functioning. A preoccupation with body parts and sensations is clearly the essence of the organizing process. Various forms of focus on the body range from somatic symptoms to sharply distinguished perceptual experiences in different personality states of multiples. As with psychosomatic indicators, many features encountered in multiple personalities are usefully considered as somatic sensations or states that have not found psychic representations that can be integrated within the ongoing fabric of personality.

The Transformation of Primary Sensation and States

As a therapist first assumes a place in the life of the organizing personality, it will likely be in a transforming role. Bollas's (1987) discussion of the "transformational object" contributes fundamentally to an understanding of the listening context of psychotherapy. Earliest experiences of parenting involve the transformation of bodily functions and mental states. Bollas points out that Freud (forgivably) failed to take note of the fact that the analytic situation itself constitutes an "acting out" of the early transformational experience. A person arrested in an organizing state is presumed to have suffered deficits and/or traumas in the early transformational processes. While the person may sometimes be quite ready to have the deficits (usually various dependency needs) responded to by the therapist, the traumatized areas pose more of a problem. Early parental omissions and commissions missed their mark in some way, resulting in various affective and cognitive constructions that are not integrated within the entire personality structure. An awareness that the transformational processes themselves may enhance or thwart the therapeutic connection with organizing personalities suggests a new kind of listening concern. The therapist must be content to set aside verbal and even interactional approaches in deference to the more crucial role of promoting micro-transformations of various early developing self states through contact or interceptive pacification until the mutual cuing of the analytic couple can become an important factor. Bollas (1982), following Winnicott, has subsequently developed his ideas to include a therapeutic regression to dependency, which includes attention to primary cognitive-affective and sensorimotor experiences in the presence of and with the aid of the analyst.

The Establishment of Mutual Cuing

Sensitive noninterfering work with all varieties of organizing personalities may be expected to lead toward mutual cuing processes between basic personality dimensions of the therapist and elemental aspects of the organizing personality. In the multiple personality, as the therapist responds to each different self and attempts to understand the various selves and, in turn, their relations to one another and to various experiences of others, a reliable communication system (largely nonverbal or paraverbal at first) will begin to evolve. Searles (1979) has depicted psychoanalysis with this level of personality organization as consisting of the formation of a "therapeutic symbiosis" — a symbiosis *de novo* — followed by successive phases of individuation. Both members of the analytic couple have the eventual task of individuating from the symbiotic union in such a way as to be able to honor the other's separateness and individuality. Searles's notion of the therapeutic symbiosis can prepare the analytic listener for the gradual emergence of a mutual cuing process based upon the establishment of ways of handling needs that each has in the relationship. Only after the holding (Modell 1976) and containing (Bion 1962, 1963) functions are smoothly in operation as a symbiotic relatedness pattern can the individuation process be expected to go forward in multiple personality work. The functional integration of various aspects of self slowly proceeds as the therapist is consistent in addressing the person as a single unitary self. I have suggested that various "personalities" be addressed in the spirit of always recognizing each as a part of the whole person. None of us is ever so integrated as to be totally without multiple self states.

Fusion and Confusion of Identities

Elemental organizing processes usually do not include reliable differentiation of self or various selves and/or others. Klein's (1952, 1975) discussion of infantile greed and envy may help to specify expectable positions that the organizing person may assume vis-à-vis the therapist. More importantly, her concept of projective identification points to an expectable blurring or indistinctness of early self-other relatedness, which is bound to be a part of the listening situation with organizing personalities or with organizing states in persons primarily integrated at other levels. While the essence of creativity is the projection into the parameters of the world a vision or belief that is then taken back into the self as reality, relatedness on the basis of projective identification is likely to have significant interpersonal effects that can eventually become the focus of careful clinical scrutiny. Frances Tustin's work with autistic states (1981) formulates ways in which young children may wall off, encapsulate, or confuse their identities with mother. She has developed fascinating treatment techniques for making contact with people in such states.

The Movement toward Transitional Activities

Various objects and activities may become part and parcel of the processes of sensorimotor and cognitive-affective experiences and transformations in organizing states. Relationships with inanimate (hard and soft) objects and part-aspects of the therapist and others may be understood as a beginning concrete means of manipulating or controlling various sensorimotor and/or cognitive-affective experiences. Winnicott (1953) has written of the first "not-me" possession as a transitional object that simultaneously symbolizes mother in her absence while it remains under the child's manipulation and control. Winnicott broadens "transitional" to include many other phenomena that have in common the quality of representing something uncontrollable in a controlled guise. The worker with multiple personalities will quickly understand many representations, transactions, and personality features serve this transitional function. Transitional use of a talisman, photos, tape recordings, gifts, and other less tangible phenomena can be expected to mark the transitional phase in therapy with organizing states.

Disruptions in the Personality Functioning
of the Therapist

Empathic contact with elemental organizing processes inevitably entails disruptions in the personality functions of a parent or therapist. Giovacchini's (1975, 1979a, b) penetrating focus on the disruptive effects that "primitive mental states" regularly have on the personal and professional integrity of the therapist points to very special listening problems. Giovacchini speaks of "the impact of the delusion" to refer to both the positive and negative effects that the person's experiences of reality have on the comfort and identity of the therapist. His discussions of the problems involved in maintaining, losing, and regaining the analytic stance prepare the clinical listener for disruptions in his or her personality functioning when working with organizing and multiple personality states. Giovacchini indicates that often interventions and maneuvers must be undertaken by the therapist so that the therapist can continue functioning as a therapist. Anticipating disruptions in the therapist's personality functioning and being prepared to undertake tactics or maneuvers designed to maintain the therapeutic stance or to shore up the personality functioning of the therapist constitutes an important contribution to clinical listening with organizing and multiple personalities.

There are several kinds of countertransference to organizing states that can be expected by listeners working the organizing experience, as discussed in the following subsections.

Denial of Human Potential

The most common form of countertransference has seen organizing personalities as witches, evildoers, hopelessly psychotic, and in other ways not quite human. In this attitude is a denial of human potential and a denial of the possibility of being able to stimulate desire in such a way as to reawaken it and to analyze blocks to human relating. We hear: "I can't reach you, you are too sick. You are untreatable so we will lock you up or give you drugs to sedate or pacify you."

Fear of Primitive Energy

When an analytic listener invites the organizing experience into a transference relationship, he or she is asking that the full impact of primitive aggressive and sexual energies of the analytic speaker be directed squarely at the person of the listener. Listeners fear the power of this experience because it can be quite disorienting and, if not carefully assessed and monitored, potentially dangerous. But fear of basic human affectivity is irrational and we now have at our disposal many rational ways of inviting and managing the organizing level affects and energies. The key technical consideration is not whether the person on the basis of *a priori* criteria is "treatable," but whether the listener has sufficient holding and supportive resource available to him or her on a practical basis to make the pursuit of treatment practical and safe for all concerned.

Encountering our Own Organizing Experiences

When we as listeners invest ourselves emotionally in reaching out again and again to an analytic speaker only to be repeatedly abandoned or refused, it stimulates our own most primitive experiences of reaching out to our own mothers during our organizing developmental period, hoping for a response and feeling traumatized when the desired response was not forthcoming. Our own "psychotic mother" transference can reappear projected onto the analytic speaker as we attempt to provide systematic and sustained connection for people living organizing states. How each of us as an individual practitioner develops staying power is the crucial question. Our own therapy is essential as is consultation with colleagues during trying phases of this work. Attempting to work the organizing experience without adequate resource and backup support is like a single mother trying to manage a difficult or sick baby while holding down a job to support herself, caring for several other children, and trying to live some life of her own. We need support to do this very taxing kind of work.

Empathy Leading to Breaks in Contact

After the preliminary phases are well under way, that is, after the two have established basic working rhythms that are comfortable and safe, and after the listener has been able to discern and bring up for discussion the specific ways in which the speaker engages in the searches for contact and then cuts off contact, we notice the speaker begins excitedly to see in outside contacts as well as in the analytic hour how the breaking of contact is being regularly accomplished. Speakers in analysis are often excited by the therapeutic process at this point because for the first time in their lives something is finally making sense about themselves. They begin a valiant struggle to maintain contact nearly everywhere they go, especially with the listener. Then we notice a tendency on the part of the analytic listener to begin withdrawing into inattentiveness, preoccupation, or even drowsiness. This type of countertransference activity, which tends to occur only well into the treatment process, represents the listener's empathy for the terror that contact provides for the speaker. That is, the speaker for the first time in his or her life feels that he or she is hot on the trail of something that promises human satisfaction—sustained contact. But in the person's enthusiasm to achieve as much contact as possible as fast as possible, it is the listener who senses the internalized danger and in some way is deliberately (consciously or unconsciously) slowing things down a bit. This countertransference reaction can be spoken to the speaker so that the two may gain a fuller appreciation of the joys and dangers of human contact.

Once again the developmental metaphor may help us to conceptualize the transforming and/or integrating functions that the psychotherapist or psychoanalyst serves for the multiple personality. The basic task of the neonate appears to be that of organizing and integrating a wide variety of sensorimotor and cognitive-affective experiences in relation to (m)other. The child who is empathically met (contacted, intercepted) in moments of sensorimotor or cognitive-affective extension is able to use people in his or her environment as the organizing, synthesizing principles and to move toward the development of the symbiosis with the (m)other. A child whose extensions are not met in timely fashion or whose peaceful states are intruded upon carelessly will remain to some degree perpetually caught in a searching, organizing, unintegrated state. Development of good intelligence and good social skills may constitute what I have called a "mimical self" or a later constellation of a "false self" or "social self," which is more or less successful in imitating or adapting to the demands of the world, but the person remains in certain important respects outside the pale of human relatedness. A personality arrested at or regressed to organizing states may or may not show signs of attempts at secondary restitution (psychosis) either through exaggerated affects or nonconventional thinking. Recent observations have suggested that there are many more persons functioning at the organizing level than has been previously recognized. One variety of these heretofore invisible organizing features is recently appearing on the clinical scene as the multiple personality.

SUMMARY AND CONCLUSIONS

The remarkable recent increase in reported incidence of multiple personality disorders has stimulated many questions regarding how to understand these altered state phenomena and what approaches might provide optimal therapeutic or analytic responsiveness. Four developmentally derived listening perspectives were summarized that are thought to be ways of listening and responding to four major levels or styles of personality organization. The expectable listening features for neurotic, narcissistic, borderline, and organizing states were defined. In principle, an individual's personality might be dominantly organized in one or another style or mode, but the multiple selves phenomena are thought to be derived from early cognitive-affective organizing states or affect-ego nuclei. By implication, listening to multiple self states in terms of constancy, selfobjects, or scenarios is likely to detract from the therapeutic process.

Four complementary etiological hypotheses have been considered: (1) limited early integration, (2) warped or deformed self-consolidation, (3) overstimulating disruptions, and (4) replicated intrusions. Simultaneous consideration of all four possibilities is a safeguard against biased or naive clinical listening. Considering the profoundly allegorical and narrational context of psychotherapy and psychoanalysis can prevent faulty listening, which stems from an exclusive concretizing emphasis on abreaction of traumatic memories and affects.

Optimal listening and responsiveness according to the listening perspective approach places an emphasis on the relatedness dimension. That is, the mode of self and other relatedness being experienced and lived at any given moment will determine the therapist's choice of response. Meeting, intercepting, or *contacting* various affective-cognitive states in moments of sensorimotor extension is taken as the optimal mode of therapeutic responsiveness for working with features of personality "in organization."

Eight expectable dimensions have been defined to enrich the listening context in work with the organizing features found in multiple personalities.

1. Reflexive mental states passing into and out of awareness with hallucinatory vividness.
2. Utilization of nonhuman imagery.

3. Preoccupations with somatic sensations.
4. Transformations of self states.
5. The establishment of mutual cuing.
6. Fusion and confusion of identities.
7. The movement toward transitional activities.
8. Disruption in the personality functioning of the therapist.

The key to transformational analytic work with multiple personality formation is the analysis of the organizing or psychotic transference. Organizing transference is a structure that spontaneously appears just as the person orienting for human contact begins to feel the threat of the engagement. "Something happens" (often silently, invisible to the therapist) so that the developing interpersonal contact is ruptured or not sustained. Therapeutic technique is aimed at finding ways of interpreting the transference that motivates contact rupture. The interpretation is a variant of, "Your past experience tells you it is not safe to stay connected to me, but that simply isn't true. You can connect to me, take things from me, give things to me, and permit us both to enjoy the relationship."

The current emphasis in research and lore on an invariably traumatic or seductive etiology and the importance of fostering a revival of memories with emotional abreactions has been challenged. Broadening the therapeutic or analytic approach through the elaboration and utilization of listening perspectives is justified on epistemological, scientific, and clinical grounds. The treatment of multiple personality requires a thorough understanding of how to work with the organizing or psychotic transference and resistance. Viewing the emergence of various affect-ego states as a creative way of expressively elaborating oneself in a psychotherapeutic setting goes a long way toward removing the magical, mystical, or pathological emphases that have proven confounding in past work with multiple personality formations.

PART III

THE DUAL RELATIONSHIP IN PSYCHOTHERAPY

6

The Problem of Duality

INTRODUCTORY COMMENTS: THE RISE AND FALL OF THE "DUALITY" CONCEPT

In 1973 The American Psychological Association Code of Ethics, in an effort to curb sexual exploitation in the psychotherapeutic relationship, opened Pandora's box when it coined the term "dual relationship." Since then, like Pandora's miseries which spread evil throughout the world, every aspect of the psychotherapeutic relationship has been colored with continual concern, frustration, and doubt. The faulty shift of ethical focus from "damaging exploitation" to "dual relationships" has led to widespread misunderstanding and incessant naive moralizing which has undermined the spontaneous, creative, and unique aspects of the personal relationship which is essential to the psychotherapeutic process.

The atmosphere in the community of practicing psychotherapists which has been created by ethics committees and licensing boards now amounts almost to hysterical paranoia. It is as though some sort of witch-hunt is afoot, and no practicing therapist has a clean conscience when guilt is being dished out about the subtle potentials of dual relating! The bottom line is that dynamic and systems-oriented psychotherapies cannot be practiced without various forms of dual relating and every therapist knows this. But we have wrongly been told that dual relating is unethical.

The good news is that the pendulum has started swinging back and a hefty dialogue clearly lies ahead of us. The American Psychological Association (APA) Insurance Trust maintains that not all multiple roles are dual relationships. But the implication is still that "duality" may be unethical. The recent code of ethics for the California Association of Marriage, Family, and Child Counselors categorically states that "not all dual relationships are unethical." And the revised (December, 1992) APA Code of Ethics at last returns us to sanity:

> In many communities and situations, it may not be feasible or reasonable for psychologists to avoid social or other nonprofessional contacts with persons such as patients, clients, students, supervisees, or research participants. Psychologists must always be sensitive to the potential harmful effects of other contacts on their work and on those persons with whom they deal. . . . Psychologists do not exploit persons over whom they have supervisory, evaluative, or other authority such as students, supervisees, employees, research participants and clients or patients. . . . Psychologists do not engage in sexual relationships with students or supervisees in training over whom the psychologist has evaluative or direct authority, because such relationships are so likely to impair judgement or be exploitative. . . . Psychologists do not engage in sexual intimacies with current patients or clients. . . . Psychologists do not accept as therapy patients or clients persons with whom they have engaged in

sexual intimacies [and] do not engage in sexual intimacies with a former therapy patient or client for at least two years after cessation or termination of professional services. . . . The psychologist who engages in such activities after the two years following cessation or termination of treatment bears the burden of demonstrating that there has been no exploitation, in light of all relevant factors. [p. 1.17]

Thus, after twenty years of grief, the term *dual relationship* as an ethical definition has been entirely eliminated from the revised APA code. The current ethical focus is on remaining mindful of the ever-present possibility of damaging exploitation. But the malignant concept of dual relationship that the APA introduced and has now eliminated has infected ethics committees, licensing boards, and malpractice litigation everywhere. We still have a major battle ahead to undo the severe damage done to the psychotherapeutic relationship by the pejorative use of the term *dual relationship*.

THE CASE FOR DUAL RELATIONSHIPS

As the pendulum swings back, such writers as Kitchener (1988), and Tomm (1991) argue that dual relationships need to be considered more carefully. Here are the main points that have emerged to date. (1) Dual relating is inevitable and offers many constructive possibilities. (2) Dual relationships are only one way an exploitative therapist or an exploitative client may take advantage of the other. (3) Metaphors are mixed when duality is treated as a toxic substance that "impairs judgment." (4) A priority of emphasis on the professional *role* serves to diminish personal connectedness, thereby fostering human alienation and endorsing a privileged role hierarchy. (5) Exploitation in relationships is always exploitation and unethical, regardless of whether it occurs in a dual context. (6) Multiple connections that cross boundaries between therapy, teaching, supervision, collegiality, and friendship can be celebrated as part of the inevitable and potentially beneficial complexities of human life. (7) The power differential in any relationship can be used to empower the personal and/or professional development of both parties as well as to exploit them. (8) A frequent therapeutic goal involves helping students, supervisees, and clients understand and negotiate the multiple and shifting layers of human relatedness and human relational systems. (9) It is preferable to humanize and to democratize the therapeutic relationship rather than to encumber it with unnecessary trappings of professional expertise and higher authority. (10) The therapeutic role can be misused by cloaking it in paternalistic, patronizing attitudes of emotional distance and myths regarding superior mental health of practitioners. (11) Incompetent and exploitative therapists are the problem, not dual relating. (12) What is needed by therapists is classification and discussion of the subtle kinds of exploitation that can and do occur in professional relationships, not a naive injunction against dual relating. (13) To categorically prohibit dual relationships reductionistically implies that there is no continuity or overlap in roles in relationships and that therapy can be separated from the person of the therapist. (14) Dual relationships are inevitable and clinicians can conduct them thoughtfully and ethically, making whatever happens "grist for the mill." (15) Dual relationships represent an opportunity for personal growth and enriched human connection that benefits both parties. (16) Human connections evolve spontaneously and change over the course of time naturally and unpredictably, and therapy need not block this natural process. (17) Duality provides an important pathway for corrective feedback, potentially offering improved understanding and increased consensuality. (18) Duality opens space for increased connectedness, more sharing, greater honesty, more personal integrity, greater responsibility, increased social integration, and more egalitarian interaction. (19) Dual relating reduces space for manipulation, deception, and special privilege, gives more opportunity to recognize each other as ordinary human beings, and reduces the likelihood of persistent transferential and countertransferential distortions. (20) Interpersonal boundaries are rarely rigid and fixed, but rather fluctuate and undergo continuous redefinition in all relationships, including the therapeutic relationship, which deliberately focuses on developing consciousness of boundary fluctuations and discussing such changes. (21) Dual relationships represent, after all, the exact kinds of complex interpersonal situations that our professional skills were developed to study and enhance, so as to increase the beneficial possibilities of human interactions and transformations.

Since these points have been discussed at length by the writers mentioned above, I will move on to other areas that I believe need to be elucidated. Being trained as a psychoanalyst, I will bring to bear on the subject various considerations of duality that have emerged over time in the psychoanalytic literature. These ideas seem relevant to consider in all dynamic and systems oriented therapies. I leave it to others to bring forward ideas that have emerged from their own areas of specialization.

PSYCHOANALYTIC CONSIDERATIONS OF DUALITY

Duality: The Essence of Transference Interpretation

The very heart and soul of psychotherapy, transference, and transference interpretation, by definition, always constitute some form of dual relationship. Freud's initial definitions of psychoanalytic technique (1912, 1915) revolve around the "love" relationship that begins to form between physician and client in the course of psychoanalytic free association. Freud suggests the image of an opaque mirror to describe the neutral stance that the analyst seeks to achieve vis-à-vis the patient's neurotic conflict. Freud's images make clear the ultimate impossibility of ever attaining perfect mirroring or perfect neutrality. Despite the analyst's attempt to form a real relationship based on mirroring and neutrality, relationship expectations brought from the client's past would inevitably begin to make their presence felt. The decisive moment in psychoanalysis, and in all derivative psychotherapies, is that in which the duality is at last recognized and successfully interpreted by the psychotherapist. There exists at this moment the "real" relationship that has evolved over time between two people. But another reality is suddenly recognized and defined by the transference interpretation. In the former reality the analyst has a caretaking, curative role and the client has an obligation to relate to real needs of the analyst including fees, attendance, and respect for the setting that supports and protects the personal and professional life of the analyst as well as the client. But when transference reality can be discerned and discussed by two, the therapist functions in a completely different relationship to the client—one of professional interpreter of the emotional life of the client, which is brought to the real relationship set up by the analytic situation. At the moment of interpretation the analyst steps into the role of a third party viewing the realistic interaction of the two and comments on a heretofore hidden reality—the transference, or the resistance, or the countertransference.

The Working Alliance

Over time the nature of this dual role of the analyst has received considerable attention in the psychoanalytic literature.

Greenson (1965), acknowledging the "real" developing relationship, speaks of "the working alliance" to acknowledge the *realistic collaboration* and mutual respect of two. Greenson's formulations stand as a correction of the faulty belief that the client's attitudes and fantasies are mostly transference distortions – when in fact a significant real relationship develops quite apart from the professional task of transference interpretation.

"Acting Out" Childhood Transformations

Bollas (1979) further clarifies the nature of the real relationship by pointing out that Freud (unwittingly and forgivably) designed the psychoanalytic listening situation in order to "act out" with his patients the earliest caretaking roles of parenting, so as to promote the transformational aspect of psychotherapy. The transformational role of the analyst is a realistic role distinctly different from that of transference interpreter. Psychoanalytic transformation occurs by means of this dual transforming/interpreting relationship. Following Winnicott's (1975) developmental approach and Modell's (1976) notion of the "holding environment," Bollas places the transformative element of psychotherapy less in a context of interpretive correction and more within a context of the therapeutic experience as it actually, realistically evolves. He refers to this transformative process as "psychoanalysis of the unthought known."

Transference Experience Arises from Realistic Relating

Schwaber's (1979, 1983) clarifying work arises from an orientation emphasizing the subjective aspects of self. Her ideas focus on the role that the *reality* of the analyst and the analytic relationship play in evoking transference. She, following Kohut

(1971, 1977), emphasizes the reality of the ongoing nature of the relationship that evolves in the psychoanalytic listening situation. Transference from past experience is to be discerned on the basis of something the analyst actually did or did not do and the emotional reaction that the analyst's actual activities elicited. Schwaber highlights the real relationship based upon the analyst's effort to listen and to respond as empathically as humanly possible. Transference is then thought to be perceivable against the backdrop of failures in the analyst's empathic understanding. That is, the analyst actually engages or fails to engage in real interpersonal activity, the disruptive results of which the analyst could not have possibly foretold. According to this view, the working through of the "selfobject" or narcissistic transference constitutes a new edition, a novel interpersonal reality that the analyst and client have now to address with new and different understanding and interpretation. Thus, not only is transference discernible by virtue of aspects of the real relationship coming up for discussion, but the working through is seen as an entirely new and evolving form of personal relationship.

The Transference Neurosis

The notion of cure in psychoanalytic theory revolves around Freud's definition of transference neurosis. The (neurotic) conflicts from the past come to be actually reexperienced in the present and are experienced by the client as the realistic situation. They are, by Freud's definition, complex unconscious features never fully interpretable as such. The ultimate unresolvability of the transference neurosis is widely misunderstood by those who wish a happy sunset at the end of analysis. But in Freudian analysis there are always interminable aspects to analytic work and the transference neurosis in certain respects lives on indefinitely (for discussion see Hedges 1983, Chapters 3 and 4).

Mutative Interpretation

Strachey (1934) quotes Melanie Klein as saying that analysts are generally reluctant to give mutative interpretations (those that promote change) because full instinctual energy would thereby be directed *realistically* at the person of the analyst. This situation is feared and avoided by analysts who fail to interpret so the full power of transference comes into focus in the here and now. Thus, the two key curative agents in psychoanalysis—the establishment of the transference neurosis and the mutative interpretation—both function to bring past emotional experience to bear on and to intensify the *reality* of the present interpersonal relationship. These two realities will never become completely sorted out. One's past emotional life forever colors present relationships. Thus, psychoanalytic doctrine holds that the duality between the realistic present and the transferential past can never, in principle, be eliminated from human relationships. Psychoanalysis serves the purpose of shedding light on many aspects of these dual realities.

The Corrective Emotional Experience

Another line of psychoanalytic thought revolves around the notion of "corrective emotional experience" (Alexander 1961). Various realistic and active procedures may be introduced into the relationship for the purposes of promoting or maintaining the analysis (Eissler 1953, Ferenczi 1952, 1955, 1962). But the need for such reassurance, suggestion, or gratification later will have to be analyzed as transference. According to this view, the client's emotional past was flawed and the therapist is (realistically) going to be able to provide a better (corrective) emotional experience. The analyst by this view may actually step out of his or her usual role as analyst and "do things," intervene in active ways to help the client relate to the therapist and to stay in therapy.

Classical analysts who oppose active techniques maintain that the refusal by the analyst to engage in active, helpful interventions (which serve to strengthen the ego by support and suggestion) is what makes psychoanalysis different from all other "more supportive" psychotherapeutic and counseling techniques. Analysts who advocate the need for active intervention under certain circumstances implicitly recognize that the therapeutic action of psychoanalysis requires various forms of duality to become effective. This line of thinking asserts that psychotherapy and counseling, as distinguished from classical psychoanalysis, definitely and inevitably include the duality that characterizes the more active psychoanalytic techniques. It took Bollas (1979) to point out that even classical technique implicitly includes a setting in which transformational experiences from early childhood are acted out in a supportive way by the analyst. Dual relationships thus form the backbone of all dynamically oriented psychotherapies.

7

In Praise of the Dual Relationship

ESSENTIAL DUAL RELATEDNESS IN DEVELOPMENTAL PSYCHOTHERAPY

It is a moot question whether psychotherapeutic clients today are more primitive or disturbed than in the past or whether our therapeutic knowledge now enables us to see more clearly the more regressed aspects of human nature. In either case, the facts are that people who come to psychotherapy today present for analysis many very early developmental issues that have come to be called "borderline," "narcissistic," and "character" problems.

In general, there is a greater subjective sense of reality in the analytic relationship the further down the developmental ladder one finds the issue being attended to in psychotherapy. Winnicott (1949) points out that the earlier in development the impingement on the infant's sense of "going on being" is, the shorter the span of the ego—meaning the less that can be considered at any one moment in time. Thus, when early developmental issues arise in therapy, less reality testing is available, and only a greatly narrowed picture of the world and the analytic relationship is possible. In today's psychotherapy, many early developmental issues are activated. Consequently, a narrow, concrete subjective experience may well take on a fully formed reality sense, when in fact only a small segment of the overall reality context is being considered.

At the psychotic or primary organizing level of human personality there is the risk of a complete breakdown of the sense of complex shared realities when the "transference psychosis" emerges in the therapeutic relationship for study (Little 1981, 1990). All people have deep layers of psychotic anxiety that may need to be activated at some point in therapy. This means that in any analysis a psychotic core may emerge for brief or extended periods of time during which the client's usual capacities to test reality and to abstract from broad experience may be impaired such that the analyst may become part of a delusional transference experience—possibly one that can threaten the therapist emotionally and realistically.

At the opposite end of the developmental spectrum, psychoanalysts learned early that symbolic interpretation serves in (oedipal, 4- to 7-year-old level) neurosis to permit a return of the repressed, which is recognized as one's own self that has been declared to be nonexistent for so long. In neurotic issues the capacity for reality testing and high-level abstraction and symbolization make the work easier to think about and safer for both parties.

At the selfobject (narcissistic, 3-year-old) level the analyst is perennially responsible for and often blamed for realistic empathic failures. Technically, the analyst takes responsibility for the activities in question, at which time the person in analysis can generally be helped to distinguish between interpersonal realities as they have actually occurred and the emergence of selfobject transference. Kohut (1977, 1984) is clear that actual, realistic, resonating understanding is the key therapeutic feature at this level. Interpretive verbalizations ("summarizing reflections") follow realistic interactional understanding. Kohut's selfobject transference concepts (1971, 1977) demonstrate clearly that blurring of self and other boundaries is prerequisite to being able to analyze the narcissistic transferences based upon self-other failures in early childhood that left the self with structural defects.

At the level of symbiotic (borderline, 4- to 24-month-old) issues, dual realities are more difficult to tease out. It requires considerable time and actual relating to establish interpersonal symbiotic scenarios as visible in transferences that become somehow replicated in the therapeutic relationship. In my work I have dealt extensively with the complicated interactional sequences and dilemmas that therapists encounter in responding to symbiotic (borderline) transferences (Hedges 1983b, 1992). Interpreting the countertransference becomes a critical aspect of responding to the many projective identifications encountered in this work.

Thus, at each of the four major levels of self and other relatedness the dual relationship mechanism is required for psychotherapy, although just how duality operates is different at each developmental level.

THE NECESSARY INTERPENETRATION
OF BOUNDARIES

The theoretician exciting the most interest today in clinical circles is Winnicott (1958, 1965, 1971), who, from his studies of the early mother–child relationship, demonstrates clearly the way the boundaries between the two mix and mingle and how this mixing and merging must be replicated when studying early developmental issues in the transference/countertransference relationship. Infant research (Stern 1985) further underlines this mixing of boundaries at early developmental levels. Little's (1990) deeply moving account of her own analytic work, which led to a complete psychotic breakdown in her analysis with Winnicott, demonstrates this aptly. No one makes clearer than Winnicott the importance of the actual reality of the therapist and the setting. His work demonstrates that the therapist *must be realistically available* to the client for long periods while restricted areas of the personality have an opportunity to expand. In his focus on early developmental issues he demonstrates that interpretation can only follow actual involvement and improvement. This kind of duality is essential to the transformation of all primitive mental states.

LOSS OF REALITY TESTING IN THE "NEGATIVE THERAPEUTIC REACTION"

When aspects of the organizing (psychotic, schizoid) level become activated, the person in analysis often develops the *conviction* of special, privileged understanding regarding the reality of the therapeutic exchange. Reality no longer is a matter for mutual discussion, or for consideration by various standards of social consensus, or for contradictory or varying viewpoints. "This is real, don't give me any bullshit, you are shooting secret cosmic rays from behind your chair at me." "This is incest, you have damaged me irreparably by allowing me to feel close to you." "Because you have stepped out of your neutral role and given me advice, opinion, suggestion, or help, you are in a dual relationship with me. I cannot seek consultation with a third party as you have asked because I would be ashamed at how I seduced you into actually helping me grow. You are the guilty party because you have the power and should have known that revealing personal aspects of yourself and reaching out to me in realistic and 'helpful' ways would be experienced by me (in transference) as incestual and abusive. Your 'good nature' and 'willingness to help me grow' are devious things you do for self-aggrandizement, to make your own ego swell with pride. You have exploited me for the sake of your own ego, your narcissism. You have damaged me by overinvolving yourself in my therapeutic growth. I demand recompense for the violations you have indulged yourself in and the damage you have done. You seduced me (or let me seduce you). Now you will pay." No amount of objective feedback, attempts at rational discussion, or weighing of considerations are possible at such a shocking moment and there may not be another moment in which these psychotic transference convictions can be discussed before an ethical complaint or a lawsuit is filed.

At the moment of the negative therapeutic reaction symbolic speech and discourse are replaced by destructive concretization. Rage or lust is mobilized and with it a clarity of understanding about reality that is subjectively experienced as right, good, monolithic, absolute, and beyond dispute or discussion. A moral crusade characterized by vengeance and righteous indignation is on. The therapist is the enemy, the perpetrator of crimes, the exploiter. Evidence is gathered, much as one gathers evidence to support a paranoid pseudocommunity, in order to support and bolster his or her views against the alleged misbehavior of the therapist. If no moderation or mediation softens the position before accident intervenes, we see suicides, destructive mutilation and homicides, as well as legal and ethical claims facing the therapist *as a result of good therapeutic mobilization of unconscious organizing affects*. The therapeutic activation has succeeded. But the cure has failed and the therapist is in realistic danger. Our focus for the future must be on how to understand and prevent such dangers.

Freud has formulated that the failure to de-idealize the analyst in time leads to a "negative therapeutic reaction" (Freud

1918, 1923, 1933). The dual relationship becomes not one in which transference and countertransference realities can be secured and discussed as a special reality that two can share as somewhat different from or resultant from other aspects of the real relationship, but as *the* reality that the person in analysis is privileged to know, a reality in which the wickedness and self-interest of the (parent) therapist is believed to have gotten out of hand.

As our experience with the emergence of psychotic transference (even in better-developed personalities) expands, the need becomes increasingly clear for the presence of a case monitor of some sort to follow the course of treatment so that when reality controls are lost by the client in psychotic transference, a third party who is knowledgeable about the course of the treatment and who has some relationship with the client is able to intervene to prevent such a dangerous and destructive negative therapeutic reaction.

Since all people have experienced an early developmental (organizing or psychotic) period with constricting limits and constraints, all people are subject to psychotic anxieties and transferences — meaning that the therapist is, in principle, never safe from the destructive emergence of an abusive psychotic transference that is experienced as very real by the client and aimed at the therapist's person. No amount of good judgment ahead of time is fail-safe protection against such potential disaster. Viewed from this angle it is always an error to trust the good will, good nature, and truth searching qualities of the client since they can suddenly be reversed in a psychotic episode.

The analyst is always in danger of becoming the target of psychotic anxieties that cannot be surmounted. If the patient was abused as an infant or young child, this abuse will likely emerge as some form of primary identification in the psychotic transference. The subjective experience is so real it cannot be interpreted successfully and the therapist becomes the victim. Therapists facing misconduct charges regularly report that they "never would have dreamed therapy could have produced such a miscarriage. She [the client] seemed like such a trusting person of good will, and of upstanding moral character. She was so involved in her therapy, so respectful of her analytic partner. How could such vengeance and hatred be directed at me, the very person who has probably done more for her in terms of opening herself up than anyone she has ever known?"

This is the problem. The therapeutic work did succeed in loosening the moralizing and idealizing defenses and in easing up the stifling rigidity of the symbiotic character structure. Indeed the traumatized, annihilated true self began to emerge with all of its raw, infantile power, lust, and rage, but while it was still identified with its aggressor in a very primitive way. The transference interpretation not only succeeded, but when the therapist (according to transference script) failed, the structure opened to the murderous psychotic rage of infancy. The idealizing tendency that has made for such an angelic self and unshakable idealization of the analyst collapses suddenly, and the way things have been going the analyst is in deep trouble if he or she has in any way trusted the good nature of the patient and extended various active interaction measures that can appear to a third party as "not avoiding an unethical dual relationship."

THE DANGERS TO THERAPISTS
RAGE ON UNCHECKED

As our therapeutic tools for bringing out early traumas improve, practicing psychotherapists are headed for deeper and deeper trouble. The dual nature of psychotherapy cannot be denied or minimized and the active role of the therapist required in working with earlier developed layers of the personality moves the dynamic psychotherapist inexorably toward an ill fate. Social consciousness raising increasingly holds the teacher, minister, physician, and psychotherapist accountable for their activities. Deep working, well-intentioned psychotherapists face the danger that their best, most well-conceived efforts to help will be experienced as violent or incestuous intrusions that they "should have known" about in advance and "should have" taken measures to forestall.

Perhaps we should ask where the phrase "should have known" appears in any single piece of responsible therapy research or even in a single theoretical tract on the nature of psychotherapy? Such a claim is completely untenable and unsupportable. The literature on predicting violence and suicide has repeatedly demonstrated how poor our best-trained experts are at ever predicting even very strong variables. No one who seriously practices in-depth psychotherapy is likely to use such a phrase as "should have known." What may evolve in psychotic transference is never known in advance. Who are those who would tell us what we should or should not have known? After the fact, like Monday morning quarterbacks, they sit in armchairs saying what we should have known or done; meanwhile, strange and idiosyncratic transference configurations unfold hourly in our consulting rooms.

The misplaced focus by licensing boards and ethics committees on dual relationships when damaging exploitation is the issue has meant that therapists can no longer simply consider what such events as attending a client's wedding, attending a lecture or social event in a client's presence, offering a helpful book or cassette, giving or receiving token gifts or touch, or sending a birthday or sympathy card may mean to a client in the context of the therapy. Rather, the dual relationship witch-hunt has come to mean that we must concern ourselves with what precautions to take so that legal and ethical questions can never arise. The only tool we really have at our disposal in psychotherapy, the spontaneity of ourselves, has thus been tarnished and is in danger of serious damage.

Given the absurd state of affairs currently prevailing, the orientation now required by therapists who think developmentally and who work dynamically (1) begins with the realization that in-depth psychotherapy always depends on the successful evolution of a dual relationship, (2) realizes that heretofore questions of meaning and interpretation have been foremost in our practice, and (3) concludes that now (considering the dual relationship panic) we must reorient our thinking to protect ourselves from accusations that could dangerously be held against us for doing exactly what we aim to do—exploiting the potential of dual relatedness for the purpose of studying human nature and freeing our clients from the bondage of the past. What a fine kettle of fish this is!

Fortunately, the pendulum has begun to swing back to a position where we can begin relying once again on clinical considerations rather than naive moralizing and absurd misconduct rulings to guide our therapy. But for the present we are stuck having to water down what we do for fear of censorship by ethics committees and licensing boards. We are clearly in the midst of a major crisis in the practice of our discipline.

Our growing expertise in elucidating the deepest, most primitive and crazy aspects of our clients and of ourselves is expanding at the very moment when the therapeutic dimension we most depend on—dual relatedness—has come under social, legal, and ethical censorship. It is by no means clear how we will come to grips with these and many related issues.

Regulatory boards and ethics committees in their eagerness to provide rules for the practice of psychotherapy have rapidly moved toward positions that, if allowed, threaten to obliterate the essence of clinical work, which relies on the dual relationship. Viewed from this vantage point our fear of the boards and therefore our tacit support of their trends registers a resistance on the part of therapists to enter the new terrain of enriched psychotherapeutic relatedness.

UNAVOIDABLE DUALITY

The essential duality involved in psychotherapy can be considered from many angles. The views on duality presented here serve to contrast (1) the real, moment to moment, spontaneous, mutual need-fulfilling aspect of the actual, contractual relationship that evolves over time between two people, with (2) the symbolic, interpretive relationship in which two gradually come to stand apart, as it were, from their real, spontaneous relating and speak in such a way as to characterize from a third-party point of view the manner and quality of their relating. Two create pictures and stories that describe (as if from an outside or objective point of view) what is happening between them and why. This interpretive, third-party, symbolic relationship that two share enables each to speak his or her subjective reactions arising from within the real relationship in such a way as to consider the emotional load (left over from past emotional relationship) that each may be adding to their ongoing appreciation of the other and the relatedness.

The essence of the interpretive art at the symbiotic, borderline, character level is a confrontation of the person's refusal to have such a dual relationship with the therapist and therefore with all emotionally significant others (Hedges 1983, 1992). The merger sense that lies at the root of virtually all clinical syndromes in treatment today resists treatment by relegating the reality of the therapist and his or her personality functioning to one of relative unimportance. This resistance functions to prevent the actualization of the symbolic duality that makes human development possible. The decisive interpretive move with symbiotic (borderline) issues comes when the therapist can say, "But I am not you and I am not your wished for (or feared) other. I am a real person relating to you. I am unique, different from anyone you have ever known. I have shown you that I can relate more or less as you wish me to. But for myself, I do not think or react as you might expect or wish me to. It is not necessary for you to be disappointed, enraged, or hurt as you once were when you were on the verge of discovering your mother was a separate person. Differentness is something that can be celebrated. It is possible for you to learn to relate realistically to me and to others in ways that are different from your experience of the past. You are perfectly capable of seeing the two of us as we realistically relate to each other and to form ideas and feelings about us and our ways of relating."

NECESSARY SUBJECTIVITY

We no longer believe there is any such thing as an objective analyst (Natterson 1991). No one knows in advance how transference and countertransference will unfold and therefore unconscious transference and countertransference feelings cannot be limited and regulated in advance. This is especially true for the evolving countertransference that is projected onto the therapist at the level of the spontaneous interaction that recapitulates the early (borderline) mother–child symbiotic relationship. What evolves as a second relationship to the one based upon conscious contract is a joint fantasy relationship that two collaborate in creating (Spence 1982).

Natterson's (1991) text illustrates clearly how patient and analyst communicatively achieve an intense oneness and fusion, how subjective features from the analyst's past come into play in the countertransference, and how at the same time each is able to individuate and differentiate more completely from the experience than either was able to do before their work together. Natterson shatters the myth of the value-neutral therapist, exposing it as a fictive assumption. He makes clear that

all human two person transactions share fundamental meaning: *each party attempts to influence the other* with his or her view of the universe, to persuade the other of the rightness of his or her view. . . . this basic power orientation of dyadic relationships makes it natural for moral influences to be invariably significant components of the therapists' activity. [p. 28, italics added]

The interaction of the basic beliefs of patient and therapist are inseparable from the human fantasies and yearnings of each. Natterson views the psychoanalytic encounter as a dyadic impingement in which each person influences the other. "Their respective fantasies and desires, values and goals, are engaged in continuous struggle, through which both persons are continuously changing. This intersubjective experience should be regarded as the basic precondition for any theoretical understanding of psychotherapeutic processes" (p. 29). Natterson's brilliant work highlights the duality between the real relationship and the emerging transference/countertransference relationship.

It is time that we be clear that the nature of transference, countertransference, resistance, and interpretation as we have come to understand them, *de facto* rest upon the existence of a dual relationship. It behooves us to remember that all beneficial effects of psychotherapy arise in consequence of the dual relationship.

8

Duality as Essential to Psychological Cure

AN ANTHROPOLOGICAL INSIGHT INTO HOW PSYCHOTHERAPY "HOOKS INTO THE FLESH" THROUGH DUAL RELATIONSHIPS

The French anthropologist Claude Lévi-Strauss in a chapter, "The Effectiveness of Symbols," (1949) undertakes a penetrating definition of the psychoanalytic task, revealing from an anthropological and sociological viewpoint the necessarily dual nature of the psychotherapeutic endeavor.

Lévi-Strauss reviews the first available South American magico-religious text, an 18-page incantation obtained by the Cuna Indian, Guillermo Haya, from an elderly informant of his tribe (original source: Holmer and Wassen 1947). The purpose of the song is to facilitate unusually difficult childbirth. Its use is unusual since native women of Central and South America have easier deliveries than women of Western societies. The intervention of the shaman is thus rare and occurs only in the extreme case of failure to deliver and at the request of the midwife.

The song begins with the midwife's confusion over the pregnant woman's failure to deliver and describes her visit to the shaman and the latter's arrival in the hut of the laboring woman, with his fumigations of burnt cocoa-nibs, his invocations, and the making of *nuchu*, sacred figures or images carved from various prescribed kinds of wood that lend them their effectiveness. The carved *nuchu* represent tutelary spirits who become the shaman's assistants. He leads the *nuchu* to the abode of *Muu* (inside the woman's body). *Muu* is the goddess of fertility and is responsible for the formation of the fetus. Difficult childbirths occur when *Muu* has exceeded her functions and captured the *purba* or soul of the mother. The incantation thus expresses a quest for the lost soul of the mother, which will be restored after overcoming many obstacles. The shaman's saga will take the woman through a victory over wild beasts and finally through a great contest waged by the shaman and his tutelary spirits against *Muu* and her daughters. Once *Muu* has been defeated, the whereabouts of the soul of the ailing woman can be discovered and freed so the delivery can take place. The song ends with precautions that must be taken so that *Muu* cannot pursue her victors (an event that would result in infertility). The fight is not waged against *Muu* herself, who is indispensable to procreation, but against her abuses of power. After the epic saga, *Muu* asks the shaman when he will come to visit again, indicating the perennial nature of psychic conflict that can be expected to interfere with childbirth.

Lévi-Strauss comments that in order to perform his function the shaman is, by cultural belief, assigned supernatural power to see the cause of the illness, to know the whereabouts of the vital forces, and to use *nuchu* spirits who are endowed with exceptional powers to move invisibly and clairvoyantly in the service of humans.

On the surface the song appears rather commonplace

among shamanistic cures. The sick woman suffers because she has lost her spiritual double, which constitutes her vital strength. In traveling to the supernatural world and in being aided by assistants in snatching the woman's double from a malevolent spirit and restoring it to its owner, the shaman effects the cure. The exceptional aspect of this song, making it of interest to anthropologists and psychoanalysts alike, is that " 'Muu's way' and the abode of Muu are not, to the native mind, simply a mythical itinerary and dwelling-place. They represent, literally, the vagina and uterus of the pregnant woman, which are to be explored by the shaman and nuchu and in whose depths they will wage their victorious combat" (p. 188). In his quest to capture her soul, the shaman also captures other spirits, which govern the vitality of her other body parts (heart, bones, teeth, hair, nails, and feet). Not unlike the invasive attention of the psychoanalyst, no body part is left unattended to.

Muu, as instigator of the disorder, has captured the special "souls" of the various organs, thus destroying the cooperation and integrity of the main soul, the woman's double who must be set free. "In a difficult delivery the 'soul' of the uterus has led astray all the 'souls' belonging to other parts of the body. Once these souls are liberated, the soul of the uterus can and must resume its cooperation" (p. 190). It is clear that the song seeks to delineate the emotional content of the physiological disturbance to the mind of the sick woman. To reach Muu, the shaman and his assistants must find "Muu's way," the road of Muu. At the peak moment when the shaman has finished his carvings, spirits rise up at the shaman's exhortation:

> The (sick) woman lies in the hammock in front of you.
> Her white tissue lies in her lap, her white tissues move softly.
> The (sick) woman's body lies weak.
> When they light up (along) Muu's way, it runs over with exudations and like blood.
> Her exudations drip down below the hammock all like blood, all red.

The inner white tissue extends to the bosom of the earth.
Into the middle of the woman's white tissue a human being
    descends. [Holmer and Wassen, cited in Lévi-Strauss, p. 190]

"*Muu*'s way," darkened and covered with blood, is unquestion-
ably the vagina and the dark whirlpool the uterus where *Muu*
dwells.

    Lévi-Strauss comments that this text claims a special place
among shaman cures. One standard type of cure involves an
organ that is manipulated or sucked until a thorn, crystal, or
feather appears, a representation of the removal of the
malevolent force. Another type of cure revolves around a sham
battle waged in a hut and then outside against harmful spirits.
In these cures it remains for us to understand exactly how the
psychological aspect "hooks into" the physiological. But the
current song constitutes a purely psychological treatment. For
the shaman does not touch the body and administers no
remedy. "Nevertheless it involves, directly and explicitly, the
pathological condition and its locus. In our view, the song
constitutes a *psychological manipulation* of the sick organ, and it
is precisely from this manipulation that a cure is expected"
(p. 192).

    Lévi-Strauss observes that the situation is contrived to
induce pain in a sick woman through developing a psychological
awareness of the smallest details of all of her internal tissues.
Using mythological images the pain-induced situation becomes
the symbolic setting for the experience of conflict. "A transition
will thus be made from the most prosaic reality, to myth, from
the physical universe to the psychological universe, from the
external world to the internal body" (p. 193). The mythological
saga being enacted in the body attains sensory and hallucinatory
vividness through the many elements of ritual — smell, sound,
tactile stimulation, rhythm, and repetition.

    What follows in breathless (hypnotic) rhythm and rhyme
are more and more rapid oscillations between mythical and

physiological themes "as if to abolish in the mind of the sick woman the distinction which separates them, and to make it impossible to differentiate their respective attributes" (p. 193). Spirits and events follow one another as the woman's total focus becomes the birth apparatus and the cosmic battle being waged there by the invasion of the shaman and his spiritual helpers who bring illuminating light into the birth canal. The presence of wild animals increases the pains that are thus personified and described to the woman. Uncle Alligator moves about with bulging eyes, crouching and wriggling his tail. He moves his glistening flippers that drag on everything. The Octopus arrives with sticky tentacles alternately opening and closing, contracting and expanding passageways. The black tiger, the red animal, the two colored animals are all tied with an iron chain that rasps and clanks against everything. Their tongues are hanging out, saliva dripping, saliva foaming, with flourishing tails and claws tearing at everything.

According to Lévi-Strauss the cure consists in making explicit a situation originally existing on an emotional level and in rendering acceptable to the mind pains that the body otherwise refuses to tolerate. The shaman with the aid of this myth encourages the woman to accept the incoherent and arbitrary pains, reintegrating them into a whole where everything is coordinated and meaningful. He points out that our physicians tell a similar story to us but not in terms of monsters and spirits but rather in terms we believe like germs, microbes, and so forth. "The shaman provides the sick woman with a *language*, by means of which unexpressed, and otherwise inexpressible, psychic states can be immediately expressed" (p. 198). The transition to the verbal system makes it possible to undergo in an ordered and intelligible form an experience that would otherwise be chaotic and inexpressible. The myth and its hypnotic power enable the woman to release and reorganize the physiological processes that have become disordered in the woman's sickness.

THE DUAL RELATIONSHIP CURE

Lévi-Strauss explicitly contextualizes this shamanistic cure as psychoanalytic in nature. The purpose is to bring to a conscious level conflicts and resistance that have remained unconscious with resulting symptom formation. The conflicts and resistances are resolved not because of knowledge, real or alleged,

> but because this knowledge makes possible a specific experience, in the course of which conflicts materialize in an order and on a level permitting their free development and leading to their resolution. This vital experience is called *abreaction* in psychoanalysis. We know that its precondition is the unprovoked intervention of the analyst, who appears in the conflicts of the client *through a double transference mechanism* as (1) a flesh-and-blood protagonist and (2) in relation to whom the client can restore and clarify an initial (historical) situation which has remained unexpressed or unformulated. . . .
>
> The shaman *plays the same dual role as the psychoanalyst.* A prerequisite role—that of listener for the psychoanalyst and of orator for the shaman—*establishes a direct relationship with the patient's conscious and an indirect relationship with his unconscious.* This is the function of the incantation proper. But the shaman does more than utter the incantation; *he is its hero, for it is he who, at the head of a supernatural battalion of spirits, penetrates the endangered organs and frees the captive soul.* [pp. 198–199]

The shaman, like the psychoanalyst, is thus enabled by the dual relationship to become (1) the transference object induced vividly in the patient's mind, and (2) the real protagonist of the conflict, which is experienced by the patient as on the border between the physical world and the psychical world. In this dual situation in which pain is deliberately induced by the practitioner, the psychoanalytic client eliminates individual myths by facing the reality of the person of the analyst. And the native woman overcomes an organic disorder by identifying with a mythically transmuted shaman.

Lévi-Strauss notes that the shamarita cure is a counterpart to psychoanalytic cure. Both induce an experience through appeal to myth. The psychoanalytic patient constructs a myth with elements drawn from his or her personal past. The shamanist patient receives from the outside a social myth. In either case the treating person fosters the emergence of a storyline that cures by giving language to experience. The effectiveness of symbols guarantees the parallel development in the process of myth and action.

Lévi-Strauss provides a fascinating argument that aligns shamanism of ages past with the modern activities of psychoanalysis and psychotherapy. His arguments go considerably beyond Freud and into areas being explored in psychoanalysis and psychotherapy today in which an inductive property of symbols permits formerly homologous structures built out of different materials at different levels of life—organizational processes, unconscious agency, and rational thought—to be understood as profoundly related to one another. Lévi-Strauss points out that the individual vocabulary of the cure is significant only to the extent that the unconscious structures it according to its laws and thus transforms it into language. Whether the myth is a personal re-creation or one borrowed from tradition matters little; the essential structure of language and the unconscious is the locus of the power of the symbol. Any myth represents a quest for the remembrance of things past and the ways those remembrances are structured in the unconscious. *"The modern version of shamanistic technique called psychoanalysis thus derives its specific characteristics from the fact that in industrial civilization there is no longer any room for mythical time, except within man himself"* (pp. 203–204).

The purpose of reviewing this anthropological analysis of psychoanalysis and psychotherapy as knowledge of the symbolic function inherited from shamanism is to highlight the inherently *dual* relationship involved in psychological cure. The shaman/analyst is first of all realistically involved with the person in conscious and unconscious ways so as to evoke a second-order relationship, the mythical transference in which the shaman/analyst becomes hero, protagonist in an inner drama, a conflict, a quest for possession of the soul. The drama proceeds by putting private experience into symbols that have the power to transform the inexplicable, the unintelligible, the inchoate, and the irremediable into a series of epic narrations that two can share together. It is only the extent to which the shaman/analyst succeeds in establishing a real relationship that the epic journey in search of the soul through mythic transference, resistance, and countertransference becomes possible.

If an attorney should happen into the hut midway in this woman's process to cure with papers for her to sign, she no doubt would produce a stillbirth or die in childbirth from inability to stay with the symbolic. He would, of course, be on hand to bring action against the shaman for negligence. A judge and jury with no way of understanding the power of the symbolic or the subtle operations of transference could hardly be expected to show much mercy for the poor shaman left with only the incantations bequeathed him by wise forefathers, a handful of hand-carved stick figures, and cocoa incense. Perhaps his songs, smoke, and hocus-pocus will be viewed as harmless enough. But that he had formed a dual relationship with the woman, had become by virtue of his social role an authorizing personage in her life, and furthermore was actually fraternizing with her family and midwife, thus (no doubt) exploiting the hapless victim for personal aggrandizement of his narcissistic needs—may indeed be dimly viewed by administrative judges as he is charged with responsibility for stillbirth, a faulty delivery indeed.

Or should this woman by chance attend a recovery or incest survivors group midway in the move to the symbolic she may come to recognize the very real sense of penetration she feels from her shaman/analyst and begin reliving traumas of the past that have been revived by this penetrating therapeutic relationship of the present. The therapeutic relationship may become so terrifyingly real that she enters a negative therapeutic reaction with her heretofore idealized shaman. She soon is encouraged by well-meaning group members to file suit against him for failing to maintain his boundaries by his attending her wedding, sniffing cocoa incense with her, failing to stop her from reading his journal articles, and not preventing her from attending his classes at the local university. The shaman is judged negligent because he "should have known" that dual relationships are damaging. He should have known that she would in the long run prove insufficiently motivated, insufficiently endowed for the process, or easily derailed by accidental outside influences so that she would be unable to move to the level of the symbolic required for cure. The tragedy: the dual relationship that is the primary vehicle requisite for carrying the symbolic cure had been put securely in place, but patient constitution, concentration, or motivation to effect a transition to the transferential symbolic proved insufficient. Outside instigators empathically tapped into her negative psychotic transference feelings toward the shaman and urged her to file a complaint to avenge herself—as it turns out, for childhood abuse now attributed by transference to the shaman.

Those who know little or nothing of the subtleties of psychological cure can only point to what remains from aborted processes and rush in with judgments. How are we who are charged with the sacred function of utilizing the power of the transferential symbolic for benefit of suffering humans to protect ourselves from tribal administrators who have little or no knowledge of our function and no awareness that our art involves wielding the symbols of the gods in *real* relationships such that people forget the difference between ordinary reality and the mythic in order to bring to bear the power, function, and effectiveness of the symbol for the purpose of relieving psychological and physiological suffering. Caught midway when only the reality aspect is so far in play, or stopped short because the willingness or capability to enter the symbolic is lacking, we can indeed look like negligent fools! *But if we give up the dual relationship we relinquish the wisdom of the ages!* Then we become reduced to the same sense of impotence of those who seek to reaffirm their self-identifications and power by sitting in judgment over people and processes they cannot hope to understand.

PERSONAL OPINION

For over twenty years my primary business has been consulting with therapists and analysts about difficult clinical work. I have witnessed a rising swell of horror and fear among professionals as stories circulate about atrocities perpetrated by governing boards under the name of "administrative justice" and acts of ethics committees that appear to be operating as kangaroo courts. If even a small number of the reports that reach me are accurate (and I believe they are) we are all indeed in a precarious position.

The shocking findings of the social consciousness movement regarding real abuses by therapists have taken us all by surprise. Our professional organizations have reacted as quickly as possible in order to recognize the hazards of damaging and exploitative dual relationships and to take measures to rectify wrongs and to prevent future abuses. Only now are there beginning signs that boards and ethics committees are coming to appreciate the extreme subtleties and complexities of dual relationship issues.

I have hoped to bring to the attention of the community of practicing therapists the central position of duality in our work in order to challenge thinking further so that injustices can be prevented and so that future regulatory efforts can take into account the inevitable blurring of boundaries that transference and countertransference interpretation necessarily entail.

I offer the following suggestions for consideration in evolving safeguards against abuse while honoring the dual relationship inherent in the practice of psychotherapy.

1. When any direct or indirect contact outside the formal therapeutic setting exists between therapist and client, a consultant should be sought out regularly (at two- to six-month intervals) to evaluate and comment on the course of therapy. This is especially important in training programs where the trainee is likely to see or hear much that will necessarily color the therapeutic relationship. It would also seem critical in small communities where various forms of outside contact are inevitable.

2. Any roles that might be unavoidable outside the formal therapeutic relationship need to be kept somehow in the public eye. Some provision for periodic review with a third party should be obtained to evaluate how the therapy is proceeding.

3. In the name of protecting privacy and confidentiality, all *appearances* of dual relationship that might potentially be seen by third parties and conceivably by reported boards and committees for open investigation should be avoided. It is understood that "pure" work is to be preferred over "complicated" work but that work with various outside influences and complications (spouses, insurance companies, employers, government agencies, etc.) tends to be the rule rather than the exception. Complications cannot be assumed to be damaging exploitations. Multiple roles do not constitute unethical relationships that are exploitative and damaging. But avoidance of appearances and third-party consultation can help keep the distinction clearer and work to avoid confidentiality breaks through investigation.

4. Qualified experts should render opinions to regulating bodies. At present most individuals serving on regulatory boards and ethics committees, so far as I can tell, do not possess

advanced specialty training that qualifies them to make judgments about the subtleties of the dual relationship necessarily
involved in depth transference and countertransference work
without outside expert consultation. If this is true, then these
individuals are operating unprofessionally and unethically. For
most purposes persons serving on regulatory boards and ethics
committees need not possess advanced expertise in the dual
nature of transference/countertransference work to be able to
identify therapist's abuses of the professional relationship. But
(a) when subtleties are involved, (b) when therapists have sophisticated and enlightened rationale for various interventions
based upon the dual nature of transference work, or (c) when a
therapist's professional reputation and personal life are to be
profoundly affected by claims that they do not honor as valid,
we cannot afford as a profession to allow people without advanced training and professional expertise to stand in judgment
of matters they cannot possibly be qualified to understand.

One way to correct the current threat that therapists live
under as a result of cries and accusations of unethical dual
relationship is to create panels of expert consultants who can
demonstrate advanced understanding of the complexities of
transference/countertransference relationships. Experts in
panels of three could be called upon to evaluate aspects of
investigations in which subtle aspects of dual relationship are in
play and to render expert opinion to regulatory boards and
ethics committees.

5. An alternate approach to the expert consultant model is
for the therapist needing protection to have some recourse to
settling the dispute in civil court where discovery and due
process is guaranteed—as it is generally not under administrative
law. We know that all too often ethics committees and governing boards are prey to political pressures and various prees-
tablished biases so that a therapist acting in good faith and upon
sound judgment may not get fair treatment. Governing boards
are certainly in a dual relationship position! Consumer interests

and fear of publicity resulting in adverse political effects are too apt to color judgments against the therapist when subtleties of depth work are involved. While a judge and jury certainly do not constitute peers in terms of depth understanding, at least there is some hope of an unbiased, unpolitical, fair judgment. With either the client or the governing board as plaintiff and the governing board acting as judge and jury the therapist *de facto* loses the civil rights guaranteed by the Constitution of the United States. As it stands in most states, therapists have no civil rights and no recourse to due process. We are potential prey to political pressures and victims of governing hierarchies without recourse to adequate defense.

6. Some therapists have pointed out that a jury certainly does not represent peer opinion, so that arbitration panels of persons sophisticated in aspects of depth therapy are to be preferred over civil courts.

DEFINING QUALIFIED EXPERTS

The position I have taken is that there are many kinds of transferences, countertransferences, and resistances that operate silently in psychological treatment. Cure itself is dependent upon the successful discernment and utilization of dual relationship variables. There is no provision in any currently existing licensing law that I am aware of that ensures training or licensing as a psychotherapist involves expertise in understanding and interpreting transference and countertransference phenomena. The California Research Psychoanalyst Law[1] does, however, specify compliance with a set of nationally and internationally recognized standards for such training. Expertise in

1. Business and Professions Code *Research Psychoanalysts* Chapter 5.1 (added by Stats 1977, Ch. 1191) Section 2529 2529.5.

transference, countertransference, and resistance analysis as reflected in this law is thought to be attained by exposure to (1) extensive (five years) didactic training *beyond* ordinary licensing requirements, (2) a minimum of 400 hours of personal didactic transference analysis, and (3) a minimum of three apprentice training cases with at least 50 hours of supervision each for a total of 200 post-licensing supervisory hours studying transference, resistance, and countertransference phenomena as they operate in three specific cases and two years of case conference supervision. When an individual becomes certified at this level and practices analytically for an additional five years, he or she attains the status of training analyst and is *only then a fully qualified expert* with enough experience to teach, supervise, and analyze others in the refined aspects of transference interpretation. This is the level of training and experience recognized the world over by psychoanalysts that constitutes expertise in transference and countertransference analysis.

Other schools of psychotherapy have yet to codify in law what comparable level of experience might qualify one with expertise to make judgments in this highly technical area of knowledge. Can we name any single board or ethics committee member with ten years of comparable advanced training and practice that might ethically qualify him or her to render the professional opinions now being made in this area? Administrative judges have no training at all and yet cavalierly remove licenses based on their evaluation of subtleties that in the profession require roughly fifteen years of advanced training to assess. A person would certainly not have to be a registered psychoanalyst to have sought out extensive and intensive training and practice in understanding the power and subtleties of transference and countertransference, but to date this law stands as the only public recognition I am aware of as to what such expertise might look like, or of how qualified individuals might be legally and ethically identified.

CONCLUSION

I do not wish my remarks to be misunderstood as accusatory in nature or tone. Blame is hardly appropriate at the level of peer review or professional regulation. We have been rapidly overtaken by a rush of new and important social consciousness issues. I have already suggested it may be our own reluctance to enter deeper therapeutic involvement, which so many of our clients desperately need, that accounts for our fear at present.

I hope my thoughts on the inevitability of the dual relationship in psychological cure will sound a precautionary note in quarters where it is sorely needed. I am calling for a more careful examination of the nature of duality, not only for therapist protection but, more importantly, in order to focus our attention on the dual nature of our work so we can develop even further its importance and potency for the benefit of those who seek out our professional skills.

PART IV

PSYCHOTIC
ANXIETIES AND
THE ORGANIZING
EXPERIENCE

9

The Organizing
Transference

MIMICRY AS A BASIS FOR THOUGHT

The organizing transference arises from experiences the neonate or intrauterine infant undergoes in trying to organize reliable channels to the environment that ensure the safety and continuity of physical and psychological life. When the child is reaching out or extending in some way to form a channel or path to the maternal body, either inside or outside the uterus, the interpersonal channeling or connection is facilitated when that extension is met (reinforced) in a timely and satisfying manner. Winnicott's (1949) formulation is that the infant needs to maintain a sense of "going on being." Any impingement on that sense prematurely activates the psychic system and forces the child to begin thinking precociously. From approximately four months before birth to four months after birth the infant's neurological system alternates from rest to activity. The child actively arranges numerous sensorimotor experiences. The child may be looking, listening, or experimenting with movement, sounds, or touch.

Under optimal circumstances the infant is not required to problem solve as a response to impingement, intrusion, or trauma. But when there is impingement into the sense of comfortably going on being, the child is forced to react, no matter what the nature of that impingement is. Such things as an Rh factor, the presence of some undesirable chemical, or a shortage of food or oxygen in the placental blood could each provide a considerable impingement for a fetus. Psychological studies suggest many ways that the mother's psychic life and her relation to her environment before the child's birth may impinge on the child's comfort and sense of safety, thus activating alerting mechanisms and thought processes. Any intense or prolonged environmental stimulus or deficit could impinge on the psychic world of an infant.

Winnicott holds that impingement forces the infant to begin thinking, to begin problem solving, before that infant might otherwise have done so, before that infant may be fully ready. Under such circumstances, a child's basic thought patterns are responses to (persecutory) impingement. Winnicott had witnessed many childbirths and sees no reason to assume that birth, per se, need be traumatic. The baby has been in cramped quarters with limited possibilities for some time. The baby is ready to leave. There is an exit. The exit is large enough and the baby's musculature is adequate to traverse the birth canal. The process can occur and so the baby transitions from one sort of environmental circumstances to another. The baby is prepared for birth, already having experienced many tolerable frustrations with the intrauterine environment. Traveling down the birth canal may even be satisfying and positively stimulating in various ways. Midwives maintain that putting the child immediately onto the mother's belly and letting her own instinct to move to the breast occur, is also activating. In other mammals the licking of the baby's body seems to stimulate deep tissues and to enliven the newborn. So there may be many aspects of the birthing experience that are stimulating to the child, or soothing and comforting.

However, says Winnicott, an unusually long or unusually intense birth experience may provide a trauma that can serve as a prototype in thinking about early impingements. If baby's first thought (*in utero* or postnatal) occurs in response to an actual traumatic intrusion, then the first thought mode upon which all later thought modes are based is persecutory. Winnicott addresses the Kleinians who speak of observing persecutory anxieties in clinical situations. Winnicott believes that these anxieties exist because persecution (impingement) *has already occurred*. There is a fear that persecution will happen again. The child experienced primordial impingement or persecutory intrusion with the result that the basic pattern of the child's mind became interrupted and organized around anticipating or guarding against intrusion. The child scans the environment for more persecution because that is the foundational experience. Such a child was deprived of a secure "going on being" experience until the perception and motor equipment naturally evolved to tolerate gradually increasing frustrations, delays, and other maternal shortcomings. In an optimal situation by the third, fourth, and fifth months, a mother and a baby are interacting in many ways. But a baby who has experienced traumatic intrusions perennially maintains a guard against further intrusion and in doing so has already lost much of its potential flexibility.

Even in optimal situations, Alice Balint (1939) still holds that the infant's first thought processes arise in relation to trauma, even if they be minor ones. The subtext of her paper is that primates have an innate capacity to mimic. Human babies mimic their mothers in order to gain understanding and mastery over what is happening to them. Before cause and effect thinking can occur, thought originates based upon primary identification at a gross body level (mimicry). An infant sees the mother smile and the baby smiles back. Mothers imitate the baby and the baby reciprocally imitates the mother in an endless circle leading toward the mutual cuing process of the later symbiotic period of development.

Hedges (1983a, 1992, 1994c) speaks of the "mimical self" as an expectable aspect of psychic and somatic experience at the organizing level. People who retain organizing modes of interacting as a significant feature of their personalities live with mimicry as an important way of being in the world. One woman spoke of having a series of cassette tapes, one to tell her what to say and do in each situation of her life. To the extent that any part of the personality retains early modes of organizational striving, mimicry of human life and activity—in contrast to contacting, engaging, or resonating emotional interactions—may predominate.

Anna Freud (1951, 1952, 1958) and Winnicott (1952) emphasize the role of maternal care in augmenting the protective shield during the period of early infantile dependency. Khan (1963) has introduced the concept of *cumulative trauma* to take into consideration early psychophysical events that happen between the infant and its mothering partners. The concept of cumulative trauma correlates the effects of early infant caretaking with disturbing personality features that only appear much later in life. Cumulative trauma is the result of the effects of numerous kinds of small breaches in the early stimulus barrier or protective shield that are not experienced as traumatic at the time but create a certain strain that, over time, produces an effect on the personality that can only be appreciated retrospectively when it is experienced as traumatic.

Khan points out that the developing child can and does recover from breaches in the protective shield and can make creative use of them so as to arrive at a fairly healthy and effective normal functioning personality. But the person with vulnerabilities left over from infantile cumulative strain trauma "nevertheless can in later life break down as a result of acute stress and crisis" (p. 56). When there is a later breakdown and earlier cumulative strain trauma can be inferred, Khan is clear that the earlier disturbances of maternal care were neither gross nor acute at the time they occurred. Anna Freud (1958) has similarly described instances in which, "subtle harm is being inflicted on this child, and . . . the consequences of it will become manifest at some future date" (p. 120).

Psychological theory and infant research (Stearn 1985) are rapidly adding ideas to help us think about what the experience of the infant may be like during the organizing period. These concepts help us grasp the kinds of early mental structuring that can be listened for in the analytic situation: (1) Basic primate mimicry and primary identification give rise to the "mimical self" (Hedges 1983a). (2) Later adaptation to the maternal environment gives rise to the "false self" (Winnicott 1960), seen most clearly in the later symbiotic bonding period. (3) Khan (1963) formulates a kind of stimulation experienced by the infant as intrusive strain trauma causing an adverse reaction of the infant, which sets off an adaptation in caretakers resulting in what can be thought of as an internalized vicious circle of mutual misadaptations.

In listening to a person living a pervasive organizing experience or to a person living out a pocket of organizing experience, how might we begin to identify aspects of their experience that might be considered transference from the organizing period?

CONSIDERING WHY SYMBIOTIC BONDING
DOES NOT OCCUR

One way to begin thinking is to consider that babies come into this world ready to attach themselves to a (m)other.

Bowlby's (1969) work on attachment has shown that human babies naturally seek attachments that make the human emotional exchange possible. If the child does *not* move toward bonding, if the child fails to bond in an overall way, or if parts of the personality are left out of the bonding dance, there must be a significant reason why this otherwise natural, expectable process did not occur. It is helpful to picture an infant extending through vocalization, perception, or movement—striving for a connection, seeking warmth, stimulation, nurturance, or a sense of comfort and safety. If the mothering person, for whatever reason, is not able to meet these extensions in a timely manner or does not know how to, or is unwilling to, or meets extensions with negative response, the extensions withdraw and/or atrophy. The baby simply does not reach in that way anymore because there is no gain, no percentage, or perhaps even pain associated with that kind of extension.

In Freud's (1895a) earliest paper considering issues of primary repression at a quasi-neurological level, he suggests that an attempted pathway that goes unrewarded by pleasurable experience or that meets with painful experience is intentionally blocked against future extension, as though a sign were posted there, "never go this way again." Bioenergetic analysts (Lowen 1975) think in terms of various systems of involuntary muscular constrictions that become chronically fixated, creating body rigidities and blocks in the flow of natural energies so that future extensions are blocked because they are experienced as painful.

The reason all people in various ways can be said to retain psychic and somatic modes of organizing experience is that there is no such thing as perfect mothering. Current infant research suggests that mother and baby may only satisfactorily connect thirty percent of the time (Tronick and Cohn 1988). In these earliest months every baby has reached out needing, wanting, and questing in various ways. Her quest may not have been met because no environment can possibly meet all of these quests with perfect timing and empathic attunement. So various experiences occur that teach every baby to avoid or to withdraw from certain forms of contact where appropriate environmental response is absent or negative.

It is helpful to picture a rooting baby who gets so far as to have her mouth almost around the nipple when "something happens" (internally) so that rhythmical sucking never starts. The receipt of nourishment, comfort, and safety from contact with mother is foreclosed. The mouth stiffens and the baby loses the nipple, or perhaps pushes it out or turns away, arching her back and screaming. This image comes to mind when we hear of a person approaching a therapist searching for human connection. The person extends, reaches out yearning for human contact. Then "something happens." They're suddenly just not there. Their questing personal presence in the room has somehow vanished, though their mimical conversation and activity may continue. Many if not most practicing therapists, presumably due to their own history of bonding experiences, fail to notice for long periods of time that the person they are with has silently left the room, vanished from the interaction. Mimicry prevails, so the person "passes" as interacting, when he or she is not at all engaged or involved emotionally. It becomes helpful to distinguish behavior that serves as grasping, clinging, or attaching from patterns or modes of interpersonal interacting that constitute reciprocal emotional connection or engagement.

Franz Kafka's literary work portrays organizing themes throughout. He himself must have lived significant organizing experiences to be so exquisitely sensitive to them. In *The Castle* the hero searches endlessly for a way to reach that nipple up on the hill, the castle. He does not even have an identity beyond the initial "K." He believes that he has been sent for and that he is needed as a surveyor, one who defines boundaries. But the castle is elusive, endlessly denying him human recognition. K. extends himself in one way after another, attempting to reach the castle, to prove that "I was sent for, I am wanted, and I have a job here which involves living in the castle village and drawing boundaries." Kafka could not bring himself to finish the book, perhaps because this story was about his own life traumas. But in soirees he read it to friends and told them how the book was to end. All his life K. searches for a connection to the castle without finding it, always frustrated, always almost making it, just about having the castle within grasp. But each time suddenly and inexplicably "something happens."

The phrase "something happens" is of great importance because when people living organizing experiences extend themselves for contact it often lacks an explicit sense of agency, of "you" or "me." The experience is more one of, "I'm reaching, wanting, grasping, almost connecting, or attaining and then something dissolves, something happens." The subjective experience is more one of an impersonal force operating to attract and then, when the possibility of connection is felt or is within grasp, the attraction dissolves, vanishes almost imperceptibly. One woman talks about a wind coming up and all is lost. In Kafka's proposed ending to *The Castle*, K., on his deathbed, has all of his friends gather around him. He still has never been able to directly contact the castle. Suddenly an unexpected messenger arrives from the castle with a cryptic note. The note, in effect, says, "You may stay and work in the village, but not because you were sent for, and not through any merit of your own, but for extraneous reasons." This is the essence of the organizing or psychotic experience: not feeling quite human, not having an identity, not feeling received by the human world. People living organizing experiences often say, "I'm weird. I'm different. I'm not quite human. I'm like a robot. I don't belong. I live in a glass bubble. I exist behind a glass wall that separates me forever from others." They somehow know that the experience they are living has never entered into an interpersonal bonding dance that lets people experience themselves as fully human. People living organizing pockets know that this part of their personality is strange, crazy, psychotic, or weird, and that it cannot find human resonance.

In Kafka's *The Trial* he poses the question, "What is my guilt?" In the end the protagonist bares his chest to the knife. His guilt is for being alive, for wanting more than his mother had to give him. In "On the Origin of The Influencing Machine in Schizophrenia," Tausk (1919) thought to ask his psychotically disorganized patient, "Can you draw me a picture of this machine which so unbearably influences you?" She drew a picture resembling a human body. Searles (1960) writes about the pervasive influence of the nonhuman in organizing experiences. There is not a resonating, rewarding experience of human life at this level. There are only objects, forces, operations, images, and powers, but not "I" or "you" as agencies.

IDENTIFYING ORGANIZING TRANSFERENCE

Identifying transference experience from this level of development begins with the assumption that if psychological attachment, the bonding dance, has not occurred or has only partially occurred, there is a reason. And whatever the reason, it occurred historically in the earliest months of life. Evidence of closed-off psychic channels for human connection and somatic constrictions that make extensions painful is retained in the personality and in the body structure in ways that can be observed in later life as the organizing or psychotic transference. This earliest of transferences represents learning experiences of the infant that occurred whenever he or she emotionally extended or reached out and was somehow turned away, not met, or negatively greeted. The questing activity was met with environmental response that taught the infant not to strive in that way again. The "never go there again" experience effectively marks organizing experiences that later can be identified as transference.

Psychoanalytic work has been characterized from its inception by its focus on bringing into consciousness previously learned, "automatic" or unconscious emotional responsiveness patterns. Psychoanalytic studies have aptly demonstrated how earlier emotional relatedness experience can be observed as structured modes of relatedness that become transferred into later interpersonal interactions. Psychoanalysts ask, "What is keeping this person rigidly held within a certain almost compulsive way of being, of experiencing, and of relating to others?" With people living organizing experiences, the transference structure can be seen as systematically functioning to limit or to prevent sustained human emotional contact. The person learned as an infant that emotional contact is dangerous, frightening, traumatic, and/or life threatening. Relatedness learning during the earliest months of life becomes organized around limiting the extension or reaching-out experience and preventing all forms of contact felt to be frightening, unsatisfying, or unsafe.

In sharp contrast to (borderline) people living out later developed internalized symbiotic relatedness modes and who are terrified of rejection and abandonment, people living organizing experiences are terrified of interpersonal connection. At every moment of longed for and sought for contact, some (psychosomatic) image or experience of a traumatizing other suddenly intervenes to make sustained contact impossible. This is why the working-through process in analysis is accompanied by such intense physical pain. It is as though the minute the infant puts mouth around nipple and starts sucking, some form of terror or poison was the experienced result. Overlearned aversion reappears later as transference. A person may be terrified of any human contact that is likely to cause him or her to reexperience that early massive and very painful trauma. What follows are three examples of how an organizing experience can appear and how we as listeners can gain some grasp of the organizing transference experience.

A Transference Illustration:
Raging at the Therapist

The first case example is from a woman therapist who has been seeing a female client for three years twice a week. An intense therapeutic relationship has developed. The client is a very bright and sophisticated woman, a professional. She lives in the world very comfortably in regard to everyday matters, but she suffers privately from having a "multiple personality." The most troubling switch is when she, without apparent reason, goes into a rageful self. Her therapist sought consultation in a crisis after she got a telephone call following their last session saying, "I'm not coming in any more because there's something wrong with our relationship." The therapist inquires about the nature of the problem. She says, "I can tell you feel there's something wrong with my relationship with Naomi." Naomi is a lesbian woman the client has developed an intimate relationship with. She continued, "You don't think that it's right, or you think there's something wrong with Naomi. There's no point in our going any further so long as you think that way." She's angry, shouting at her therapist, and then she lists a number of other things. "You don't listen this way . . . and you're not that way . . . , " a tirade of angry complaints and accusations leveled at the person and the practice of the therapist that she had never heard before.

Her therapist is in a state of shock, feeling she may never see her again. She is not even clear about what might have been said to upset her. She cannot link her abrupt disruption to anything. The therapist asked, "What makes you think I don't like Naomi? I've always been supportive of your relationship with Naomi." But the client is certain she disapproves of Naomi and of the relationship. So far as the consultant could ascertain the thera-pist has no such negative feelings about the relationship and has no personal biases against lesbianism. In fact, the therapist seems glad her client has found a friend. The therapist is in crisis because she has been able to schedule a telephone appointment with her but is anxious about how it may go. She tells the consultant that her client is basically not lesbian. She's had three or four relationships with women but they've been relationships in which she is looking for soothing contact with a woman, possibly in order to feel mothered. She can't develop relationships with men because she doesn't know how to relate to men. She's confused and frightened by men. She's talked at various times about how even though she's having a sexual relationship with a woman, she doesn't feel that she's lesbian. She doesn't feel like other lesbians. The client feels certain she's really not a lesbian. At one point the therapist had said, "I really don't think you're a lesbian either."

It occurs to the consultant that this could be where the organizing transference became attached, that is, in the therapist's attitude that she's not lesbian. The consultant asks, "How have you developed your view? From all you have told me of her relatedness capacities, she's emotionally three months old. We have no idea what lesbianism means to her, and we have no idea what her future may be. She has developed no real sexual identification yet and therefore, no stable gender identity." The therapist immediately resonates with that. It seems the client is experiencing some breach in empathy. She has determined that her therapist has an attitude that she's not really a lesbian. Now she claims the therapist disapproves of Naomi and of her relationship with Naomi.

Her therapist has learned how to work the organizing experience very skillfully. For many months the two have worked over many connecting and disconnecting experiences in other relationships, although she has not been able to work the organizing transference directly with her therapist—at least not until now. In a series of parallel transferences the two have been studying the ways she connects and disconnects daily with people. She says, "I *feel* fully connected with people. I see people. I talk to people. I move in a social world. Superficially I do very well, but at some other level I know I'm not connected." She has the conviction that her mother "gave me away" in the seventh or eighth month *in utero.* And that what she has been striving for ever since is to be bodily reconnected to mother, to be sustained in a physical relationship. The suggestion is that there was once a connection, but that mother broke the connection. The analytic speaker has no idea how to make or to sustain mental connections.

She has presented one critical traumatic memory. When she was perhaps 2 or 3, she and her mother lived in quite poor circumstances — in maybe one room with a bathroom down the hall. Her mother would often take her to the bathroom with her, and so the child witnessed her mother's miscarriage. Her mother pulled out the bloody fetus and flushed the unborn baby down the toilet. It was a vivid memory. The consultant asks the therapist, "Do you suppose her mother also tried to abort her, because that seems to be what's coming up in the transference? I remember one man who had an endlessly recurring dream desperately hanging onto the edge of a cliff, clinging to one root, about to fall to his death at any moment. His mother later confirmed that she had used a coathanger several times in an attempt to abort him during the pregnancy. His struggle to stay alive was vividly represented in the recurring dream. Do you suppose her memory is a screen memory? Or is it something she actually witnessed? My hunch is that the memory stands out so vividly because she believes 'that's what mother did to me. Mother flushed me down the toilet. Mother broke the contact and flushed me down the toilet in the same way.' Perhaps that's what she experiences you are doing to her right now. She has somehow succeeded in experiencing in transference that you're aborting her. She is using something in your demeanor toward her friend Naomi in order to project the organizing transference wish to abort her into the therapeutic relationship."

The deceptive thing, and the reason this example is clear, and the next one even more interesting, is that when a therapist first starts tracking these organizing experiences in transference they frequently look like symbiotic (abandonment) material. The speaker says, "I'm leaving you because you failed me. You abandoned me and I'm never coming back." Yet, upon closer examination, we begin to realize that as the organizing transference begins to fit into place, the person waits for a moment in which she can recreate the organizing rupture in the relating. She re-created it by screaming accusations at her therapist about her attitudes and how bad she is as a therapist. Her intensity and abruptness as well as her departure from ordinary reality appreciation has left the therapist shaken. She says, "I've never been this shaken with this woman before. I'm worried I'll never see her again. I'm worried she'll never come back." It's not too difficult to infer, under the circumstances, that an unconscious fantasy may exist on the therapist's part of getting rid of her. She then says, "Oh, you know, there's another thing. I have been delaying all week returning her phone calls. She called me. I think, 'I've got ten minutes and I can call her. No, no, no. If I call her tomorrow I'll have 15, so I'll call her tomorrow.'" So she's aware she's pushing her away in that way. The therapist also said she had the fantasy of "Well, you know, she's threatening to be very difficult lately, and the truth of the matter is, if she didn't come back I suppose it wouldn't be the worst thing in the world for me." The client may have picked up some ambivalence in the countertransference that she reads as abortion fantasies, miscarriage fantasies. This is her way of accomplishing the disconnection, first inside herself and then with her therapist.

There are two ways we may study the presence of the organizing transference "rupture in relating"—in its passively repeated form and in its actively mimicked form. In the present example we might first infer that when the baby needed something, mother attempted in some reasonable way to give the baby what she needed but it wasn't right. Mother's attempts failed somehow. So the baby began screaming. We then picture this mother, who with limited resources didn't know how to respond to the baby screaming. Maybe the child had an earache or whatever. Not being able to bear the tension, the mother leaves the scene so the child learns "when I scream mother leaves." So the analytic speaker now screams at her therapist with the expectation that she too will leave her. Her way of accomplishing the rupture is to scream. When the consultant suggested this to the therapist she quickly reviewed every relationship the client has had with a man. At the point in the relationship at which the client begins to feel connected to the man, suddenly she switches into this "other personality," which is a "screaming bitch" and starts screaming and yelling obscenities and accusations at them and so they can't stay around. She accomplishes the break by screaming accusations.

But the activity of actually accomplishing the break belonged to mother and so is somehow identified with, mimicked. According to this line of inference, did mother scream at the baby for misunderstanding her needs in the relationship, for not being responsive to mother's attempts to care for her? We don't know exactly how the primary identification with the mother who broke the contact operates from this limited material but it provides clues to future analytic understanding. The therapist is still left worrying, "But what am I going to do with this disconnection?" Since the therapist has been traumatized, like the mother may have been with the child's needs, she too seems almost ready to flush her down the toilet.

An alternative formulation might use Fraiberg's (1982) notion of *pre-defense*. In observing interactions of neglected and abused children with their parents Fraiberg notices three fundamentally biological reactions that serve to (defensively) control the stimulation: aversion (i.e., flight), freezing, and fighting. This woman's screaming at men and at her therapist might be considered a fighting response in the face of anticipated abusive overstimulation and contact rupture that the organizing transference threatens to generate. The following two vignettes will illustrate the flight and freeze tendencies.

These interpretive hunches connect immediately with the therapist. Then she is ready to talk with her client about it all. The consultant warns, "Don't rush into this material because one thing we know is that when people are in organizing states they can't handle much at any given moment that is abstract, that is verbal. Just be with her for now. You've learned from her rantings. You've seen the small window to her soul from your own shocked experience, which no doubt in some way represents her trauma as an infant. But if you start to talk about it too soon, you'll be introducing ego functioning into space where ego doesn't belong, which may have been her mother's worst empathic error. If so, then you become her psychotic mother by trying to be too helpful!"

On the way out, the therapist says, "I just never know what to expect from these organizing people. I've been really gearing up for the worst." The consultant responds, "Well, maybe you will have a difficult experience with her when you talk with her on the phone today. These people have a way of making it very hard on us." The therapist says, "But you know, it also occurs to me that maybe when I call her, at the other end, there will just be this still, quiet little voice that says, 'Hi, I've missed you.' "

The following week the therapist reports exactly that. She was able to stay with the client and help her feel how awful it was to think that her therapist in some way might disapprove of Naomi or think that a lesbian relationship wasn't right for her. The rupture had been repaired, the connection remade so the client could continue to stay in therapy. But the crucial transference experience that appeared is by no means understood or worked through. This episode represents her first tentative foray into working the organizing transference directly with her therapist. Now the heat is temporarily over and the therapist has a clearer view of the nature of her disconnecting transference replication. The organizing transference seems to be worked through in a series of waves or episodes. The therapist will be more prepared to act quickly next time. The interpretation will perhaps be possible in the non- or preverbal way the therapist stays with her in her rageful self and invites her to stay connected and to live out together her terror of being with the therapist rather than to disconnect or rupture the connection with rage.

A Transference Illustration: Flight from the Therapist

The second example of organizing transference involves a woman therapist who has been seeing a client for three or four years. This client has been driving an hour-and-a-half each week to see her therapist. The therapist says, "so there's a long umbilicus." The client has presented as tenuous in her ability to maintain relationships. In the last six months she has talked frequently about terminating therapy because of money and distance. She canceled her sessions in bad weather and during the winter holiday rush. On several occasions the therapist has empathically tried, "Well, okay, I can understand how busy you are and how far it is. You have accomplished a number of things in therapy, so if you want to consider termination we can talk about that." She even suggested helping her find a therapist who was closer. But that all became taboo. The client was allowed to talk about termination, but the therapist was forbidden to talk about it.

On the occasion in question the client called during the Christmas holidays and without any warning canceled all future appointments. Her therapist made several phone calls in unsuccessfully attempting to reach her. She sent a Christmas card. She did everything she could to reach out to her. The therapist thought, "Well, maybe it's best that she stop and this is her way of stopping. Maybe I shouldn't be pursuing her." This *laissez-faire* attitude may be appropriate for listening to more differentiated forms of personality organization but is clearly not empathic when working an organizing transference in which the client cannot initiate or sustain connection and is frequently compelled to break it. This therapist is an empathic and intuitive woman and so remained persistent in her attempts to restore the connection. They finally did connect by phone and the therapist discovered what happened. The client said, "In the last session I was telling you about my friend Valerie and you turned away. Then I knew you didn't care for me so there wasn't any point in my coming back."

As the incident was discussed in consultation, the consultant encouraged the therapist to review recent events in order to get some content about what was going on with Valerie. Concrete images about contact ruptures serve us well in understanding organizing experiences. It is often important to ascertain exactly what was being talked about, and why turning away to pick up a cup of tea was seen as a rejection. The woman has been slowly backing away, but not letting the therapist back away. The therapist can't talk about termination but the client was waiting for the moment when the therapist turns at a critical moment so that the rupture of the organizing transference can be attached to the therapist's turning-away activity. The consultant says, "She's found a way to live out the organizing transference of mother disconnecting. This is the window to the organizing experience we are waiting for. We wait for the moment in which the reenactment of the turning away, the breaking of contact, the rupture of experience happens in the transference."

This episode might be mistaken for a symbiotic-relating scenario or narcissistic breach in empathy—"just when I needed affirmation from you, just when I need something from you, you turned away." It could be seen as splitting; it could be seen as abandonment; it could be seen as selfobject failure. But the consultant had heard developments in the case several times before, enough to realize that there was a deep organizing component. In response to the consultant considering the rupture as disconnecting transference, the therapist said, "You know, she's been married for twenty years. So I had always thought of her as basically symbiotic or borderline in her object relations. But now I recall a number of instances with her husband in which she must have been in an organizing pocket and experienced her husband in transference as the psychotic mother." But now the rupture of relating had actually been recreated with the therapist. The therapist says, "It's funny, during this time period she had moved. She called my recorder to leave her new phone number on it. And, you know, I didn't take the phone number off the machine before I erased the message." So the analytic listener is ready in some sense to let her die, too.

The therapist was fired up with these ideas because they seemed to make sense and to organize in her mind many past incidents. She's ready to go back and talk to her client about all of this. The consultant cautioned her not to rush and explained why. The therapist tunes in quickly and says, "I feel like, where we're at right now, is we're both laying down in a playpen and I have to wait for her to come to me." The consultant reminded her the baby has to be allowed to find the breast but it must be available to be found. The transference to the psychotic mother will be reenacted again and again so there will be ample time to interpret. But the therapist can use her new understanding to simply be with her client in new ways. She was reminded of what she already knew from her studies of the organizing experience, that abstract verbal interpretations per se will not touch this very early transference. Interpretation at the organizing level must be a concrete activity, often manifest in physical gesture or interpretive touch *at the specific moment when the analytic speaker is actually in the act of pulling away from contact, of (transferentially) creating a rupture.* Viable interpretation of the organizing transference involves an actual, physical, concrete reaching out of one person toward another in such a way as to communicate, "I know you believe you must break off our personal engagement in this way now. But it is not true. You have, as an adult, the ability to stay here now with me and experience your long-standing terror of connectedness. How can you manage not to leave me now? Can we manage to remain in contact for just a few more minutes?"[1] Clients often deliberately and perhaps wisely conduct the early phases of therapy at quite some distance from the therapist by spacing appointments far apart or arranging long and difficult drives. They often sit at a distance from the therapist. They know that closeness can only be experienced by them as traumatic. Thus, the invitation to sustain contact must be cautiously offered.

The therapist had arranged this consultation because she was concerned about her own anger. In the midst of all the client's coming and not coming, calling and canceling, connecting and disconnecting, the therapist had become enraged and said she was "just ready to kill her" when she sees her on Thursday. She even made a slip and said, "I have an appointment with her on Saturday." The consultation group laughed to think she doesn't want to see her so soon as Thursday. She's an excellent therapist, and of course she really does want to connect, but it is easy to understand the countertransference ambivalence. Ruptures in relating, which organizing transferences necessarily entail, stir up organizing experiences in the therapist (See chapter 11).

---

1. All forms of physical contact have been avoided in traditional psychoanalytic psychotherapy. However, it becomes clear that when the organizing rupture in contact is being actively lived out that the client is in an extremely concrete state of mind and adequate empathic contact may involve token "interpretive touching" in the specific manner just suggested. Elsewhere I consider the many and complex issues involved in this concretized form of interpretations (Hedges 1994b).

A Transference Illustration:
Frozen in Impotent Rage

In the third example of how organizing transference works, an emerging theme of an otherwise very well-developed woman has been related to the organizing period. This example is from a much later working-through period of the analysis (with a male therapist) and occurs in a personality much more capable of verbal abstractions than the previous two. The woman's mother, during the baby's first few months of life, was afraid to pick up her baby for fear of "breaking" her. It's been discovered through several years of intensive psychotherapy that there were many strengths this mother was able to stimulate in this child, but at the deepest psychic level there are connecting difficulties. The emergent theme over several weeks was the analytic speaker's rage that occurs on a fairly regular basis in social situations when she knows that the person she's interacting with can indeed do more for her, and be more there for her but somehow flakes out. In short, her rage is mobilized at people when they have more potentially to offer than in fact the person is actively living in the current relationship.

In a key session she develops the theme further. Early in the marriage, she says, her husband was far more warm, far more giving, and far more available than he is now, and she is angry that he isn't more available when she knows he can be. She becomes exasperated to the point of feeling utterly helpless and frozen. By the same token, she indicates that what attracted her to a close friend was that this other woman had so much to give. The friend is well traveled and well read. She is alive, active, versatile, a good conversationalist, and much more. But, in a recent example, when her friend had a bit of the flu and refused to get out of bed to go to her son's very first baseball game, "then I don't see her any longer as what she could be or might be for

me, if she can't be there for her own son. I become angry and
disillusioned with her. Now I know what has been bothering me
so much lately about her in our relationship. Too often she
cancels, flakes out, or blobs out when I know she doesn't have
to, when I know she has far more to give but is choosing not to.
I become completely immobilized in impotent rage."

In the discussion of various examples that have occurred
with her husband and her friend, she said, "Now I'm finding that
not only when I'm enraged at the other person for not living up
to their potential do I not get what they have to offer me; but I
also see that when I'm enraged I am totally unable to take in, to
get, to make use of that which they can in fact offer me." She
referenced some examples from previous transference experiences in therapy where she, in complaining bitterly about the
therapist's seemingly endless unavailability over the holidays
and weekends, was so preoccupied in her hours leading up to the
holidays that she was unable to make use of whatever good
experiences might be possible in the sessions. Her comment is,
"Something always happens." The emphasis here is on the
subjective statement of the disconnecting experience being impersonal. It's not, "I'm disappointed with the other." Or, "The
other lets me down." Or, "The other fails to live up to his
potential." It's "We're interacting and then *something happens* and
the potential that is there isn't being lived out, and I fall into a
lost state of sadness and grief, which is usually manifest in
instantaneous but frozen rage."

At this point in the session the client realizes she has lost or
repressed a further insight regarding her husband and friend
that she was very excited about only a moment before when she
connected to it. But just as quickly as the insight came, it fled
and she was very disturbed for some time about having lost this
insight.

Late in the session she provides another example of some
neighbors whom, when she first began to get to know them, she
experienced as somewhat available. Now she experiences them

more as users than givers. And while, she acknowledges, this latter is no doubt also true in ways, she cites several instances in the beginning of their relationship in which the neighbors were very supportive, very helpful, very outgoing. But the man in the couple began on occasion to have other things that kept him away from doing things with them. And the woman began not being able to have lunch with the client often or visit over coffee. Before too long there were enough gaps in the relationship that it became unbearable to her. She says, "It's easy to say they aren't meeting my needs. I'll have to go elsewhere." But she realizes that this is not entirely the case. They do have some things to offer, but because they're not offering all that they can, she feels that "mysterious unbearable pain" again.

After a few thoughtful moments she said, "It sounds like a reason to break contact." The therapist quickly replied, "No, it's the *way* you break contact." The client then said excitedly, "That's exactly what I lost. I was trying to formulate the problem with my husband and my friend in terms of how I break contact but I couldn't quite get there. If I'm always living in what a person could give me but isn't, then several things happen: One, I have reason not to relate to them. Two, I'm not relating to them at all but I'm relating rather to my fantasy. And, three, they do have something to give or I wouldn't be relating to them, but in my distress and frozen anger I'm completely missing what they have to give to me. I break the contact by being sad and enraged, complaining about what I'm not getting."

At this point she slowed down and indicated that she was emoting very deeply, that she felt she'd reached a very profound point. "I know somehow that this can change my life if I can finally get hold of it. If I can find some way of fully knowing about this, I will be able to change many things." Her therapist said, "It seems as though you have located the mechanism regarding how the contact is broken and how it relates to the early experiences of your mother who, much of the time, was there so that you knew full well what things she could provide.

But when she was preoccupied, or not willing or able to give, or frightened about how she might harm the baby, she bowed out leaving you stuck, knowing that she could give more but that she was not giving it. No wonder she reports that you were such a good baby and slept a lot! The content of the transference is, 'You could be giving me more but you're not.' " Then the client said, "Now I know why my daughter seems to be left out of this dynamic. You know how I've always said with her it's somewhat different? Well, the difference is that I'm not expecting to be given to by her. I understand that her role isn't to give to me and so I'm much freer to relate to her without this pain coming up. The few instances in which I do lose it with her, I may feel that she's not giving me her full cooperation as freely and fully as I know that she can. But, in fact, I am able to take a great deal from her by simply being with her – by being present while she is losing her baby teeth, or brushing her hair. I go to softball league with her and I receive through just watching." Her therapist said, "You do take what she has to offer." She responded, "Yes, but it's often very indirectly, just by enjoying being with her. Whatever she does is so wonderful and beautiful that it's a very rich experience just being by her side."

The client then comments about last week's Thursday session. "I was concerned that you didn't know about my feelings of caring for you and how grateful I feel to you for just being here with me. I get a lot from you by just being with you even if you don't have a lot to give on a certain day." (The therapist had an eye infection on that day and his spirits were a little off. It was something she detected and expressed concern about within that hour.)

"Now," she continued, "I find I'm a little scared about knowing all of this. Things keep clicking in my mind – more and more examples. It's like my whole life is built on this single mechanism. No wonder I wasn't happy when John, my supervisor, failed to tune in to me completely when I knew he could. If I finally identify this, I may be able to change. I am excited, but

I think I'm mostly very scared. I think the scare is that I won't remember this, I won't be able to take hold of it. I won't be able to make it my own."

The therapist said, "No. The scare is that you will remember it. You are in the process of deep change and as you are changing you are coming face to face with a terror you have avoided all your life. The terror of having to encounter a real live person who has some good things to offer but who may not, for a variety of reasons, be willing or able to give fully in all areas. Sooner or later in every relationship you encounter this situation and it brings back the sad and rageful reactions you had to your mother during your earliest months of life. So you have been unable to continue relating or you have given up the relating when the conditions are not met right. What you are scared of is actually allowing yourself to negotiate the uncertainties of relationships and to survive the positive possibilities as well as the painful disappointments, which are bound to be a frightening and powerful consequence of fully knowing and living out what you are now discovering."

Each of these three examples serves to illustrate how the rupture of the organizing experience is repeated in transference. In each instance multiple interpretive possibilities exist. The decisive moment of organizing transference interpretation is not visible in any of these examples—in the first two because the relationship had not yet arrived there, and in the third because the *in vivo* interpretations had already begun and the client was in a later stage of "owning" the interpretative work, though she expresses fear of losing it. Examples of the actual interpretive and working through process will be provided in Chapter 10. The presence of Fraiberg's (1982) three "pre-defenses" of aversion, freezing, and fighting is suggested in three case vignettes presented and may be seen as the clients' ways of achieving a rupture in contact that, due to transference projections, is threatening to become overstimulating.

10

Working Through the Organizing Transference

THE CONCEPT OF TRANSFERENCE PSYCHOSIS

The specter of madness has haunted humankind for centuries. But the systematic study of insanity arose only in the nineteenth century, coinciding with the industrial revolution and rise of urbanization. Whether the increased awareness of insanity arose because more craziness was being produced by the changing conditions of human life, or whether the increased social demand for more coordinated cooperation in working and living situations brought insanity more into public view, is a question that remains unanswered. Relabeling the problem "mental illness" has been credited with leading to more humane treatment for people suffering with various pronounced forms of mental disturbance. But now after more than a century of intense scientific and clinical study of various symptom clusters or syndromes, a radical paradigm shift is emerging in the way that psychological organization is conceptualized (Hedges 1992). The word that best describes the new conceptual approach is *relatedness*. Jacobson (1954, 1964) was the first to describe her psychoanalytic work with "more deeply disturbed" individuals as a study in the way people represent themselves in relation to others. Numerous "self and other representation" studies followed until it became evident that human mental life itself could be considered as systematically organized in layerings of representations of the way people experience and represent themselves in relation to the various ways that they represent others through different phases of human development. According to this metaphor each layering arises out of or is built upon the ways that previous experiences of self and other representation have been laid down in psychic memory. Memory itself has come to be considered a function of the way a person's experiences of self and others have come to operate. According to this view the most important features in the human environment are other humans with whom the developing child has significant intimate daily contact. Mental structure itself is thought to arise from and to be dependent upon early relatedness experiences. Mental efficiency, cognitive and affective styles, memory organization, social skills, intelligence, and creativity itself are the product of early relatedness experience and bear the indelible mark of those whom we were first attached to and first learned to love and hate. Relatedness intelligence is thought to develop in early childhood and to provide the foundation for many possibilities and restrictions in our capacities for satisfying and fulfilling lives.

The relatedness thought paradigm conceives of early relatedness experiences as having established psychic representations that serve as memories associated with physical constrictions and psychological restrictions that limit, distort, and undermine our capacities for joyful, loving, and creative living. Our understanding of madness thus has a new face. Human madness is universal and it relates to unfortunate experiences we each had as infants that have left us with a series of greater or lesser limiting relatedness assumptions that have systematically exercised a devious and destructive influence upon all subsequent layerings or levels of our psychological organization.

While poets and philosophers have long been fond of pointing to universal forms of insanity, the first psychological writer to suggest that a *forme fruste* (morsel) of intense delusional belief can be seen in almost every case of psychoanalysis was Hammett (1961). The term *transference psychosis* was suggested by Gitelson to Reider (1957), who uses the term more descriptively and etiologically, feeling the term is less dynamically precise than its Freudian analogue *transference neurosis*. Rosenfeld (1954) describes how psychotic manifestations are linked to the psychoanalytic transference so that the patient includes the analyst in the delusion. Little (1958) uses the term *delusional transference*, saying, "In practice one finds certain patients who cannot use transference interpretations; the difference between these and other patients is qualitative not quantitative" (p. 134). By 1981 she collected her papers on the subject in a book entitled, *Transference Neurosis and Transference Psychosis: Toward a Basic Unity*. Transference psychosis then becomes a developmentally earlier transference manifestation that contrasts sharply with transference neurosis.

Wallerstein (1967) summarizes the Freudian concept of transference neurosis as follows:

> On both clinical and theoretical grounds the transference neurosis has long been established as the central technical and conceptual vehicle of psychoanalysis as a therapy. The usual course of psychoanalysis and of the development of this regressive transference reaction is characterized by the familiar reactivation within the analysis of earlier (i.e., infantile) experiences and also of earlier (i.e., infantile) modes of reacting to and mastering those experiences. At times this reactivation within the analytic transference can (temporarily anyway) sufficiently

lose its "as if" quality to become near delusional. Classical analysis is, however, usually protected against such extensive reality disorientation by the split, described by Sterba (1934) into an observing (introspecting) ego alongside the experiencing ego. It is this observing part of the ego which in its guardian function enables one constantly to maintain distance from, and exert reality mastery over, the transference illusion. [p. 551]

Little (1958) points out that in the delusional transference or transference psychosis the saving "as if" quality is gone. At the moment of experiencing, the analyst *is*, with a strong sense of authenticity, the idealized and deified as well as the diabolized parent. Ferenczi (1912, 1919) first describes how actual hallucinations can be evoked in and by the analytic hour and shows how some patients are overwhelmed by impulses and act out their psychic content in the analytic hour. Wallerstein (1967) presents two analytic cases in which, in the unfolding of the transference, the expectable split in the ego did not occur and the ego was "overwhelmed by the intensity of the liberated affects" (p. 577). Reider (1957) points out that psychotic episodes in psychoanalysis occur under two circumstances: either a previous psychotic state is reenacted, or an identification with a psychotic person is reenacted. Wallerstein's cases illustrate both kinds of circumstances. He calls for "setting forth more explicitly the range of specific circumstances under which these ego vulnerabilities occur and the intrapsychic functions they serve" (p. 584).

Since that time various writers have addressed these issues in terms of the traditional concerns of psychoanalysis, but only now are we in a position to let our attention turn to the issues as they emerge within the new relatedness paradigm, within the context of the earliest self and other representations. Hedges (1994c) has put forth a series of dimensions along which the ego's earliest experiences can be listened to in psychotherapy. But the central therapeutic approach, as with the establishment of the transference neurosis, relates to that moment when the delusional transference or the transference psychosis is activated within the analytic relationship. There is much to be said about the nature of this organizing-level transference structure and how it can be framed for analysis. Here the focus will be on the working-through phase and how the therapist may position him or herself to empathically interpret psychic extensions of the client. How empathy can be expressed regarding the wall or block to interpersonal experiencing is the central technical problem and requires precise thinking and precise timing.

EGO VULNERABILITIES AND HUMAN TOUCH

Hedges (1992), in an extended discussion of psychoanalytic empathy, raises the central questions of "empathy with what, and what forms will it take?" Kohut's (1981) last talk at Berkeley is cited wherein he calls for the elaboration of a developmental line of empathy that extends from complex verbal-symbolic activity with advanced issues of the Oedipus complex downward developmentally toward increasingly concrete forms of postural, facial, and gestural empathy. In a symposium, "Touch: The Foundation of Experience," Brazelton and Barnard (1990) trace the philosophical, epistemological, interpersonal, and curative aspects of touch throughout the ages, concluding that human experience originates in empathic forms of actual physical touch. As depicted by Michelangelo on the ceiling of the Sistine Chapel, touch is critically involved in conveying the divine spirit of the Logos to the human soul. Symposium participants agreed that the critical feature of human touch, which conveys the human spirit from one person to another, is the motivation of the one touching.

Hedges (1994c) discusses at length a specialized form of

interpretive touch that is appropriate – and at times necessary – for extending human empathy to the earliest organizing levels of self and other representation, to reach the earliest ego vulnerabilities. He takes the position that the earliest task of the infant is to organize channels of contact to the maternal body and later to the maternal mind. People pervasively living organizing-level experiences in later life or people attempting to revive for analysis a pocket of organizing-level ego vulnerability have experienced an arrest in psychic development during a time in their lives when physical contact with the maternal body was the only way that the infant mind could be effectively contacted. As a result, the organizing or psychotic block is a somatic one – an internalized fear of emotionally reaching out and touching others or allowing touch by others in ways that were experienced in earliest infancy as traumatic. At certain (well-defined) critical junctures with such people, the analytic regression takes them to a level where any attempt at distinguishing psyche from soma fails – where psyche and soma are truly the same experience.

Successfully framing for analysis the somatopsychic organizing-level internalization entails meeting the person at the level of the arrest – which means at the level of physical contact. Such interpretive touching is not for the purposes of making either the person in analysis nor the analyst feel soothed, comforted, or safe per se. Rather, the invitation to make interpersonal contact on a token physical level – when offered at the exact moment that the internalized rupture in contact is activated – can serve as a physically concrete, empathically timed, interpretive response on the analyst's part.

The offer of physical connection in effect says, "I understand that in your primordial past when emotional contact with others was a present possibility that you somehow experienced what was offered as traumatic. We are here to study what went wrong during that period so that you have been forever cut off from various kinds of human interaction and personal fulfillment. Throughout your life whenever the possibility of intimate interpersonal contact has been offered it has been necessary for you to move into a 'fight, flee, or freeze' pattern [Fraiberg 1982] because your learning experiences had taught you that human contact is frightening and dangerous. I am here with you now. You experience our being together and feeling close as a primordial threat which you must avoid at all cost. This is not true. We have been together for a long time. Certain kinds of trust and continuity have developed between us. We can stay together and enjoy human closeness. You do not have to fight me. You do not have to flee contact. You do not have to freeze in fear. We can make contact with each other that is wholesome and fulfilling for both of us. Can you hold my hand now? Can you work to overcome your overwhelming urge to split away? Can you stay with me a few minutes so that we can both know that we are human, that we care for one another, that feeling close is a good feeling, that contact with each other can be safe?" For many people this will be the first time since infancy that an invitation to be together has been offered in such a way that it can be accepted – albeit not without fear and trembling and not without a difficult follow-up working-through process.

BEYOND THE UNTHOUGHT KNOWN

At the organizing level the discoveries of somatopsychic blockages are not unthought known, they are puzzling, traumatic, and unknown. That is, the internalized compulsion to break contact, in whatever form that rupture takes, forecloses knowledge of how one withdraws because it is pre-defensive and exists at the somatic level of neurological conditioning rather than at a more clearly psychic level. The known is at best that the connecting other is somehow dangerous and that connections are to be avoided – much as any prey knows danger situations that are to be avoided – though it may not have explicit knowledge of what it feels like to be in the hawk's talons or to struggle for its life. The subject can only struggle to somehow control the danger emanating from intersubjective contact with the other – through imitation, and various manipulations involving moods, guilt, and demand, because the impetus is basically a defense or a fending off of threatening stimuli associated with survival.

Whatever desperate maneuvers the person uses or however he or she experiences the other impinging – it is reasonable to assume that the function of the activity is self-protective. The neurons function on a quasi-instinctual avoidance of threat basis, thereby making it impossible to observe and to analyze whatever personal reactive potentials might emerge in the absence of defense. The activity presented to us does not tell us the withdrawal story, only the pre-defense used to fend off reexperiencing the original sequence of primary neuronal activity involved in the first terrified flight from (dependency) circumstances that are judged or misjudged as similar to the potential interpersonal connection of the present. The activity that can be observed is inevitably an outward-directed response to what the other is doing or not doing rather than to potential internal dangers or potential overstimulation. That is, the pre-defensive activity is directed toward the persecutory object's activities, real and/or projected.

Freud (1920) set the stage for understanding this externalization process when he envisioned an organism with outward-turned sensory receptors developing an energized protective shield. The defense activity against external impinging stimuli is effective enough so that soon the organism begins to project the impinging internal stimuli onto the outside in an attempt to control them with the protective shield as well.

The persecutory pattern and the modes of breaking contact are not where the action to be understood, to be analyzed, is. Their function is pre-defensive avoidance. The technical problem is how to stop the pre-defensive action and let the terrifying organizing transference sequence unfold. The original impingement, according to Winnicott (1949), is into the continuity of being, into the infantile sense of "going on being," into the sense of being alive and safe. Because the early impingement intrudes into life's continuity the infant is obliged on the basis of a survival instinct to react. And the pattern of this primordial reaction constitutes the first thought pattern. Since it is in response to impingement, this primary governing template, which influences all subsequent thought, is necessarily experienced as persecutory in nature. The persecutory template then exists as a fundamental foreclosure mechanism that operates with many faults until later in life when it can be analyzed. One of the faults is that the person is always on the lookout for certain classes of impingements, projecting them onto situations that may have similar cues to the original one but are not the same. Another thought fault occurs when the person is monitoring the environment for certain classes of cues that spell danger and tends to miss whole other classes of danger situations, thus setting up a vicious circle of maladaptation and leaving one a sitting duck for real exploitation coming when one is not tuned into danger situations that common sense would otherwise warn one about. A third problem is the wholesale importation of some form of fear response (learned in connection with infantile sensorimotor capabilities and under conditions of total dependency) into situations of later life that might be characterized by more diverse and reliable sensorimotor modes and the capacity for psychic independence.

Behavioral conditioning studies have manipulated in numerous research experiments an array of proximal and distal cues to positive and negative reinforcement situations, showing without a doubt that mammals are readily conditioned to all types of peripheral cues. The classic example is Pavlov's dog, but conditioning studies have demonstrated a series of kinds of learning and extinction curves involving extremely complex sequences and combinations of cues to which subjects "neurotically" and "psychotically" become conditioned. Harlow's cloth monkeys and rubber spiders are the best known. But Pavlov's dogs and Harlow's monkeys are only the simplest kinds of experiments from a massive body of elegant conditioning research. They stand out in the public imagination because their lessons are clear and graphically portrayed. One trial conditioning is commonly observed when strong aversive stimulation is provided—and this singular fact is of great interest to the present discussion.

In understanding conditioned fear of interpersonal contact, we have yet to appreciate and specify the wide variety of dimensions involved. Bion (1962, 1963, 1977) and Grotstein (1981) speak of predator–prey anxiety, and the critical dimension of binocular vision. Lacan (1977) speaks of human evolution according to complex visual environmental cues. Tomatis (1991), the French audiologist, envisions human evolution as an ear that has grown a body—highlighting the importance of the auditory. Patrick Suskind's imaginative novel *Perfume* as well as infant research into smell suggests the power of olfactory stimulation in organizing early mind. All these basic conditioning examples point to the critical and central place of infantile sensory perception in conditioning the organizing-level transference structure. All of Kafka's literary work (e.g., 1926, 1937, 1979) abounds in sensory imagery.

Fraiberg's pre-defenses point to the biological means of managing impinging stimuli that become experienced as threatening. These modes likewise become incorporated into the early transference structure. We have reason to believe that considerable conditioning occurs before birth and we are able to observe it directly in the hours, days, and months after birth. Stern (1985) cites infant research to demonstrate that in the earliest months perception and response is amodal. For example, a sharp auditory stimulus may cause the baby to close its eyes in an attempt to flee the sound. Infant research demonstrates that sensory input of all types is responded to globally and amodally at first. The distinctions in the sensorimotor modalities we commonly think of only slowly evolve out of a much more general and interrelated stimulus–response system operating at birth. Such fusions and global sensorimotor responsiveness also appear when the organizing transference structure is being experienced.

This is all to say that what cues are being conditioned to what traumatic impingements in infancy is a complex matter, and it is anybody's guess what is happening at the time of early experience. Khan's (1963) concept of *cumulative trauma* makes clear that even the best-trained infant observers do not know how to observe or interpret cumulative strain trauma at the time it is occurring because such stimulus–response sequences often operate invisibly and silently in infancy. Only retrospectively when childhood disturbances or adult breakdown under stress occur can it be inferred that damage was being done to the child that could not be seen at the time (A. Freud 1958).

What was learned, what was conditioned in infancy was a pre-defensive reaction, a genetically determined or reflexive behavioral means of blocking out classes of environmental cues that were present proximally and distally in the original infantile trauma situation. Faulty responses to cues may have been further mislearned because of fused, global, or amodal perception and motor response operating in early infancy. In psychoanalysis, what lies beyond the defense is a set of sequences of terrifying responses, which Winnicott (1974) has sketched out in broadest terms in his "Fear of Breakdown" paper. Green's (1986) formulations regarding the dead mother must be governed by similar considerations. Because the impingements of commission or omission are persecutory in their effect in infancy, the only way to manage the stimulus was to withdraw and to defend in whatever way the organism could manage. "I have learned to be in relationships by learning mechanisms of disconnection from the other in order to feel safe and to comfort myself." To understand the contemporary relational attempts of the adult subject or the relational activities of the interacting other does not tell the story. The intersubjective field is foreclosed by pre-defense. Knowledge of the prerelational past is required but, in its details, forever unknowable in principle. Its effects can, however, be charted and defined in a systematic exploration of the transference psychosis.

FRAMING THE ORGANIZING TRANSFERENCE

In framing the transference psychosis for analytic study, there is much room for a Kleinian (1952, 1957, 1975) understanding of splitting and projective identification, as well as Tustin's (1972) formulation of confusional or entangled autism, which resembles Mahler's (1968) symbiotic psychosis. But such considerations are developmentally later than the organizing transference that blocks the infant's movement toward projection and projective identification. That is, the infant reaches out. To the extent the extension is received and experienced as pleasurable the reaching in this manner is reinforced and a channel is found to the maternal body and mind. Conversely, if the reaching is not actively rewarded, is ignored, or actively punished in some way, a block to ever reaching in that way again is conditioned. Between these two extremes there is a world of sometimes finding, sometimes not finding—along with whatever result is conditioned to whatever proximal and distal cues that may be present in the moment. That is, Tustin's confusional or entangled autistic child did connect enough with the externally perceived mother to have its psychic mechanisms confused with hers through early splitting and projective mechanisms. Her encapsulated autistic child was once connected at the physical level and at the sensuous level, but the sensual connection was ruptured prematurely and traumatically so that the child could only build a wall that served to keep out incoming stimuli that might have built a sensuous bridge to the mother's psyche. One might further consider other oral-level compulsions involving food, addictive substances, and tactile (sexual) sensations. Here one might imagine that there was once a reaching, and a certain finding. The overall fate of the finding is recorded in the way the symptom operates on the one hand to find, bring, and conserve needed and comforting aspects of the object, and on the other hand to expel, repel, and destroy the aversive and unwanted aspects of the connecting object.

In analytic listening framed in terms of confusional or entangled mechanisms, a part of psyche was presumably once open to early interpersonal connecting and to the development of splitting and projective identification mechanisms. But a part of psyche had an eye to biological safety and so maintained enough distance and disconnection to avoid anticipated dangers—even though there may have been a faulty or globally determined assessment of the central or peripheral cues in the persecutory situation. The action that is later displayed responds to these faultily interpreted cues and focuses on the external environment because there is no way the internal terror responses can be viewed, since they may have occurred only once and then been foreclosed from reexperiencing by the blocking of the fear response. That is, the pre-defensive safety mechanisms function to keep things out of the psyche, to keep life at the somatic level, to prevent elaboration through reflection. This means not only that knowledge and experience in these areas cannot be elaborated through subsequent experience, but that allied experiences remain distorted because they are isolated. But most importantly it means that the foreclosed potential experience is not part of Bollas's (1987) "unthought known" to be recovered as memory because it was never actually known—only fleetingly and instinctually apprehended in a gross and globally perceived manner and reacted to with helplessness, terror, withdrawal, and total blocking.

Bollas's unthought known references early preverbal, pre-representational mother–infant experiences that make up the basic working knowledge of our personalities but have not become the subject of systematic thought until the psychoanalytic relationship brings the experiences into the realm of the experienced and thought. The foreclosed area of the organizing-level experience remains essentially unknown but marked with dread. That is, the unthought known is made up of living modes of interaction, affects, and moods that conserve early experience with others. The foreclosed area contains only dread and terror of vaguely experienced unknowns related to dependency connections—such as the fear of breakdown of functioning, the fear of an empty or persecutory environment, and the fear of starvation, abandonment, and death. When any cues similar to the proximal or distal cues present in the original learning situation present themselves in subsequent experience, an instinctive pre-defense of fight, flight, or freeze occurs, preventing contemporary assessment and response to what may be more objectively happening in the moment. The predefense is a struggle for survival and held onto tenaciously.

Primordial memories that conditioned the predefensive responses are from such an early developmental period that they globally fuse and confuse the sensorimotor modalities involved and the nature and source of stimulus cues arising from inside and/or outside the body, whether the attributed agency is self or other, or even whether the central sensorimotor focus possesses an attracting or an aversive quality as it is confounded with peripheral and nonrelevant cues. If we needed a working definition of psychosis this would certainly be it. Transference psychosis results when the analyst becomes a part of this confusional, delusional perceptual motor system—as is inevitable in the working-through process of intensive psychotherapy and psychoanalysis. And when symptoms and memories are constructed to express the primordial, life-threatening trauma they take on a realistic hallucinatory vividness of life and death proportions. This vividness of recovered memories corresponds to the phenomenon of dreams that have hallucinatory vividness—the key fact of importance upon which Freud built his first theory of mind and the unconscious (1900, Chapter VII).

ORGANIZING TRANSFERENCE: CUTTING OFF THE PASSIONATE LINK[1]

One woman during a phase of the working-through process of the organizing transference had the following experience. She and her family had been away for the weekend with another family and had quite a nice time. This was during a deep period when she and her analyst were maintaining contact with each other seven days of the week and had been doing so for several weeks. She had been back from the weekend for a day and was concerned that her friends she had taken the trip with had not yet called her to "check in." She was further concerned when she could not reach them, feeling the panic of being out of contact with them. Her husband thought nothing about it and even chanced the comment of, "Well, don't worry about it. They're probably just sick of being with us and need a few days off!" Realistically, she knew that this was the case, but inside she felt a terrible panic because a close and intimate connection was not being sustained.

Her thoughts drifted to a conversation of the previous day regarding her younger brother who arrived when she was 18 months old. That conversation centered on the problem of what happened when mother turned to the new baby to take care of the baby and how she lost her mother in the process. This particular discussion had been occasioned because for the last

---

1. This is a follow-up episode from the analysis of the woman in the third vignette in Chapter 9.

two weeks the client was feeling emotionally shut off from the analyst despite (or as it later turns out, because of) the intense seven-day-a-week contact. The event that had stimulated the closing down or shutting off had occurred at a Saturday session. When she arrived at her analyst's office she saw another woman whom she did not know in the secretarial portion of the office. Her fantasy was that this special Saturday session was not so special and that the woman was a close friend, or perhaps a date of the analyst, who was waiting for him. She felt the analyst was not really emotionally present because he was simply waiting for the time to pass so that he could be with the person of his choice. (This was in fact not the case. The woman was a student doing some work in the office that day. But this piece of information never came to light.) During the two-week interval since, much of the concern had been on the emotional closing down. Although she knew that right now her analyst was more available emotionally to her than ever because of his willingness to provide the possibility of intense contact, nonetheless it was at this point of greater availability that she found herself cutting off, walling off. There had been much talk about her mother's involvement with her younger brother throughout the years, and then how the situation was no doubt made worse when a sister came along only 18 months after her brother.

Today, however, she comments that long before her siblings were born there was a third party whom she believed had the power to take mother's attention away—her father. She spoke of her mother's style of relating, which she could remember throughout her childhood. When mother was angry or felt confronted, she would simply close off in a sort of walled off, sullen way. She remembers as a child she often did not know what she had done that had made her mother angry. She knew she had done something, but it was not clear what because her mother would close off and would not talk. She supplied a piece of new information today. Her mother once told her that in the later phases of pregnancy with her, and into the earliest months of the child's life, there was extreme marital discord. Now she can imagine that during these early months of life when father would enter the room or be present, that her mother's overall emotional availability would be suddenly closed off, shut off—as has been her mother's lifelong character style.

In silent, slow tearfulness she then recounted another episode that has happened this past week with a close business colleague whom she frequently gets together with to share their mutual concerns and business activities. They had scheduled two meetings during the week that she was very much looking forward to when he called. He said that he had been unexpectedly required to leave town and would be taking a flight out Tuesday afternoon. Was there any way he could get together with her on Tuesday before he left? She had some time and he rearranged his schedule so that a Tuesday meeting could be scheduled. She said, "I tried not to take it personally, but nevertheless I did. As soon as he said he had to cancel the two meetings I was looking forward to, there was no way I could hear that he wanted to be with me and was doing a great deal to rearrange his schedule so that he could meet with me before he left town. It was as though that was all incidental." She experienced a total collapse inside around his canceling the meetings. She is very tearful now and the sensation is that the relationship will never be the same again. This parallels the sense that she had with her friends today. Because the contact was not there exactly when she needed it, she collapses into feeling somehow they would be lost forever. This feeling parallels her sense that the analyst has other concerns with other people and is also lost forever. She experiences a tearful realization that there would never be another person "there for her" in the way and at the time she desperately needs them.

The picture then emerged of her lying in her crib reaching to mother, but mother not being able to respond because she was herself emotionally unavailable. She then became aware of painful body sensations. The lower part of her body became tight and stiff as though she were digging her heels in. This seemed like a way of filling out the picture that with the upper part of her body she could reach to her mother, to her analyst; but the lower part of her body was refusing. The analyst commented that what seemed lost forever was the passionate link. Even though she knew with her business colleague, with her friends, with her analyst, that she did have a good relationship and good connections, when third parties seemed to detract attention, the internalized sensation was one of the passion being lost forever. She could feel the cutting off process as "something happening" in her body. This was linked to her historical sense as an infant that when father would enter the room, mother might remain physically present, mother might even be doing her motherly tasks, but somehow the passionate link between mother and baby would be lost with her not having any power to restore it.

The analyst's question was whether this seems more like the infant's cutting off the passionate link and finally putting herself to sleep in the face of helplessness, as a way of withdrawing to take care of herself. Or was this the infant identifying with the mother who was traumatizing the infant by being passionately cut off from her relationship with her baby? At present it seemed like both factors were operating, she said. The analyst made the specific point of labeling her experience "delusional," making very clear that, in fact, her fears did not reflect social realities. She has many loving relationships, many people who care for her, who are passionately involved with her and she with them. But under certain circumstances what comes crashing down is this horrible, internalized sense that the passionate link is lost and that it is lost forever. While historically the emotional abandonment seems related to the presence of third parties (primarily father), and while third parties can still serve as a trigger, the most salient feature is the connection that mother somehow ruptured. For reasons that were not clear to the baby, mother would suddenly close off, affectively disappear, leaving her in a position of desperate and painful reaching out with no return response.

The infant's sense of timelessness and forever was discussed. In infancy it must have seemed as though the passionate link could never be regained. Furthermore, since this was the way that the loss of the passionate link had been internalized, in all subsequent significant relationships, whenever there was a significant relationship affected by a third party or some emotional preoccupation the internalization would quickly destroy the passionate link and make it seem as though there could never be anything other than the excruciating pain and then the lifelessness that has always been. The question for further examination is how through time this shutting-down mechanism, apparently developed in relation to mother's emotional abandonments or preoccupations in the presence of third parties, has come to serve as a way of limiting her sense of connection with important people. After all, there is always some third party lurking around to point to as the "cause" of shutting down the relating—just when sustained availability is a possibility.

At the close of the session, she said, "This sounds like terrible news. But somehow I'm feeling very relaxed." Her analyst countered with, "It's not terrible news at all. It's a relief to finally have this more clearly defined than it ever has been. The bad news is that we still have some working through to do. So there is still pain ahead. But as with frightening and confusing things in the past, you have learned that knowing about them, no matter how painful it may be, is to be preferred over not knowing about them. Now you can be aware of how fragile the passionate link is and how subject it is to being destroyed internally by the mere presence of a third party. This is a valuable thing to know." The client agreed.

11

The Development
of a Transference
Psychosis: Sandy

Sandy, a 31-year-old woman who for a number of years always had a great deal to tell me—many stories, many interesting vignettes—arrived one day full of stories she was eager to relate. In the waiting room, she suddenly began to feel something else—an intense desire to be very emotionally present this hour. She somehow understood at that moment that the stories she had wanted to tell me would be her way of not allowing herself to be psychically present in the room. She keenly felt the disappointment of letting go of the exciting stories she wanted to tell. She slowly began to sink into a very quiet, frightened place. She had been working for some time on trying to allow herself to be more emotionally present, to be fully alive in the room. She wanted to feel herself and to feel my presence, but she had so many things to talk about this was generally difficult for her to accomplish emotionally. On a few occasions she had had a glimmer of it.

On this particular day as she settled down on the couch,

Sandy reported starting to feel chaos. With the internal chaos came tears of fright. I stayed with her fears and was able to support her experiencing the chaos of wanting to remain emotionally present but not knowing how. She was able to clearly differentiate this fear from other kinds of fear she's had before. When I indicated that this frightened, chaotic place was a place that she had been working for a long time to allow herself to experience, the tears came profusely. Sandy had interpreted my comments as reassuring her that no matter how frightened and confused she felt at the moment, this was an okay place to be. I pointed out that it was not simply a matter of being okay; the chaos and fear she was feeling for allowing herself to be emotionally present with me were very real at this moment, which she reaffirmed. It held a sense of present reality that was very different from what she would have experienced if she had gone ahead and told the stories she had intended to tell.

For about ten minutes she stayed in a quiet state of fear, making occasional quiet comments about physical sensations and her awareness of troubled breathing. Occasionally I checked in with her to see how she was doing, with her reporting that she was still present and feeling emotionally related to me but frightened. She contrasted this more quiet, tearful, chaotic fear with a number of previous regressive experiences that she has had in which she has felt wildly out of control, terrified, sinking, and falling—in much more urgent and frantic forms. She could see now how those were ways of defending against this place of quiet terror, of allowing herself to be emotionally present with another person. At one point when I checked in with her, she said, "I feel like I'm slipping away." Whereupon I extended my hand and said, "Can you stay? Can you stay here now?" She reached her hand toward mine and for a brief moment the two of us felt that we had retained our emotional connection with one another. Her comments were to the effect that this was the first time in her life anyone had ever invited her to stay with them or ever asked her to remain present.

No sooner than she had said that, she began to close in a little more tightly on my hand. She turned on her side, facing more toward me and, with her other hand, grasped my hand. I had the distinct sense that something had changed from the experience of simply being together from the first moment our hands had met. Gradually it became clear that her presence was leaving the room. Upon inquiry she replied, "I'm slipping away, I can't stop it. Something's happening to remove me from you." She began talking about the stories, the unrealness, and how the way we spent our time today had been more real. But once her emotional presence had started to slip away it was beyond her power to keep herself present in the room any more. The emotional contact, which was real, chaotic, and frightening, had gradually melted into a sense of being together and calm. But that sense in turn set off a retreat. The onset of the retreat was marked by her reaching, grasping, and clinging to me, as if for reassurance. But the very contact itself and the grasping set off a sense of uncontrollable slipping away.

Now I had an opportunity to point out the similarity between the way she was grasping my hand with both of hers, and how sometimes she clings to me physically in a hug toward the end of hours. I said, "This clinging, attaching sense is very different from the real chaos and the ensuing fulfilling moment of contact we had before you began to slip away, when you were able stay for a few intense connected moments when I asked you to."

I likened this clinging, grasping, attaching physical contact, which is reassuring, to the stories that she so often excitedly tells, which are also reassuring to her. But both the stories and the clinging contact have a certain unreal sense in that they do not contain the real terrifying emotions of being with another person in the present, nor do they contain safety and calm.

Rather, they seem to mask or foreclose the true terror and difficulty of being together, as well as the comfort that can also be real. Her comment was, "Then those reassuring feelings are not quite real." I agreed that they were a way of not allowing the more real feelings of fear as well as comfort to be experienced. She immediately said, "I now feel ashamed of the way I have been using physical contact because it seems so phony." I asked, "Whose mother is speaking now?" She responded that it was the mother who frightened her, who broke contact with her, who accused her of being somehow bad. I commented that she had been abusively shamed for many things, for being dramatic, phony, and manipulative. But that that is not the case. The fears she felt at being alive, vulnerable, and present today had not been received by her mother. Her real presence, with her genuine needs for love and connection, had been deflected by her early mother, causing her to withdraw and/or to assert herself more frantically (as in clinging or storytelling) in an effort to be received, to feel loved, comforted, and safe.

At the end of the hour Sandy was tempted to reach for the customary goodbye hug. Yet she felt awkward about it, realizing that the hug would never quite be the same again. The reassurance it had held for her was in some sense a false reassurance, in comparison with the moments of presence and contact, which were terrifyingly real and so reassuring in a very different sense.

Several months later, as the approach to understanding the organizing transference began to occur, there was a great deal of panic and confusion. In order for the organizing transference to become more visible, seven-day-a-week contact had been maintained for three weeks. The contact included four days of regular sessions and three days of scheduled brief telephone contact or office appointment. After working through some of the difficulties in maintaining contact, there had been a week of fairly good contact. By "contact" it is meant not merely the loving attachment that she had been able to feel for some time, but an emotionally interactive engagement. She had been pleased that the week had gone well and that she had felt emotionally in contact with me around many important issues. The two days of phone contact came, which happened to be Friday and Saturday, and then a special session was scheduled for Sunday. The contact that had been sustained throughout the week had undergone some shakiness during the two days with only telephone contact. During the Sunday session there was initially some limited but good emotional contact. After a period of time she began to be aware of pulling away, of trying to be close again, and then of pulling away again.

During this delicate period I found myself watching very closely for the exact moment at which Sandy might begin a full-fledged withdrawal. At the moment I began to feel her presence leaving, I reached out my hand and asked, "Could we hold onto each other this way?" At first, she was reluctant because it seemed that she was needing to withdraw. But after a little urging she made hand contact. For a few moments there was a real sense of being together and sharing an experience. I remarked on how difficult it was for two people to be together and to sustain an emotional experience with one another. She shortly reported that she was slowly and silently receding, that she was "withdrawing inside." There was nothing she seemed to be able to do about it, she said. She was pulling away. She was frightened and panicked, but clearly withdrawing. Soon the hands that were held together seemed meaningless and she left the session discouraged, feeling that the weekend disruption had made it impossible for her to sustain the sense of connection, that she was physically constricting and closing off. She stated, "Sometimes I can feel much closer to you when I'm not here. Sharing closeness together is hard to do."

I had the impression that my being present only for phone calls on the weekend days reminded her of the countless times her parents, particularly her early mother, had withdrawn from contact, setting up an intense need to clamor for what she needed. But the clamor was objected to by the parents and she was viewed as spoiled, overly needy, phony, or manipulative. The cycle that had become slowly represented in the analysis began when the child's needs were not responded to. This, in turn, led to increased intensity of demand, which the parents had found intrusive. Finally it seems she would retreat into autistic isolation. In many overt ways her parents could be there for her and were able to provide basic physical care. But it seemed they never could enjoy being with her and harshly responded to her frantic expressions of chaos and fear that their flawed parenting set up in her. It was as if their emotional deprivations had set up an intense fear of breakdown, emptiness, and death. Their promise of availability coupled with their emotional unavailability was a betrayal of the child's emotional needs.

By the following day she came in practically bent over double with severe pains in her neck and lower back. She had already been to two doctors that day and received several tentative and potentially dire diagnoses, from possible meningitis, to a severe virus, to a chronic chiropractic condition. For the next three days she was under medical care and stayed at home taking pain pills and other medications. Sessions were held by telephone, with the main discussion being around the intense pain and the withdrawal. While medical possibilities must be ruled out, we both shared the conviction that the severe pains and somatic constrictions somehow reflected the movement of the analytic work. She was inclined to see the disruption (abandonment) of the weekend as causal. I raised the possibility that the week of good contact followed by the brief Sunday revival of connection seemed causal. That is, contact itself is the feared element because it brings a promise of love, safety, and comfort that cannot ultimately be fulfilled and that reminds her of the abrupt breaches of loving care in her infancy.

The following weekend phone contact was maintained. Some domestic difficulties arose between her and the longtime boyfriend with whom she lived. She made it to her sessions on Monday, Tuesday, and Wednesday, and was very glad to be back. She talked a great deal about what was going on. There was some residual weakness left from the illness the week before, but mostly the focus was on "how on earth am I going to be able to continue to stay in the relationship with Marc!" By Wednesday she had been looking at apartments and was on the verge of moving out. Throughout the relationship this had been a pattern. At various times when there would be difficulties in the relationship, it would seem necessary for her to leave. The fantasy was to go somewhere where she could simply be alone, pull away into herself, and feel closed off, comfortable, and safe.

By the end of the Wednesday hour, while there had been obsessive concerns about her relationship with Marc and about whether to move out or not, there was a certain sense of closure. She said, "I think I'm just not fit to live with anyone because I can't get along with anyone. It's like I just can't relate, I can't stay connected, and when I do, it goes badly. I finally have to withdraw into a safe place where I can feel whole and alive by myself."

That night she had a horrible nightmare. She got up in the middle of the night and typed up the dream as follows:

This dream was totally vivid and real. It was happening in the here and now, in the very apartment I live in on this day's date. I couldn't really tell the difference between what was going on in the dream and what was going on in my life. Marc and I are fighting or I'm fighting with him and it's the very fight that we're in right now. I'm in the kitchen trying to talk to him. I'm trying to explain and I'm getting more and more hysterical. I look at him. He has short hair so that he looks quite different. He walks calmly away from me and into the living room. I am hysterical. He is calm. I say, "Do you need me to go to your company picnic

with you?" I know that he does. He looks at me calmly and says,
"No." He has decided that I shouldn't go with him, that he
doesn't need me to go. He's totally calm. His neck in the dream
is very different from his neck in real life. I know he doesn't look
like that with his hair short. I start going after him, all the while
aware that I'm being hysterical. He's still totally calm. He begins
walking up the stairs. There vaguely seem to be others, family
members, in the background. He proceeds upward, ignoring it.
Totally calm. He goes to the study. Then I retreat to my room
looking out, aware that there are other people in the house.
Everyone in the house is calm except me. I'm crying and hysterical.

All through that last part of the dream there's an overlay of
children's Golden Books. I don't know where or how they are
there. It's more of an image. When I wake up hysterical I feel the
Golden Books symbolic of lifelong struggle. I wake up crying and
silently screaming and flailing my arms and my legs and kicking.
I am aware in the aftermath of the indignity of the whole scene.
For whatever reason, whether or not it's my fault, I am the one
who is raging and hysterical, with Marc being totally calm. I love
him and I want to make the connection with him desperately
and no matter what I do it fails. The little voices in my head,
both in the dream and now, are saying, "Yes, but it's because you
are so infantile and hysterical and don't know how to connect
that you have created this situation." But the stronger knowledge, both within and during the aftermath of the dream, was
that this relationship is set up to perpetuate the indignity, the
hysteria, and the frustration of my early life. I make constant and
futile attempts to connect, while he remains interested but
dispassionate, with the rest of the family in the background
listening to my hysteria.

I also wonder whether the short hair and the fact that
he looks very different in reality than in the dream is symbolic of the fact that his true self and thoughts are different
than I would like to believe they are. That unmasked, he is not
who I think he is. The indignity of it all is what seems so
powerful in the dream. This seems like a replica of my child-

hood where all of the necessities were more or less taken care of. There was only a moderate amount of mistreatment and even some semblance of love. But there was an overall emptiness and neglect that was abusive. I am done in by my love, because I do love him as I did love my family. The image of the man with his hair short being so different from my image of him haunts me.

During the remainder of the session the interaction was marked alternately with periods of understanding between us, and moments during which Sandy, in confusion, would say, "You know I don't understand all of this. You know I'm not getting it." At some level things were being processed. But at the level of deeply understanding the dream discussion she did not feel that she really did.

After the dream was associated to in various ways the concern from the previous day reemerged as to whether or not she should get an apartment so as to find a retreat where she could be safe and comfortable. I asked if it would be possible for her to apply the dream to understanding the therapeutic relationship. That is, if the dream were representing a transference situation, what would that look like? She thought for a while but was not able to connect the dream to the analytic relationship, although as my interpretation unfolded, she understood it. I suggested that I was represented in the dream as her boyfriend. She immediately said, "Yes. It seems like it was your neck and short hair in the dream that I was seeing, not his." I interpreted the dream as a picture of the childhood situation, which was being transferred not only into the relationship with her boyfriend but also into the analysis. I thought that this dream presented a version of her living disconnection.

I recounted the week of connection, the disruption of that connection through the Friday and Saturday phone call days, and how difficult it was to regain the connection on Sunday. I reminded her that even the Sunday connection was nip and tuck until I had reached out and asked her to try to stay present and connected. I recalled that she had in fact been able to sustain it, but that in less than ten minutes she had felt herself inexorably being drawn away. She had felt her entire body constricting and herself withdrawing, so that even though hands were in contact, her soul had withdrawn from the interaction. I interpreted that the dream picture represented what was going on in those moments of withdrawal, that, "from an objective standpoint you and I may be able to agree that we were in connection and that then you slowly broke the connection. But the dream picture tells us what your subjective internal process was like. That is, you experienced me not needing you, not enjoying you or your love, and then pulling away from you in much the same way that your parents did. And in the dream as your boyfriend did. I calmly left you and went off to study for the weekend, oblivious to your needs." The nightmare gives a vivid picture of how the withdrawal happens after contact is achieved.

At this point she remarked that her boyfriend often complained that even when they did have moments of closeness and intimacy, immediately afterward she would start some kind of a fight. I commented that the fights were a cover-up or a defense against this more terrifying, painful, and dangerous contact situation, remembered from earliest childhood. "The Golden Book overlay of the dream suggests that this is the story of your childhood. Golden Books tell the way life is supposed to be. Your Golden Book tells you the way life was and somehow is still 'supposed to' be. There were people in your environment, your mother, your father, and your family who had a great deal they could give you, and they did give you basic physical care. But when it came time for emotional interactions they cruelly turned their backs, leaving you grasping at straws in a wild hysteria and finally withdrawing to your closet for safety. You were always made to believe that problems in relationships were your fault."

It horrified her to think that her withdrawal is her internalized reaction to *the connection* rather than her reaction to the other turning away. That is, she has consciously perceived her becoming hysterical because the other person was not connecting. But the dream, viewed as a transference representation, suggests what happens when, in fact, she does connect. There had been a week of good connection followed by a slight disruption, a strong reconnection, and a pulling away. Within twenty-four hours she was in excruciating physical pain and agony and remained so for several days, being physically traumatized by having made the connection, which was then experienced as traumatizing.

She replied, "Then you really don't think I should get that apartment?" By this time, I was quite clear about the meaning of the moving out fantasy. I pointed out how in the past, as in the present, the moving-out fantasy has served as an autistic retreat for achieving a means of surviving and gaining a sense of comfort when she cannot safely connect to a person whom she needs.

I had been considering Tustin's (1981, 1986) formulations in attempting to understand her. Tustin thinks that the infant and mother are in a sensuous relationship during pregnancy. During the earliest extrauterine months the physical sensuous relationship optimally continues comfortably until psychological bridges begin to be made between the mother's mind and the child's mind. If the mother cannot maintain the sensuous relationship with the child, or abruptly ruptures it, the child begins engaging in withdrawing autosensuous behaviors. These ideas were presented to the client informally. She interrupted, "You mean the spacing out and withdrawing I do at times?" "Yes, when sensuous connection to your mother was needed but she did not provide it, you retreated to the safety and comfort of self-stimulation." She in fact had physically withdrawn in childhood to her closet and in adulthood to separate apartment-type settings to escape several relationships, feeling — at least briefly — soothed by the aloneness.

This vignette spans perhaps six weeks of intensive contact. The actual time it took to produce the dream picture of the withdrawal was about twelve days. The intervening time was spent in intense physical agony, frenzy, and daily contact. During this period there was no interpersonal emotional connection with me. The contacts were of a frenzied attachment kind. She is correct when she speaks of her love for others, but she was also becoming aware that there is an attachment kind of love and a connection kind of love; in the latter there is an emotional engagement. She is readily able to experience desperate, clinging attachment love, but is limited in being able to experience or to sustain the mutual, emotional engagement kind of love. When she experiences others as not needing her, not enjoying her, abandoning her to their own preoccupations she becomes desperate and clinging. The dream portrays her experience of the other coldly turning his back, unconcerned about her desperation and the autistic retreat that follows the trauma of feeling unresponded to. The entire cycle is internalized and endlessly repeated.

In the discussion following the dream, the focus was on whether her boyfriend would someday be able to interact with her. That could not be predicted yet. I said, "You chose him because he was sufficiently emotionally withdrawn so that you could maintain an attachment with him over a long period of time without this threatening transference from your childhood cropping up to destroy the relationship. As you begin to find a way to be more present and to ask for more emotional connection and emotional interaction, the question remains whether he will be able to evolve with you and develop increasing connectedness as well. At the present you simply don't know the answer, because you've not been able to stay present long enough to allow him to struggle with what he needs to struggle with in the relationship in order to remain fully present."

Following an extended summer vacation break there was much news and settling down for three weeks, with the earlier working through of connection experiences seeming to her to be a long way in the past. After having worked for some months on a creative and complex marketing strategy, Sandy had presented her proposals to colleagues and company officials late one Thursday afternoon. She received an overwhelmingly positive and enthusiastic response. People were interested and asking complicated questions she had had good answers for. People really connected to her in a favorable way. She enjoyed it and took pride in her work. A group took her out for celebration drinks afterward and she felt surrounded by a warm glow.

Within hours doubts and fear began and throughout Friday and Saturday a downward spiral of self-criticism, hopelessness, and despair evolved until she went into a panic and called me at home on Saturday night. I was available to talk for about forty minutes. The panic gradually subsided and the main connecting issues from before the vacation break were brought back into focus. The details of the marketing meeting were reviewed. The admiration, respect, and warm personal connectedness she experienced by her colleagues and her superiors were interpreted by me as causal in the downward spiral. She was reminded that loving connection and self-value are forbidden and dangerous. We felt deeply connected and I alerted her to the danger of a reaction to the good connection she was now achieving with me. I agreed to call her Sunday morning.

During the brief Sunday call several reactions emerged. She was in a mild state of confusion and perplexity. Not wanting to lose the good connection she had experienced the night before, she had pulled out some newspaper articles on childhood development I had written and she spent time reading them and trying to stay in touch with the good experience of our connection. But confusion started as she read, because many of the ideas on the written page seemed to be her own ideas. Had I taken her words and made them into my own without asking permission to do so? Or had the ideas been mine, but with so much interaction had she taken them in and felt them to be her own? She cited several examples, wanting to know whose words they were. I discussed the issues with her, showing her that some of the ideas came from others who were quoted, and that both of us had taken in the ideas. Other ideas had clearly been picked up from me, but possibly there were some that came originally from her although examples were not available at the moment. I encouraged a search, indicating that I always wished to obtain permission or to credit what I take in from others whenever possible and appropriate.

Privately, I thought that the content seemed to express the organizing level uncertainty of "Whose body is this? Whose breast is this?," and heralded disillusionment with the infantile omnipotent wish that usually precedes a breakdown experience (Winnicott 1974). That is, my mind (words) should belong to her, but after the good connection it appeared that I was running away, stealing my (nurturing) self from her, and she became confused and frightened. The working-through experience was being resumed after the vacation break but with some new themes: being affirmed sets off a downward spiral, and the confusion of the source of nurturance.

She then presents a screen memory that had arrived earlier in the morning. "I was back at my parent's home. You know how I used to have my closet set up with a small desk and things for me to read and do—my retreat? Well I had something really important to say and came out of my closet and went to tell my father. Whatever it was, he immediately put it down and humiliated me in the process, so I went running back to hide in my closet." The interpretation offered was that the night before she had come out of the safety of the vacation break and permitted a regression precipitated by the gratifying marketing meeting. She had then made successful contact with me Saturday night. But while reading my articles she became agitated and confused about whose words these were. The feeling of being devalued by my differentness or "word theft" was viewed as a transference feeling demanding that she flee from the frightening and humiliating contact back into her closet. The screen memory suggested that the infantile omnipotent possession of the maternal body was abruptly and unempathically broken by her mother's narcissistic preoccupation with her own concerns, causing an autistic retreat. What she thought belonged to her was claimed by her mother, leaving her suddenly frightened and in uncontrollable confusion and retreating into herself. More adverse reactions were anticipated, I warned, as contact was being needed and being found.

By Monday evening Sandy arrived in my office dragging, looking terrible, and barely able to speak. She had been in excruciating pain all day with problems breathing and talking. She felt she was extremely ill and disoriented. Did I think she should go to a doctor? I encouraged medical coverage and also reviewed the events, saying that it has been a strain getting up the courage to begin the deep analytic work again but that last Saturday night it had begun. The total aching body, the gasping for breath, the chest pain, and the near laryngitis all seemed like reactions to the contact—her body was protesting the forbidden pleasures of relating that had been enjoyed.[1] We were touching that terrifying wall of relating that went back to the original wish to be biologically safe and in control of vitally needed substances. What became somatically internalized was expressed in the screen memory of an abusive rebuff at the hands of a narcissistic father (or crazy mother).

On Tuesday she reported that she had been to see a doctor who thought she had pneumonia. Every bone ached and she could barely talk or make it to session. There were deep heaving

---

1. The bioenergetic interpretation of such pains is that they are body memories of early constrictions in the throat and bronchial area. The constrictions, begun in infancy, represent a bodily reaction to deprivation of food and/or air and simultaneously an effort by the life force to assert in the musculature a desire to live. As this desire to be alive in human relationships is revived in the real world and in the analytic transference, the early and painful body memories assert themselves.

sighs on the couch as she expressed the fear that she was dying. She was anticipating being so bad tomorrow she would not be able to come to session. She asked if she should try to make it if at all possible. I affirmed the need to take care of herself and respect her illness and the effects of the antibiotics. I also affirmed the importance of making her analytic session if possible.

I pointed out again how the sequence seen before the summer break had been revived. There was the Thursday triumph, the downward spiral, and the Saturday analytic contact, followed by the losing of the contact with the confusion of whose thoughts were whose, and the screen memory involving total body agony, humiliation, and running terrorized in pain back to her closet after a devaluating contact with the narcissistic father.

Wednesday arrived with great pain and distress, much talk about the physical symptoms, problems sleeping, and the agonies of the week. I attempted, as on Monday and Tuesday, to contextualize the agony as the body's retreat from fulfilling contact. Agony and retreat were body memories that arose in relation to the analytic contact. But in her illness today, more than in the previous two days, she seemed totally inaccessible in any way to my words. While she listened to attempted interpretations, she could only nod her head. But nothing could be discussed or processed. She reported "slipping into a black void and nothing can stop it."

On Thursday she arrived with a pained facial expression, an antibiotic in hand, and a request for water to take it with. She continued talking in the same vein as the previous days for about ten minutes. Suddenly she asked, "Why are you being so silent?" I responded, "Because I hadn't thought of anything to say yet." This enraged her and the remainder of the hour was spent railing at me for being emotionally absent, for being narcissistically preoccupied, and for not empathically "coming after me to rescue me." My instinctive response was to be somewhat defensive to the barrage of accusations. "This always

happens. It has happened every time I have really needed you—
when I am slipping into the black void, when I have no way of
staying alive, you back away emotionally. You just vanish when
I get dependent and regressed and need you. You would let me
die." The anger mounted until she bolted out of the room seven
minutes early slamming the door saying she didn't know how
she could stay alive (it was not a suicidal threat the way it was
said).

I had been struggling not to be defensive, to understand the
mounting despair and rage. This type of tirade had been present
before but the context had never been so clear as now. But with
the hour cut short I did not get the opportunity to point out that
these kinds of rages in the past had tended to be either when she
longed for reassuring mergers or on Thursdays before the
weekend break. I did not get to say that we could certainly
schedule phone contact over the weekend if that would help.
Although once or twice I attempted to relate the present rage
reaction to events of last weekend, the reaction and the violent
accusation of coldness, distance, and narcissistic preoccupation
made all possibility of interpersonal contact impossible.

I found myself quite upset by the raging intensity of the
hour and the rageful exit, but I had experienced a similar
intensity on prior similar working-through occasions with her,
so I decided to wait out the reaction rather than to cut it short by
intervening with a call. She knew my home number; I knew I
would be at home for the three days. So if connection was
needed it would be readily available.[2]

The Monday session was missed. Again, I believed that
contact was possible if needed and so decided to wait. The
rageful exit and missed session had a dramatic, manipulative

---

2. In a subsequent consultation I questioned the possible meaning of
my seemingly not very helpful role in this difficult situation. It seemed to me
upon reflection that, as uncontained as the situation might appear on the
surface, the context and previous experience suggested that the ego function
of body memory recall was in operation and needed to be heard out.

flavor, making the evolving situation all that much more interesting for understanding the unfolding transference sequence. In past understandings of the infantile situation, what I had experienced as the client's pressured manipulations had been discussed at length as an internalized residue of an infant whose needs were abusively ignored to the point of terror and a fear of dying. They had been seen as the historically meaningful manifestation of an infant fearing imminent death through neglect or abandonment and learning to do everything in its power to force people in the environment to respond to its needs, to rescue it from aloneness and psychic death. The muscular constrictions in the chest and throat were further indications of how deeply embedded the desperation was. Although a manipulative flavor was present, what seemed more important on this occasion was the clearly articulated desperation, the despair, the fear of dying, the rage at my perceived emotional abandonment, the wish to be rescued, the fury at my spoken helplessness, which was seen as narcissistic preoccupation, and the "bailing out" when true need is present. Because the sequence had been somewhat experienced previously, because it was being articulated so clearly and forcefully with meaningful transference accusations and body memory, and because I would be readily available should she attempt contact, it again seemed best to wait this out rather than to intervene in the unfolding elaboration of the primitive transference sequence.

Tuesday was spent in anger, silence, and despair. "Why didn't you save me last Thursday? I was dying. You just let me fall off the face of the earth. Why didn't you call Thursday afternoon or over the weekend? When I wasn't here yesterday weren't you worried about me? You knew I was in bad shape. Why didn't you call?" (Note: My calls in the past were always by appointment so there was no historical precedent for her expecting a call in response to analytic distress.) I tried to remain as present at the feeling level as possible, so as not to become defensive in the face of the barrage of accusation. The session teetered on some empathic engagement around the despair and rupture because of my "narcissistic" inability to stay with her "true need." In one moment of rage near the end of the hour she slipped and called me by her boyfriend's name. She was horrified and redoubled her anger, saying that now I would capitalize on the slip and use it against her.

Wednesday she sat up to confront me on the series of breaches, my brutal and insensitive personality, how I could have handled each event, and how my failings were cold and cruel.

All this occurred as is to be expected in the development and working through of the transference psychosis. The experience of the diabolized parent is strongly authentic, the analyst *becomes* the hated object of infancy (the "psychotic mother"), and no capacity for a split-off observing ego or reality testing ego is present at the moment of the experience. As on the previous two days I attempted empathic attunement with the despair and anger, but also continued to bring forth the overarching context of all the events. Sandy insisted the breach was on the previous Thursday when she needed me to be empathically attuned to her despair. I believed that the breach was internal and related to the Saturday night of the previous week when, following a long break, deep contact had been made, which was immediately broken by the confusion of words, the screen memory of father devaluing and humiliating her, and the ensuing painful body memories. The entire round of rageful accusation and painful physical symptoms was seen by me as the reemergence of an internalized primitive reaction to the treacherousness of interpersonal contact. But an analyst's attempts to be abstract in interpreting themes at the moment the analytic speaker is experiencing infantile concreteness always makes for gaps in the communication.

Unlike the previous session, small parts of my argument gradually did seem to be reluctantly taken in; but only after my patience had worn thin and I was clearly on the verge of anger myself. The countertransference feeling was clearly, "God damn it! I'm here, I'm holding on to you in this regression the best I know how. Why are you accusing me so fiercely—where is your rationality, your sense of human decency? Why do you treat me so badly?" This was, of course, not spoken at the moment because the present priority was clearly with the emergence of the organizing transference. She stated, "I always have to give in, to do it your way. I can never win. It's always been that way. With my parents, they were right, I was wrong. They were okay, something was wrong with me. My only choice is to sell out and be false." I did get a chance to point out that despite how badly injured and angry she felt, "We are not in adversarial roles like you were with your parents. We might be in a tough spot at the moment, but winning and losing are not what we are about. We are working together to allow patterns and memories of past sequences of agony to appear so that we can study how your mind operates. The last thing I would want you to do is to sell out, to give in. You've got to hold firm while we get all of this sorted out." We were slightly calmer at the end of the session.

On Thursday she resumed the couch and for half an hour a conversation with more understanding of each other's views was possible. I commented to the effect that I am who I am and that I misbehaved according to my personality, which was one matter. But her *reaction* to shortcomings of my nature provided an opportunity to see the whole sequence as a part of her mental structure. This did not mean that my behavior was being justified or that I, as the analyst, was right and she was wrong. But rather that I had my personal way of responding, which sets off primordial rage in her because my personality limitations are reminiscent of those of her parents. This was repeated and then somewhat reluctantly taken in.

I pointed out that the other person's self-preoccupation is always our enemy and has to be dealt with. In every relationship it would be only a matter of time before she found the other person's narcissistic preoccupations that would remind her of traumatic infantile encounters with her parents. Our investigation was into her reactions when she did encounter the other's narcissistic limits. What we have been seeing these two weeks in the unfolding of a mental sequence is *her*, her own personal reactions to others' narcissistic limitations.

She then reported a dream from the night before in which she discovered someone putting her boyfriend's clothes in her closet, where, she protested, they didn't belong. She saw the dream as condensing the childhood retreat from unempathic invasions into the safety of her closet, the transference humiliation and fury she so often experienced with her boyfriend, and the current transference situation with the analyst in which she felt my identity (clothes) an intrusion into her autistically safe place.

On the telephone the next morning she confided, "I'm afraid to tell you this. You know one of the injunctions of my growing up years was 'never tell anyone anything.' I'm afraid I'll lose this if I tell you. That you will somehow interpretively blow it so I don't want you to say anything about it." She explained, "By the time I left your office on Tuesday I realized that I cannot relate to anyone, that I've never been able to, and that there is no hope. Since I don't know how to relate to people I have to relate to something or die. I thought I might start relating to my body, just trying to be in tune with it and I did. When reaching you is beyond possibility, I can be with myself and, even though it is painful, I can be okay." Respecting her wishes, I only echoed what was said at the time and agreed that staying with her body was of paramount importance. The overall context of the sequence was spoken again and arrangements were made for phone contact the following evening.

After two full days of heavy social demands the next call was again filled with agony, which did not surprise me, given the inevitable strain of the anticipated social events. Sandy wanted to run, withdraw, pick a fight, but could remember there was some reason she was not going to do this. She could not remember the reason but she hoped she could stay with it. I chose to remind her that she had been able to stay present Tuesday night because she had chosen to stay connected to a sense of herself, to her body, no matter how painful that might be. The intense social interactions were upsetting enough that she was wishing to retreat to her closet and to soothe herself. Perhaps she could stay in touch with herself. Staying with the painful reactions she was having in her body at present seemed more important than leaving them. Why not curl up in bed for a while? That way she would be by herself, could reduce incoming stimuli, and focus on the physical pains caused by attempting to relate to people. It sounded like a possibility.

The next day the retreat to bed was reported as successful in that by focusing on herself she was able to feel her labored breathing and chest pains slowly diminish into physical calm, thus reconstituting a satisfactory self state. She asked, "Do you think that maybe the breach, instead of that Thursday marketing meeting, was around my reading your newspaper articles and becoming confused Saturday night?" I said, "No, that was when you began feeling the fragmentation, the slipping into traumatic confusion as a result of our connecting on the phone. Connection serves to remind you of when you were once satisfyingly connected to mother's body and then abruptly lost it. It happened on Thursday at your marketing meeting and set off the downward spiral until you called me and connected again to me on Saturday night. It is the connection that is feared because it was always somehow destroyed by your parents' narcissistic preoccupations. At present it is impossible to feel interpersonal connection without immediately expecting the traumatic and abusive turning away of your parents."

AN ASIDE ON PSYCHOANALYTIC EMPATHY

This vignette further raises an interesting and difficult issue regarding empathy. Kohut and the self psychologists have stressed the importance of selfother attunement—the analyst remaining tuned in to the subjective concerns of the person in analysis. Kernberg and others have sharply criticized this approach (see Hedges 1983b, pp. 269–270), saying that it is relatively easy to formulate an interpretation that agrees with the subjective state of the client. It is more difficult to provide psychoanalytic interpretations that empathize with the broader personality picture, but may be subjectively unpalatable or unpleasant at the moment.

When working the organizing experience this problem often becomes acute as illustrated in this vignette. One could argue that I was unempathic when I did not respond in an empathic rescuing mode to this woman's despair. When I attempted to stay with what I saw as the broader personality issues, I was accused of being narcissistically preoccupied, out of tune, and wrong. There is always a delicate balance when responding empathically under conditions of accusation. On the one hand the subjective experience of the client has a certain priority or urgency in the immediate setting. But simply going along with the client's subjective demands may mean colluding with the resistance to establishing the painful, helpless, humiliating, rageful infantile transference. Here to have simply rescued the client from reexperiencing the contact rupturing organizing transference would have been to collude in acting out the resistance. But to hold too firmly to this broader perspective runs the risk of a damaging clash of subjective worlds, which could precipitate a negative therapeutic reaction (Freud 1918, 1923, 1933). The problem of intersubjectivity as seen here involves walking a tightrope between receiving the despairing, manipulative, rageful accusations as the transference object and avoiding defending oneself from the accusations—usually ones that are going to strike home deeply somehow.

Hilton (1993) points out that when we are accused there is a three-part response that arises almost instinctively from most of us: (1) denial—"I didn't do it," (2) defense—"I did the best I could," and (3) blame–"She knows better than this, this accusation is pathological." The real problem, says Hilton, is that an accusation often is aimed, somewhat successfully, at a core wound of the accused, at a blind spot, or Achilles' heel. Until the accused is able to work through the core wound as it is active in the present relationship, it is unlikely that he will be able to give a satisfying response to the accuser who "knows" she is somehow right.

The problem of the core wound of the analyst, at which the accusation is aimed, becomes complex when considering the nature of the organizing experience. With developmentally more advanced symbiotic or borderline experience the fear of the client is abandonment, and an accusation of empathic failure means, "you abandoned me." But with organizing experience the transference is paradoxically comprised of structured terror around the issue of connecting or sustaining an interpersonal connection. That is, it is deeply empathic not to connect. Accusations focusing on the analyst's somehow letting the person down, of empathically failing, arise from the organizing level resistance to experiencing the transference, not from the transference per se. Not until the person in analysis can somehow let go of the accusation or demand, and then permit a lapse into deep yearning, helplessness, and terror, not until the utter sense of breakdown, emptiness, and death can be fully experienced in the here and now relationship, can the infantile transference be secured for analysis. Rescue by means of subjective empathic agreement in this situation would have been antitherapeutic.

Thus in an accusation situation involving organizing-level issues, the broadest psychoanalytic empathy would entail being able to navigate between the Scylla of colluding with subjectively valid resistance, and the Charybdis of unwelcome, unpleasant, unempathic transference interpretation. Hilton charts our course: (1) Avoid denial, defensiveness, and blame. (2) Use consultation to work through the core wound the accusation touches in oneself. (3) Show the person that you know how deeply he or she has been wounded by you or by the position you have taken. (4) Provide some reassurance that this particular kind of injury can somehow be averted or softened in the future—that is, that "this won't happen again to me or to someone else." This reassurance may take the form of the analyst's recognizing that there was a technical or empathic misunderstanding or mishandling of the situation by him (the usual Kohutian response). Or in the sort of dilemma presented in this vignette, the interpretation needs to include some reference to the ongoing, overall transference circumstance.

Unfortunately, at the moment of organizing transference experiencing the person is living in a concrete, nonsymbolic world of infantile trauma without his or her usual reality testing capabilities or ordinary access to symbolic logic, so that sensible and meaningful discussion is virtually impossible.[3] In the example, the dilemma revolves around the problem that "narcissism in others is always a danger. But by our coming to understand your *reaction* to my narcissistic preoccupations as a part of your mental structure, as a sequence of your ongoing mental life, we have a way of working together more effectively to understand how the pattern repeatedly shows up in your life." The client's response was, "Oh, what this all is is a piece of how my mind works? I think maybe I can get hold of that."

Someone may arise here to ask, "But doesn't healing result from the client's feeling the old pain in a new situation in which he or she can be satisfactorily met in a different and more satisfying way in the present? Can't the person feel his or her raw experience contained in an empathic way so that the experience

---

3. I have come to advocate the involvement of a third party when intense or extended working through of the organizing transference is anticipated (Hedges 1994b). A third party case monitor can be available for weekend or vacation contact, can aid in reality testing when the client is lost in concreteness, and can serve to help the analyst with countertransference dilemmas and potential legal or ethical threats.

250 Psychotic Anxieties and the Organizing Experience

can be reorganized into a cohesive and meaningful self-structure? If we develop empathic forms that are larger and more containing doesn't the healing that is required occur? Now the person is able to be in another place, a place of greater self-containment. Doesn't the analyst's overall containment provide the environment for the development of new personality tools?" The answer is yes and no. Yes, in that the new and broader canopy of interpersonal containment is needed for more complex representational relating to develop. But merely positively reliving traumatic situations in a more satisfying environment is not enough. In infancy, the first time around, love and containment might have been enough. But after organizing-level extensions have been made and found unsuccessful or painful, a psychological structure is built up that must be dismantled, analyzed, or broken down. A delusion has been created that henceforth makes relating dangerous and terrifying. In analysis the transference can come to include organizing or psychotic elements that revive the early memories of trauma in the form of transference and resistance to the experiencing of transference. In these vignettes we slowly see the transference developing. The analyst is begged to participate in the resistance to remembering the horrors of being rebuffed, humiliated, and sent back into an autistic closet. It would be easy to collude with the resistance by empathizing with the experienced abandonment or by externalizing the accusations of abuse onto others in the past. The resistance can be easily acted out in angry confrontations of parents, family members, and others from one's past who have related traumatically to the person.

"KILL THE BABY":
A COUNTERTRANSFERENCE REGRESSION

What follows is a first-person narrative of the countertransference experience that emerged at this point in the ongoing vignette.

The earliest instance of the theme that stimulated my countertransference regression occurred several years ago. I recall a vivid fantasy of this woman about ten feet away facing me in a small subdued crowd, jumping up and down enthusiastically smiling and waving, trying to attract my attention. I reported my fantasy to the client at the time. It was discussed in terms of how she had never felt seen by her parents. In fact, she never felt that she belonged to them, or to anyone else for that matter. She had always felt somehow different, set apart, isolated and separated from others, not really a part of any group or relationship. As a result of our analytic work she now feels that sometimes she "belongs" to Marc, her longtime boyfriend, and at times to me.

Sometime later the theme emerged of her interpersonal intensity. In agonizing over a series of relationships in which for some mysterious reason she felt that people seemed somehow to shun her, to silently ridicule her, to turn their backs quietly on her, to fail to reciprocate her friendly overtures, she worried that she was too intense. *Intense* was a word that seemed to summarize a set of qualities that she felt were perceived by others as intrusive, aggressive, demanding, challenging, complaining, insisting, being pushy, and so forth.

On the one hand she was proud of her assertiveness as a woman and pleased at her ability to make things happen, to express concern for others, to stand up for what is right, and to not be pushed around. But she feared that her intensity drove people away, caused people to be afraid of her, or not to like her. She is a bright woman with keen insight into people and it seemed that perhaps she saw too much, that she knew too much about what motivated people for her own good. It seems she reads people deeply in ways that make them uncomfortable or perhaps provoke them in ways. But despite these intense, somewhat abrasive qualities she has many friends, is well liked, and is respected for her integrity, vision, and insight.

In the context of an ongoing dialogue about her intensity I

had occasion to remark on several occasions how, when she first saw me in the waiting room and sometimes on leaving the office as well, she seemed to take me in, to scrutinize me deeply to the point that I sometimes found it uncomfortable. Over the years I have cultivated a habit in this business of avoiding heavy eye contact, of often averting my eyes so as not to make people feel watched. Limited eye contact with clients now feels natural and comfortable to me, especially with analytic clients who use the couch. But often she would pull for eye contact by staring and then follow up her gaze or scrutiny with questions about how I was, was I okay today, what was I thinking. I found all of this mildly invasive and uncomfortable.

On several occasions she intuited that I was having an off day and commented to that effect. Although I had not perceived any mood irregularities in myself, on two or three occasions when she was upset by what she perceived as my preoccupied mental state I was able to report back to her that later in the day others also had noticed my being somewhat bland, or unresponsive as well. I reported this to her in the spirit of validating her perceptions of my unconscious moods. I questioned the possible meanings of her extreme sensitivity. The main conclusion we drew was that as a child she was so traumatized by her parents' preoccupied, unavailable, or destructive moods that she routinely surveyed people for "where they might be coming from" at the moment. It seemed some basic survival mechanism was being noted. She needed to know if I was okay, how I was feeling, was I going to be emotionally available to her, was she going to be safe with me today, or were there hidden emotional agendas or dangers?

In time, the question of her interpersonal intensity that seemed to create some discomfort in others was linked to her need to read unconscious moods and motivations. I volunteered how uncomfortable I felt being scrutinized visually and emotionally, but understood her need to check me out each day, although the need was clearly greater on some occasions.

Early in the analysis she began to ask for hugs at the end of sessions. These goodbye hugs began in the context of regressive moments when she felt desperate and was not sure how she could leave or make it to the next day or through the weekend. Afterward on several occasions I explained my discomfort with the hugs. She assured me that hugs were human and expressed connection. I explained that while I was not committed to total abstinence of touching, like most traditional analysts, I always felt physical contact of any sort needed to be understood, and that I was always uncomfortable with physical contact that had not yet been understood. She thought analysts were phobic of physical contact and had a problem themselves, no doubt fearing overstimulation themselves or sexualization of contact by the client. Hugs at the end of sessions had nothing to do with that, she asserted. They were an ordinary part of human warmth and understanding. During periods in which she felt stronger, hugs at the end of the session could be omitted.

She did, however, experience a series of powerful sessions in which, when she was emotionally pulling away during sessions, I extended my hand and held on to her while struggling to maintain emotional contact with her as well. I later explained what I believed to be a critical and concrete aspect of touch on such occasions, as it served to help keep us together when she was losing her sense of me at the moment. In time I came to sense her desire for hugs and responded accordingly and spontaneously.

Slowly the organizing transference began to be traced or defined in how she was more or less "present" in the room, more or less available for contact. At first she believed she was present and in contact most of the time. But slowly she realized that she was almost never present in an interpersonally emotionally engaging way, and that she often had not the slightest idea of who I was. She said on several occasions, "I can feel so much closer to you when I'm not with you." This was interpreted as how difficult it was to actually establish a sense of deep and meaningful interaction with me in which she could actually feel my presence as a real person separate and different from herself. She had developed a fantasy of me, of who I was, and could carry on a reassuring dialogue with me in my absence. But when it came to knowing who I was, in the sense of being able in the here and now to interact with me, she often felt lost. She felt discouraged by this and gravely disabled.

I was able in time to draw a distinction between her feeling "attached" to me in a safe way and her being "connected" to me – able to feel open and active channels for communication and connection between two real, live, interacting beings. She was at first upset when I applied the attachment–connection distinction to hugs at the end of the hour. She did not like the idea that her reaching out for physical contact stemmed more from an attaching, clinging impulse or need for physical reassurance than from a communicating, connecting interaction. But on several occasions she clearly felt the distinction and then began to limit the hugs to more special occasions, although she clearly did not like my interpreting them as attaching without connecting.

A series of breaches occurred over time in which she felt emotionally unresponded to by me. Her view was that just when she really needed me to be emotionally present I would somehow withdraw. She believed that I could not tolerate neediness or dependency and so would withdraw or disconnect and go to a cold, critical, imperious place. I could indeed feel the abrupt disconnections, her despair, her agony, and her rage at how I was not there for her. But I could not see or experience the pattern she believed to be present. To me it seemed her agonies and disconnections came upon the heels of some connection that she had established with me, and I attempted to point this out to her.

After several breaches I learned to note that at the first inklings of rage or of an intense, invasive, or accusatory demeanor on her part I tended to become more silent because I would be puzzled, attentive, and thoughtful—not having any idea where she was coming from, or not understanding the nature or meaning of her manner. That is, my subjective sense was that we had just successfully connected, that I had been present for her. So when her response was distress or rage I was puzzled and pulled back a bit to try to understand what was happening. My caution and increased alertness would then be felt by her as cold withdrawal.

Afterward I would be told by her what I should have done or said in these moments that would have been more empathic. However, the empathic response I "should have" given did not occur to me because at that moment I had gone into a more abstract tracking mode trying to figure out what was happening. That is, when I sensed sourness, intensity, or invasiveness I tended to begin reviewing in my head the overall context of the past hours, weeks, or months while listening as carefully as possible for what the present problem was within the overall context of her personality and our interaction. While I was puzzling in this way she might insist on some sort of immediate response from me. Her demand for immediate responsiveness would catch me off balance. It seemed that under these conditions no response I ever gave was satisfactory and her rage would escalate. Although I'm not sure if any response I might have given would have been more helpful or prevented the escalation, her complaint was invariably that I was inappropriately cold and withdrawing.

In quieter times I seemed to be able to show her the connections and disconnections I was tracking and she seemed to understand them. But in the moment she would tense up. She would feel locked into a fight with me over how I would coldly withdraw, think her complaints to be transference, blame her for disconnecting, and see her as "nuts" and myself as okay and right. There had been a series of interactions that were distressing to both of us. We tended to have different views about what was happening. She believed that I always somehow withdrew when she felt needy and she had a bad reaction to it. She accused me of refusing to examine and to acknowledge that my faulty responsiveness made it impossible for her to trust me or to trust her analysis. She feared I was just going to do it again and worried that there was no point in continuing her relationship with me, that I had a basic personality defect and could not keep from rejecting her. It seemed to me that as she would feel something real in the interpersonal connection or in her body in relation to our connection, something internal would occur causing her to feel that I was cold, isolated, critical, withdrawing, skeptical, and disgusted with her for being so dependent and needy.

My overall tracking for some months had been related to the ways in which she could not allow connection or engagement between us to occur and the ways in which she closed it off when it did occur. I could hear her insistence that at these breach moments the disconnecting problem was with me not her. I could see she needed me to cop to her accusations of my inappropriate emotional coldness and withdrawal. If I did not readily accept the blame for emotional withdrawal, this further escalated her distress because I was in effect saying (like her parents always had) that it was all her fault, that I was right and she was sick, excessively needy, bad, wrong, or pathological.

I became especially interested in tracking how she managed to produce these breaches somehow using features of my personality in order to relive the anguish of her infancy and childhood. I considered the possibility that my tracking on a more abstract plane than she wanted to be heard on, could be an intellectualizing defense, a way of avoiding her connecting overtures. Perhaps my intellectualizing defense was activated when (as she claimed) she was most needy. But whether, or to what extent, I was actually being defensive, or my moods made me significantly less available to connect with, I had the distinct impression that she was using features of my personality to accomplish transferentially determined disconnections. I tried on several occasions to suggest this but was met with the firm conviction that there was a narcissistic personality flaw in me that I was trying to blame on her. If I was correct in believing that she ferreted out something in me to stimulate and/or attach organizing transference to, how was I to show her that, without seemingly replicating her parents' crime of "shifting the blame" to her and further enraging her? What was going on and how were we to sort it all out? We were both clear about a history of these disruptions that occurred on the day before weekend or holiday breaks.

The precipitating incident leading to our next distress occurred on a Friday afternoon. The week had gone comfortably with her allowing herself more body feeling than usual. I thought Friday might go well also. I was, however, aware that I was going backpacking and would not be near a phone for forty-eight hours. I might need to tell her this since she often needed to know how I could be reached on weekends. It seemed to me that I was having a good day. I was looking forward to a beautiful weekend in the mountains with close friends with spectacular autumn weather promising.

In the waiting room I felt her penetrating eyes and I averted mine (as I usually do). In the hallway she made a full turn around to take me in again, something she had not done before. I felt closely scrutinized and averted my eyes again. The past couple of months it seemed that she had been aware of watching me in the waiting room since I had made the comment about her intense eyes. On a couple of occasions there had been an exchange of what I took to be knowing smiles as we were both thinking about the eye contact and what it might be about. In an instant, as I was reviewing all of this in my mind and thinking, "It is Friday and she is forcing me to disconnect, to pull back from her intense, intrusive scrutiny. I feel penetrated and knee-jerk withdraw. She knows this about me. With the weekend coming she is attempting to either break a potential connection or prevent one from occurring by using my instinctive withdrawal from her gaze."

In my consulting room, instead of moving to the couch as usual, she turned, faced me, and asked if I'm okay. I assured her, "I am, but [and here comes the breach] when you scrutinize me it forces me to withdraw." She was enraged. That's ridiculous. How could she force me to withdraw? There it is again, and I'm blaming her for it. She wants that in writing because no one will believe it otherwise. In attempting to explain further (clearly a mistake in these circumstances) I reminded her of my aversion to her intense stare and commented that if she wanted to connect with me that's certainly not the way to do it. She was further angered. I attempted a few other rationalizations that failed and then became quiet waiting to hear it all out to see if there was some element I could perhaps take hold of. My silence was further enraging. Toward the end of the session she announced that she had a good week, was overjoyed last night, and wrote an exciting poem she brought, which she had wanted to share with me. She was happy with what was happening to her, with our work, with me, and she came to share it all with me today until I ruined it. Instead of waiting to see where she was coming from, I wrecked the session by disconnecting (she never got to the enjoyment of reading the poem).

Every session the following week she sat up to confront me. I always did this to her, just when she was ready to connect I managed to spoil it somehow. I am an unanalyzed analyst. She listed the times I had failed her and then blamed her for being somehow pathological. I have a deep character flaw that I will never get over so what's the point of her trying to relate to me. If every time when she is ready to connect I wreck it, what's the use of continuing her analysis? We need an arbitrator, someone who can show me my part in all of this.

My feeble attempts to talk about our overall context, about her intensity, about eye contact, about her using my discomfort at her scrutiny to achieve a disconnection fell on deaf ears. She was on a rageful roll and nothing I could say engaged her in thought about other aspects of what may be happening. Her body was drawn up tight, her eyes piercing, her voice tense and authoritative, her manner confident and strident. I had done it to her again and it had to stop. As she reviewed past incidents that she believed I refused to acknowledge my part in, I repeatedly attempted to correct her, to remind her that I had acknowledged how I had failed to be empathic, but that acknowledgement had not helped. I continued to ask if it is possible for us to notice how she was reacting to my empathic error. Each time she interpreted this as my trying to blame her, to hold her responsible for what I have done wrong.

The attack was amplified on Tuesday with her "pulling all the stops" on her anger, dredging up every complaint and flaw in my nature she could think of, and by mid-session Wednesday I was weakened, exasperated, and banging my hands on the arms of my chair almost shouting that I did not say she was a bad person, or that it was her fault, or that my response last Friday was the best one. I only said that we are different people with different ways of thinking and responding. I had a real personality that responded to things she did. She may be using my personal responsiveness for her unconscious purposes. I was angry that she persisted in turning everything I said to mean that I was okay and she wasn't. I was struggling not to defend myself against her harsh attacks, to find some way of validating her feelings. But she still turned my comments into how nuts I think she is, how I think everything is transference, and that I still believe I hadn't done anything to deserve her anger and disillusionment.

Toward the end of the session I was able to say as sincerely as I knew how that she was absolutely right that I started last Friday's session badly. She was quieter and, I hoped, listening to what I had to say for the first time. I tried to explain the long-term tracking I was doing. I said that when I felt her gaze and her immediate demand to know if I was okay, I mistakenly responded on the abstract plane I was considering at the moment, rather than waiting to see where she was coming from. She was having a joyous body experience, had written a poem, and wanted to share it with me. A concrete moment of happy sharing was what she wanted. My error, I said, was responding from another plane than the one she was on.

In struggling to explain how, given who I was and our previous discussions about her intense gaze, she could expect me to avert my eyes when she stared at me, I likened it to hugs at the end of the hour that I thought she had previously given an indication of understanding. I explained that if she wanted to interact comfortably with me, neither of these modes would work because they made me uncomfortable. I had shown her I could go along with what she wanted, but if her desire was to achieve a mutually comfortable interpersonal connection given who I was, those means would not achieve it. This did not make me right and her wrong, it was merely the way I was. The intensity and physical contact were simply not ways of approaching me that she could count on a favorable response to. She became quiet and thoughtful and left silently. I hoped I had acknowledged the nature of my error, and how it had indeed prevented me from being with her – and how that replicated the numerous times her parents had done just that to her, leaving her isolated and badly damaged as a result. It seemed that she was taking some of this in and she left the session somewhat subdued.

But the next day she arrived utterly devastated. She could see now that I definitely could not be trusted. All along she had believed me. She had hoped that our relationship would be different. She had believed that I could be emotionally honest, but from my response yesterday she could see that there was no hope. No hope for me, no hope for our relationship, no hope for the analysis, and no hope for her. All I could see was "an error in timing." But the fatal flaw remained, I still believed that it was her fault not mine. Further, I had humiliated her by saying I never wanted hugs, that I didn't like them, that they were all her neediness and nothing I cared for. It simply wasn't true; I had engaged warmly in those hugs, she said. Or if it was true that I hated her need of hugs, then I was dishonest when I had hugged her. I managed not to be defensively corrective of how she turned things today, but only echoed her despair and how this was exactly the despair she had experienced all her life with the emotional dishonesty of her parents. She now had discovered me to be as emotionally dishonest as they had been. The most devastating trauma of her childhood was being repeated in our relationship.

I had encouraged her earlier to go over her concerns with a consultant we both knew. I brought up that possibility again, this time as a suggestion for a way out of her despair. Near the end of the session there was a long silence and slowly tears began to trickle down her cheeks. She was able to whisper, "Betrayal, what a horrible betrayal. To believe someone is emotionally honest and then to find out they haven't been." As she left I mentioned that I would be home all weekend in case she had anything to tell me.

By Monday she was ill with asthma again. Betrayal was the theme. She reviewed her distresses with me. I was allowed to correct the "error in timing" she spoke of to my view that I was badly out of tune with her by being on a plane of abstraction, tracking long-term themes when she was wanting to have to-gether some concrete happiness of the moment. That seemed better. I was allowed to repeat my belief that we were experiencing being different people, not that I was right and good and that she was wrong and bad. We were struggling in this together but not as adversaries. She agreed but expressed that she felt I was trying to send her away to resolve this with a consultant when she had to work it out with me. I agreed that she had to work it out with me, but pointed out that sometimes a third party can shed helpful light and provide support.

Then I related the consultation I had had last week regarding my work with her. I told her I had come to understand several things more fully. She listened quietly and intently, but gave little response at the time. I reviewed how I had talked about my dilemma with her. I related that I had shared with my consultant how from her perspective it looked adversarial — and finally, despairing and bleak as she experienced the horror of emotional betrayal. I demonstrated with my hands banging the arm of the chair how I had related how angry I had been that she kept misinterpreting me as saying it was all her fault. I showed her my body freeze-frame that had been caught by my consultant of banging the arms of the chair. I quoted the empathic interpretation of my plight given by my consultant; "Mother, I hate you for not being available to me, for not hearing what I have to say, for misinterpreting my love, for not being there when I need response from you. I thought you understood me and now I find you don't." Our work had succeeded in producing a regressive trend in me that stimulated my response to my own organizing mother.[4]

Her eyes grew larger, but still she was silent. I felt she grasped that I was telling her about my regression in our situation, my helplessness and anger; about how fragile and pained I had become. I continued talking about my consultation. I relayed how I spoke about how what was happening between her and myself was of critical importance. I was tracking the disconnects on one level and she on another and we were not meeting — how frustrating it was for both of us. I mentioned that I had spoken about how I knew somehow she was doing absolutely the right thing in raging at me, but I still could not understand completely what it was all about. I told her I had been sitting in a love seat when the consultant observed another body freeze-frame at the very moment when I was

---

4. I wish to gratefully acknowledge Robert Hilton as serving as my consultant in this difficult work.

expressing greatest agony about my plight with her. I showed her how I had leaned forward and sideways (toward a fetal position) with my right thumb approaching my mouth. Our session was drawing near an end. She asked a few questions to be sure she understood what I was saying about the oral and fetal body regression I was experiencing. I communicated compassion for both of us in the dilemma we were in and the strength it took on both sides to allow this deep regression to occur at the depth it obviously was. My sharing with her my consultative experience and the depth of regressive stress our work together was stimulating in me seemed to provide some connecting link, though I couldn't tell at the time exactly how I had succeeded in reaching her.

Several hours later she left word for me to call and I reached her mid-evening. She was sobbing and barely able to whisper, her lungs and throat were unbearably tight and in pain. Her whole body ached. She said she was breaking down and began sobbing uncontrollably. She said Marc was there with her, so she was okay, but very frightened and confused. One thing kept running through her mind that she had not told me before. As long as she could remember, whenever her mother was angry, her mother would first scream and yell, but then lapse into a cold, distant, withdrawn silence. Her mother literally would not speak to her for days on end. She was never sure exactly what she had done to produce the awful silence in her mother, but it was icy and cruel. It felt like what she gets from me when I withdraw into silence. Then she said, "This other I'm not quite sure about—what broke the cold silence. But it seems like after a week or so something would happen, maybe we would be passing somewhere in the house or something, and our eyes would catch and I'd break down. As soon as I'd break down she'd be okay again. But she would hold out until I broke down. It was so cruel. How could anyone do something so unbelievably cruel to a child—holding out until she broke. And I did. I always did. I always broke first. Like it was a battle to see who could hold out the longest. And she always won—even to this day she wins. I have to speak first."

I told her I thought something had happened when I shared my own helpless regressed distress with her. She agreed. We talked about it several ways. She was calming down now, glad for the talk. It seemed that when she could see my pain, my regression, something broke. But for once it wasn't her. When I told her about my body regression in response to her she knew I was connected to her. She knew I had feelings, and that I was not her steely mother. That we were not in an awful battle over who was most sane. She replied, "Right now I feel a tremendous need to be taken care of, to be physically attended to, to be held, caressed, comforted. Like it's been a horrible trauma and I need comforting." I suggested she ask for physical comfort from Marc tonight. She asked if she could call me early in the morning.

When she called the next morning she told me that Marc held her all night. First one side of her body and then the other would get cold and be in terrible pain. He was glad to be there for her and she reminded herself that, despite her various frustrations with him, whenever she has really needed him he has come through. I commented, "He does care deeply for you and he has the patience of a mother who holds on until things are okay again."

This was not the first traumatic transference repetition with this client nor the last as we worked through this organizing transference. But in the aftermath several interesting things were said. She had lunch with a close friend and laid out the whole story of her distress with me and felt very understood. She realized for the first time that I did not have to be a perfect person to be her analyst. She expressed concern that she had made me feel so bad. I hastened to tell her that I was fine, that my regression was certainly in relation to her, but that it was as much a part of our work together as was my sharing it with her. I reminded her how mothers must be able to regress in order to be with the distress of the infant, and that we both felt a need to experience this together no matter how distressing the experience might be.

She said, "I do know that. But all those things I said about you, you know they are true."

I explained, "That was the worst part, that you know me too well."

"But," she pondered, "I don't know why I said them all to you so meanly. I have to think about that."

I said, "You had to remember, and this is the only way. I know we both wish for pictures and stories that are easy to remember, that aren't so hard on us. It would be wonderful if we could simply and easily agree that you had bad parents. It would be altogether too easy to simply confront them about their shortcomings, their cruelty, their abusiveness, the cumulative strain trauma they caused. But this painful reexperiencing kind of memory is more difficult. This cruel and abusive battle, beginning as it did from earliest infancy can only be remembered as trauma, rage, betrayal, confusion, fear, tightening in the throat and lungs, and cold and pain all over your body. The accusations directed at my shortcomings are for the damage they caused you by being preoccupied with themselves."

We then spoke of how fragile her mother must have been to have been so threatened by the relationship demands of a baby. She had always thought of her mother as cold, calculating, strong, and cruel. Suddenly she understood that it was not so — that her mother was desperately clinging to her own sanity. "She could only hold to the false life that he [father] offered. She could hide herself safely in that false life with him. If there had ever been a choice, if it were him or me, it would have been, 'kill the baby.'"

The following week her sessions were quiet, her breathing calm and even as she dozed off several times on the couch — almost asleep, thinking, dreaming, silently enjoying being with me and not having to entertain me — knowing that I was enjoying her peace and restfulness. I had the fantasy of being a parent lost in timeless reverie in a rocking chair with the new baby.

THE DELUSION DEFINED

The following Monday there was again a despairing rage. It was pointless to continue her analysis. She now knew that she could not trust me emotionally, that I was fundamentally psychotic like her parents and could never provide her with the environment she needed to continue her analysis. "You would just let me walk!" Meaning that I did not care about what happened to her, that I would simply let her walk out in all of her pain and disillusionment. I assured her I could not prevent her from walking out. But that would be a horrible loss for both of us, even as discouraged as she was with me at the moment. Perhaps it would help if she spent some time going over her problems with me with the consultant I had on several occasions urged her to see.

On Tuesday she wordlessly moved the large wing-back chair she had been sitting in, turning its back to me, and sat in silence the entire session. I could not tell if it was anger or despair she was feeling.

Wednesday she echoed the uselessness of going on with me, the hopelessness of it all. How psychotic I am and how despairing she is. I struggled to stay with her and how awful it is to feel that there is no one to trust and nowhere to turn. I had occasion to discuss in basic terms a few ideas of Tustin and Klein. It seemed what she had hoped was that I would be able to restore the intrauterine state of physical at-oneness with her mother's body. Again and again when she bumped into boundaries of myself or of others she was painfully reminded that Eden cannot be regained, that the lost maternal body is lost forever. We discussed the broadest dimensions of how a baby can be slowly led to realize that mother's body is separate and that baby will not die, that basic trust is possible even in an imperfect and failing world. In her case it seemed clear that she was abruptly and cruelly forced into the realization that the necessary and longed-for features of her world were not under her control and that she had been enraged and suffering ever since. She said she had to hold onto this rage and that she was not sure why—that she must not give in. I supported her in this saying that she should not give in, that she must stay with her intuition. But I was for the first time a bit worried that she might actually attempt to end her work with me.

Thursday she announced that she was mad. She looked more confused than angry. She declared that this situation was impossibly painful and confusing—she could not function, and she did not know how she would get through the weekend in this shape. Then came the deepest anguish I had ever heard from her, without the slightest hint of manipulative energy to berate me or to get me to rescue her from it. "I can't trust you because you're psychotic and will emotionally damage me. But I can't let go of you or I'll die." There was a brief silence as we both grasped the impact of her powerful words. The truth had finally been spoken and we both immediately recognized this central definition of the internalized emotional situation in which she had lived since infancy. We talked about it, and how significant this definition of her fundamental delusion is. It was like an enormous boil had finally broken and she was flooded with relief. I agreed to call her each day of the weekend. She immediately and spontaneously connected this central dilemma with the successful business meeting of several months ago that marked the beginning of this lengthy regressive experience. She saw how when her friends and colleagues connected with her she immediately distrusted their sincerity, their warmth, their good will. The distrust was her transference repetition to her terror of connection. A series of other memories immediately tumbled out that could be seen and understood in light of this new

Rosetta stone. It was as though a key to understanding everything in her life had finally been spoken. She said, "You kept talking about connecting and disconnecting and I suppose that is what this is, but when I put it into my own words it suddenly makes more sense to me."

I emphasized the importance of her finally being able to state the bind she was in with me: that I am crazy and may damage her but that she can't do without me. I added that at least this second time around maybe I wouldn't be so crazy as her first mother! She smiled. She recalled that some years earlier she had attended a weekend "birth regression" seminar. In fantasy she had regressed back to the womb. She had a picture of herself as a hard-boiled egg. All the other eggs were enthusiastically jumping up and down and she was hard boiled. I interpreted that this was a picture of her psychic life with the protoplasm hardened from the beginning prohibiting any emotional growth. She said, "It goes back to before conception. My mother didn't want me to develop at all. It happened even before my father appeared." Some deep tension had been relieved, a way to rethink and reexperience everything was now available. In light of this image I recalled my countertransference fantasy of a few years earlier in which I saw her amidst a group of others enthusiastically jumping up and down wishing to be seen, longing to connect, to grow.

Spontaneously she related this new discovery to a series of distressing situations that have caused her great puzzlement and pain. Now she could see them as somehow arranged by her to prevent contact by experiencing others as untrustworthy or even using the closed off or defended parts of others' personalities to get them to do things that would prove that she couldn't trust them or relate to them. On the way out she said, "And there really isn't anyone I can trust." I said, "Not in the way you have always wished to—they are crazy and may hurt you, but the problem you are stuck with is that even if you can't totally trust anybody, you do need people to relate to and to feel alive with." The reader will understand that the fundamental kernel or nucleus of her character structure had been spoken. The turning point in the analysis had been reached. Her infantile trauma had been remembered by being emotionally repeated in the analytic relationship. The internal character structure could now be subjected to a sequence of working through experiences both inside and outside the analytic relationship. The flexibility required for more spontaneous and creative living was then achievable through gaining conscious knowledge and mastery over the somatopsychic structuring of her personality. Psychoanalysis cannot restore us to Eden. But it can serve to permit us increased access to our personal powers for creatively living a more fulfilling life.

12

Countertransference to the Organizing Experience[1]

Empathic contact with elemental organizing processes inevitably entails a certain regression or what Anny Katan (1969) has called "ego flexibility" on the part of a mother or an analyst in order to be able to attend to baby's psychic movements. Katan prefers to call the normal processes of maternal adaptation to the infant ego flexibility to avoid the pathological connotations she feels are present in the word *regression*. Narcissistic injury is frequently felt when a mother or an analyst is responded to at best as a need satisfier or at worst, as a dreaded enemy, unreliable caretaker, or nonhuman intrusion. Giovacchini's (1975, 1979a, b) penetrating focus on the disruptive effects that "primitive mental states" regularly have on the personal and professional integrity of the analyst points toward very special listening problems. Giovacchini speaks of "the impact of the delusion" to refer to both the positive and negative

1. This chapter also appears in Hedges 1994c.

effects that the patient's experience of reality have on the comfort and identity of the analyst. His discussions of the problems involved in maintaining, losing, and regaining the analytic stance prepare the clinical listener for disruptions in his or her own personality functioning when working with organizing experiences. Giovacchini discusses interventions and maneuvers undertaken by the analyst so that the analyst can continue functioning as an analyst. Anticipating disruptions in the analyst's personality functioning and being prepared to undertake tactics or maneuvers designed to maintain the analytic position and/or to shore up the personality functioning of the analyst constitutes an important contribution to clinical listening with organizing issues.

Different forms of countertransference experience, that is, emotional responsiveness on the part of the analyst, are to be expected depending upon the developmental level of the issues currently being presented for analysis.[2] Thus far, four distinct forms of countertransference have emerged with clarity that characterize therapists' responsiveness to organizing experience.

1. *The belief that the person is somehow so defective that they can only be treated chemically, physically, or supportively.* This belief is not confirmed by clinical studies conducted by therapists who understand the nature of the organizing transference, and it is directly opposed by many analysts with similar experience (Sanville 1992). In my view this is a wholesale writing off of human potential and fails to take into consideration that these individuals possess full human capabilities that have been stopped short by infantile experiences that can be analyzed. There are certainly psychotic pictures that have as their basis an organic reason that human connectedness fails, but the vast majority of

---

2. See Hedges (1992) for a study of the different kinds of countertransference responsiveness that are expectable to each of the four developmentally derived listening perspectives.

psychotic states are considered functional and therefore amenable to treatment with the proper psychological tools.[3]

2. *The fear of psychotic energies being directed at the person of the analyst.* Melanie Klein is cited in Strachey's (1934) classic paper on the therapeutic action of psychoanalysis as having observed psychoanalysts' reluctance to make mutative interpretations (ones that have the power to transform). It was her belief that analysts fear encountering the full force of id energies directed squarely at themselves in the transference, which interpretation of transference and resistance promotes. We can now say that in the analyst's finding potential contact moments and seeking to bring the internalized modes of contact rupture into full emotional re-creation in the analytic relationship, the full power of a lifelong history of psychosis is being invited into the analytic consulting room with the analyst as the target of powerful psychosomatic energies. This prospect can be frightening and, indeed, with many organizing or psychotic states is dangerous and unadvisable on a practical basis. Aside from critical practical considerations that I have mentioned already and elaborate on elsewhere (Hedges 1994c), there is no reason in principle why emotions of whatever nature and intensity cannot be experienced in analysis and directed at the analyst. The analyst simply has to be prepared for the strength of their emergence.

3. *Organizing transferences stimulate the analyst's own organizing yearnings, traumas, and fears.* When an analyst repeatedly reaches out to someone and is not responded to or is responded to in intrusive or frightening ways, it tends to activate his or her own most primitive experiences when reaching out to mother and not finding her. Analysts may wish to keep the relating on a superficial level so as not to have to reexperience their own most primitive selves. Analysts may also wish to keep the targets

---

3. I have provided theoretical elaboration and clinical illustration (Hedges 1994c) as well as extended case studies (Hedges 1994d, in press).

of the psychotic energy outside the analysis or in the past so as not to have to experience regressive trends in themselves.

4. *An analytic listener may break contact out of empathy with the analytic speaker.* Well along into the therapy, after (a) suitable contact points have been identified, (b) interpretive contact has occurred, and (c) sustained contact is beginning, the analytic speaker is often quite excited by the accruing results. He or she has never before been invited to relate in a way in which it was possible to respond. Nor has the person living in an organizing state ever been effectively shown the nature of how he or she ruptures contact. Soon the person excitedly begins catching on, and bringing in numerous examples of loss and regaining of contact in daily life. At this point we watch analysts become preoccupied, thinking about other things in sessions or becoming drowsy—clearly in an attempt to put the damper on the relating. This is usually an unconscious reaction on the part of the analyst that registers his or her awareness that all of this contact is indeed dangerous for the analytic speaker and possibly for the listener as well. It is as though the speaker, in an enthusiastic move to rush ahead, is in danger of biting off more than she can chew and the analyst is instinctively finding a way of slowing things down. This can be noted and spoken, however, so that two can discuss the dangers of developing sustained contact and work on them together.

13

Therapists at Risk

TRANSFERENCE REMEMBERING AS ESSENTIAL MENTAL STRUCTURE

I often find myself musing on the concept of transference and wonder exactly when and how I first came to grasp such a strange and highly abstract notion. But I am never quite able to locate any specific moment in my past when I suddenly caught on to what transference is about. I cannot recall any instant of intuition when the whole meaning of Freudian psychology unfolded magically before me. Rather, I have come to think that transference must be something that we have somehow always vaguely known about since the beginning of our lives and perhaps since the beginning of human time. It is as though transference in all of its variations, operating as affective metaphor and metonymy, and making possible emotional condensation and displacement, is the fundamental structuring mechanism of the human mind that has taken us ten thousand years to notice.

Psychoanalysts now take for granted that human mental functioning originates in and through relationships and that human relatedness can be thought about and studied as a set of habits and patterns developed in relation to significant others in childhood. Coming to understand ourselves in these terms entails bringing to consciousness a whole set of enduring emotional attitudes developed in relation to significant others—attitudes that color the ways we experience ourselves in relation to others and to the world.

In my role as a psychoanalyst, I am often in a position to point toward the operation in the here and now of a transfer of emotion from a childhood experience onto myself or onto the current experience of the analytic relationship. It is always exhilarating when I can see from the analytic speaker's response to my verbal or nonverbal interpretation a sudden apprehension of some hidden aspect of their experience with me—when something I have been able to say or do serves to mirror a whole aspect of his or her emotional life that has been heretofore unnoticed. To suddenly "see" the operation of transference in an emotionally charged moment of interaction is always surprising and illuminating.

Transferred emotional templates operate unconsciously as mind structuring mechanisms, habits, or patternings. And their appearance in consciously defined ways of being is always evanescent and elusive, so much so that people who have not had occasion to study in themselves the operation of these invisible patterns find the concept of transference nonsensical. But if one knows how to watch carefully, suddenly a gap in the fabric of the conversation or emotional engagement opens and an entire unconscious structure or emotional meaning of the engagement comes clearly but fleetingly into view. Two people experience a sudden inhalation, a flashing insight and inspiration, a deep and intimate moment of *knowing together*, as the Greek derived word *consciousness* denotes. A heretofore invisible and elusive aspect of our emotional relating suddenly reverberates in the atmosphere around and within us as a truth: a truth somehow vaguely known, and now suddenly and starkly apprehended in the living context of our relatedness. And just as quickly as apprehended, the experience is lost, as though sunk again beneath the surface of consciousness. With time and persistence, the analytic listener and the analytic speaker come to learn how to catch brief glimpses, how to form viable narratives, how to engage in telling interactions – in short, how to construct analytic nets for capturing these elusive specters of the deep.

One would think that once an enduring pattern of being is apprehended and defined by two in consciousness, that a person could rely on this definition of the way one's mind works in subsequent interactions and relationships. And to a certain extent this is true. That is, after an extensive analysis of one's fundamental relatedness patterns, a person does carry in consciousness a basic map of familiar patterns of subjective experiencing. But the most incredible thing that has emerged from a century of psychoanalytic study is that these fundamental relatedness dimensions must be defined anew in each and every intense and intimate relationship we engage in. We might attribute this phenomenon (following quantum physics and chaos theory) to the infinite and ever-changing complexity of the human mind and its amazing resiliency and adaptability when placed in dynamic interactive contact with another completely different subjective world. A more parsimonious account might follow the work of infant researchers who note the amodal or global nature of early perceptual-motor life and the fundamental nature of total body affects in structuring enduring human personality organization – almost like a series of complex and adaptable gestalts that are subject to change at any moment and always in need of redefinition. Once transference defining begins in a person it becomes an ongoing and unending activity as the person strives to define how his or her basic patterning of emotional experience continues to operate in every relationship.

Whatever people hope to experience in psychoanalysis relates to the sudden and almost magical appearance of these moments of insightful truth and inspirational vitality in the analytic relationship. With or without words, two people suddenly and fleetingly experience a different order of interpersonal reality – an ordering that we usually only experience in dreams, slips of the tongue, flashbacks, somatic and psychic symptoms, and orgasm.

In the last century we have learned that different types of analytic nets have to be constructed in order to ensnare different kinds of emotional specters transferred from the past and in order to allow entry into this separate ordering of human relatedness.

Mutually experiencing and acknowledging how emotional themes and patterns from past relationships are inciting, impinging, determining, and/or limiting the present moment of emotional relatedness constitutes the activity of psychoanalysis and depth psychotherapy. The transference interpretation, whether verbal or nonverbal, bespeaks an intimacy and a mutual knowingness otherwise usually forbidden or considered bizarre in ordinary social discourse. Successful (or what has been called mutative) transference interpretation inexorably plunges two people deeply into an intensely stimulating interpenetration of ordinarily defined personal boundaries that human beings seldom experience except in situations of deeply aroused mutual seduction. From listening to many therapists reporting their experiences over the years, I have reason to suspect that the intense and mutual physiological arousal in analytic situations during moments of successful, deep, mutative transference interpretation is similar to that which occurs in other stimulating seduction situations. By daring to draw the full force of the analytic speaker's life history of somatic arousal directly toward him-or herself, by daring to receive deeply the emotional impact of the analytic speaker's full instinctual arousal, and by daring to feel the somatopsychic arousal of being fully connected to the deep emotional life of another human being when physiological drives, both sexual and aggressive, are mobilized and active in the interaction, the psychoanalyst provides the opportunity for a transformative experience to occur. The consciousness attained during such moments regarding the transfer of emotional experiencing via established templates or patternings may or may not be rethought later in the same terms or may subsequently take on a myriad of different forms. But the transformative power of this moment lies in the fact that the emotional patterns in question can never be simply lived out in total blind unconsciousness again. Something new is known about oneself and with that knowledge comes a certain degree of personal power and flexibility.

RESISTANCE TO TRANSFERENCE REMEMBERING

The constellation of affects and perceptions brought into focus with such great clarity and force during these moments of high interpersonal arousal have been avoided (resisted) for so long that, once reexperienced, they cannot be forgotten. This resistance to remembering by repeating emotional patterns that in infancy and childhood were experienced as traumatically under- or overstimulating is known to psychoanalysts as a special set of transferences. Different forms of resistance to remembering accompany different types of transference memories that originated during different developmental epochs. That is, psychoanalysts have come to study not only an array of transference memories but a parallel array of resistance memories that structure the human mind.

The profound and intense interpersonal emotional contact that characterizes the intimacy of psychoanalysis and psychotherapy is necessarily experienced as exhilarating, arousing, tenuous, dangerous, and frightening in various ways by both people involved. These moments of deep emotional and cognitive insight concern what we are about, how we are relating to each other, what we desire from each other, what excites us and frightens us about each other, and how all of this relates to our pasts and how our subjective worlds have come to be structured. The feelings inevitably stirred up in such an engagement echo a long chain or history of intense interpersonal contact moments in the life of each participant.

CLASSICAL TRANSFERENCE CONTRASTED WITH PREOEDIPAL TRANSFERENCE

Classical analysis and classical analytic technique were explicitly devised for and limited to the treatment of oedipal level neurotic transference structures. "The talking cure" involved the establishment of a rigid frame for free associating and an analyst who practiced stringent restraint and personal anonymity vis-à-vis the patient. As psychoanalysis has widened its scope, a series of preoedipal transference structures have come under study that have entailed departures from the classical technique. Jung, Adler, Reich, Ferenczi, Alexander, Sechehaye, and other contemporaries who have begun schools of psychotherapy like Rogers, Berne, and Lowen have recognized the need for more personal involvement on the part of the analyst when bringing preoedipal transferences into view. Even the whole popularized recovery movement might be said to focus on emotional transferences from preoedipal traumas, though the recovery movement tends to aim toward containment of, rather than analysis of, those transferences.

As our awareness of preoedipal transference and resistance structures has grown, it has become gradually obvious that there is no such thing as a neurotic in pure culture, but rather the isolation of oedipal neurotic structures stands as the first historical definition of one way that transferences and resistances operate in human personality. We now know that every stage of human development is marked by the child's solutions to relatedness dilemmas. And that these solutions remain as personality patterns through which subsequent experience is perceived and organized. Contemporary psychoanalysis distinguishes fairly clearly and reliably four distinct (though not mutually exclusive) levels of self and other experience that can be identified in analysis as different types of transference and resistance structures (Hedges 1983, 1992). In earlier chapters I have summarized these four levels of psychic development along with the kinds of transference and resistance memories characteristic of each.

In mutative transference interpretation, exactly how past relatedness experiences are inextricably woven into the present fabric of relatedness is a brief, brilliantly illuminated moment known to both. The moment is not merely *like* a seductive encounter. It can only *be* a seductive experience of the most profound magnitude–two people engaging one another until the cores of their subjective worlds are engaged in deeply personal intimate contact. For optimal psychoanalytic results, the experience and understanding entail a protracted mutual seduction of one another's caring, concern, and loving regard.

Traditional psychoanalysis, which maintained its focus only on advanced oedipal (neurotic) psychic formations, never needed to stray from formal, verbal-symbolic restraint in order to bring the symbolic structures under analytic scrutiny. But contemporary psychoanalysis, which fosters psychic transformation by focusing on issues involved in preoedipal self formation, symbiotic scenarios, and organizing channels, requires that both participants bring a full range of personal instinctual life to the analytic engagement.

MAINTAINING SEPARATENESS AND SAFETY IN THE ANALYTIC ENCOUNTER

Safeguards against incestual and parricidal involvement are provided by the eye of the third party—traditionally symbolized by the father, now codified in psychotherapy by ethics and law. A mother must be fully and instinctually involved to provide maximal reception for the preoedipal needs of her child. To the degree that a mother's emotional involvement with her young child is limited by personal preoccupations, restrictive notions about childrearing, or rigid internal defenses, what she has to offer as a symbiotic partner is likewise limited. On the other hand, the ancient taboos regarding seduction and violence toward the young teach that under- or overstimulating involvement by caretakers creates trauma and damage in formative minds.

It is the Eye of the Other as internalized in the psychic structure of parents and other helping professionals that guards against penetrating and destructive overstimulation of those seeking to expand their psychic development. Without this Eye of the Other to monitor and structure intense relationships in such a way that they are nontraumatically stimulating, the person uninitiated into the complexities of human emotional relatedness either (1) slumps for lack of stimulating response, (2) moves into activities designed to avoid the intense stimulation, or (3) receives the stimulation as traumatic intrusion (which may later need to be avenged). These three choices (freeze, flee, and fight) are open to every person in childhood, and the way the person solves the problem of intrusive stimulation will also be revived in the analysis as transference and resistance memory.

Because of the characteristic or ritualistic roles of speaker and listener routinely assumed in the psychoanalytic situation, the sequence of intense transference illuminations will emerge as more obvious, more explicit, and more often clearly spelled out regarding the unconsciously transferred emotional structures in the speaker than in the listener. Traditional psychoanalysis is formulated to imply that there is no emotional involvement on the part of the analyst. And if there is, it is detractive and should be eliminated—not spelled out, and certainly not spoken to the patient. In more contemporary work with preoedipal transferences some reciprocal exchanges around various emotional issues are to be expected. And every analyst knows the internal transformations that occur in the personality of the analyst as a result of each deeply engaging analytic relationship.

SUBLIMATION OF ANALYTICALLY STIMULATED DRIVES

The question of propriety in psychoanalysis hinges on whether the intensity of the mutually stimulating relationship has been able to evolve to the deeply intimate moment of mutative transference interpretation with both parties—or at least with the analyst—being able to sublimate the experience of drive mobilization in such a way that insight and development can spring from this loving involvement, rather than thoughtless emotional penetration and destruction. Our culture vaguely and intuitively understands the power of helping relationships to produce growth as well as damage. The universal existence of rules regarding incest (sexuality) and murder (violence) attests to universally experienced temptations. We certainly don't have laws about things that are not tempting. Recent clarification in ethics codes and laws regarding the essentially parental position assigned by organized society to helping professionals of all types further attests to a cultural commitment to curtailing unsublimated encounters with those individuals who seek guidance and growth from those more initiated in various aspects of human life.

If we did no more than simply consider the psychotherapeutic encounter in this way, we could quickly surmise that the
helping partner is always at risk of having his or her own drives
mobilized in the process of a significant helping connection, and
then at risk of somehow getting lost in the process. "Getting lost"
might entail a person feeling consciously or unconsciously stimulated by the emotional pull of the intense relatedness experience and then mobilizing rigid defenses or boundaries against
personal involvement. But defense and boundary are not sublimation. Defense means erecting an internal barrier to relating
spontaneously and instinctively to the other person—a closing
off of potential channels for personal affective connection and
communication. Likewise establishing a ritualized frame or rou-
tine boundaries for oneself represents a cognitive effort to draw
limits that protect oneself by a Carte Blanche, by a priori refusal
to receive and to be affected by the intense stimulation that
intimate relating necessarily provides. On the other hand, sublimation entails a usually more or less conscious process of
experiencing the arousal that naturally arises in consequence of
connection and then utilizing that spontaneous excitement and
enthusiasm for the attainment of creative and productive goals
in the context of the relationship. The history of our field
demonstrates how often analysts have gotten lost in defensive
activities when sublimation would have been more useful. In
fact, it might even be said that much of the technical lore and
dogma of psychoanalysis is aimed at bolstering the analyst's
defensiveness and defining ritualized boundaries to ensure non-
relating, rather than encouraging the analyst toward sustaining
a posture replete with desire and apprehension.

The current blind and naïve morality surrounding so-
called "dual relationships" further encourages therapists to turn
away from the essential therapeutic task—that of mobilizing
intense emotional constellations (formed in the distant past) in
the real here-and-now relationship with the analyst or therapist,
so that they can be experienced as powerful illusory patterns
that govern one's emotional life.

ACTING OUT TRANSFERENCE AND
RESISTANCE MEMORIES

Of course, many things can and do crop up to interfere with the unfolding of successive layerings of transference. Resistance to reliving transference memories was first seen by Freud as the patient's will to remain ill. When negative therapeutic reactions threaten to crop up, the finger of accusation is invariably pointed at the analyst in some extra-analytic arena or displaced onto some external person from the present or past. Ideally this finger of accusation is leveled at the analyst as a part of the analysis so that the disturbing affects can be secured as transference or as a resistance to reliving deep transference feelings.

But when, for whatever reason, the resistance to deep experience is great and transference experiences cannot be established with the analyst, the analytic speaker may act out the negative transference in his or her accusations of the therapist. This is not to say that we do not have incompetent, unethical, and unknowledgeable therapists among us who do not want to or who do not know how to manage intense transference and countertransference stimulation. But having consulted on many aborted therapeutic processes, more often than not I find that the therapist has been successful in mobilizing deep transference patterns in the therapeutic relationship. But because we can never know in advance what a given person's deepest patterns of emotional trauma—neglect, seduction, violence—might look like until they are actually mobilized in the analytic transference for study, we cannot know what early (and therefore borderline or psychotic) trauma may be turned toward us without a moment's notice. And since all people have experienced various forms of overt trauma or strain trauma in infancy and early childhood, a therapist is always at risk in that every individual piece of work may dredge up some unexpected piece of psychotic abuse that will suddenly and abortively be aimed at the therapist.

Accusing the therapist (or someone else) instead of analyzing the resistance and transference implicit in the traumatized
position the person feels him- or herself in, only serves to wreak
further havoc on the now self-defined and self-maintaining
victim. After the fact, and without benefit of many working-
through memories, the third-party Eye of the Other (the social
justice system) is then engaged for the purpose of avenging
experienced abuses. But no working through, no healing, no
deep contact with one's invisible personality structures ever
occurred to a person who is standing in front of a judge, a jury,
a licensing board, or an ethics committee. While there may be
times in life that an adversarial situation is necessary or even
desirable, searching for one's soul is certainly not one of them. In
situations where an analytic speaker questions the propriety of
the analytic situation, I advise extensive third party consultation
and in extreme instances a change of therapists. Filing a complaint serves to polarize positions and solidify the victim sense in
one's mind prematurely, before adequate working through has
occurred. If there is valid need to file a complaint, that can
always be done at a later time. The stakes on working through
are usually much higher. Considering the purpose of psychotherapy—that is, to revive past emotional patterns in direct
relationship to the person of the therapist so that they can be
expressed, experienced, and examined by two so that resistance
and emotional transfer can be established and worked through,
it should not surprise us if a primitive impulse derails the process,
leaving a displaced accusation aimed inappropriately, and only
too realistically, at the therapist.[1]

In considering these issues I am reminded of the recent
absurdities that have arisen with the advent of Prozac, a drug
prescribed for profound depression. We have a whole popula-

---

1. Further ways of safeguarding the therapeutic process during the
working through of psychotic transference, such as the utilization of a third
party case monitor, are discussed in Hedges 1994c.

tion of severe depressives whose lives and aggressive energies are so stifled they are seen to be in chronic danger of suicide or homicide. Clinical lore even tells us that these people do not generally have the energy to aim their full aggression at themselves or at others, but warns of potential danger when the depression begins to lift. These people are then given the new drug, which is miraculously successful at raising their spirits. The occasional subsequent suicide or homicide is then attributed to some unknown chemical side effect of the drug! Psychoanalysts and psychotherapists deliberately arrange a setting in which primordial abuse patterns can be remembered by the client's feeling them repeated in the vicissitudes of the here-and-now transference relationship. The therapeutic regression is begun and fostered by the therapist. When the abusive pattern is resurrected in relation to the analyst and the expected resistance to transference does not yield to analysis, for whatever reason, the therapeutic process is aborted with the accusatory finger pointing at the therapist. Those many naïve watchdogs who serve as the Eye of the Other conclude that Prozac caused the suicide, forgetting entirely that the treatment has addressed the issues successfully, but that not all aspects of the hidden unconscious can be fully anticipated in advance and controlled.

A psychoanalyst or a psychotherapist does not have the power to transform anyone. He or she can only provide a setting in which invisible dimensions of the person's character can come to light. The analyst cannot fully anticipate or control how the person in analysis chooses to experience the transference or what the analytic speaker may do with the transference memories once revived in present experience. Stimulating the transference to be active and present is the analyst's task. But the analyst cannot prevent the acting out of the impulses mobilized by the transference. The analyst cannot prevent the acting out of the resistance to change, especially when the primitive and intrusive psychotic content of traumatic stimulation from childhood becomes attached to the person of the analyst or when the resistance to the transference analysis is acted out in the form of accusations against the analyst or outside others. The treatment process has succeeded in unmasking the hidden abusiveness and the identification-with-the-aggressor defense. But the person in analysis is unable or unwilling, for whatever reason, to allow the primordial defensive rage to melt into ordinary human fear, frailty, and helplessness. The fault for this, if there be any fault, cannot lie with the analyst, for this deep transformative melting is not under his or her control. Transformation can only be attained by the courage and persistence of the person in analysis. Clearly the greatest risk of a psychoanalyst or psychotherapist is allowing him- or herself to be fully emotionally present, to risk living in an analytic relationship perennially enlivened by desire and fear.

CASE CONSULTATIONS INVOLVING RISKY RELATIONSHIPS

What follows are a few examples that have come to my attention that illustrate the helplessness of the analyst to effect change and how he or she has then suffered as a result of a negative therapeutic process that turned into an accusatory one. In each case, the therapist is narrating his or her experiences to me.

Consultation One: Marge (with a male therapist, fourteen years experience)

I saw Marge for two-and-a-half years ten years ago. She came to me after her children were grown and left home. She was a chronically depressed housewife in danger of alcoholism. A psychiatrist prescribed medication for her but she kept going downhill. Nothing I could do or say seemed to help. She didn't want to go to work or school to bolster her skills. She belonged to a church, which was enough group for her. She worried if her husband was having affairs on his sometimes week-long business trips. She mostly stayed home, watched television, ate, and slept.

On the day that later came into question, Marge was more depressed and despairing than I had ever seen her. Many times she spoke of having nothing to live for and of being despairing because she felt no one cared about her and that life was meaningless. The few friends she had she couldn't talk with. Marge said she was ready to end it all. Inside myself during the entire session I had to continually assess the seriousness of the suicide threat. It seemed serious. I could see that I was going to have to obtain a contract for her to call me before she did anything to hurt herself. But could I trust her even that far? Was I going to have to call the paramedics or police before I let her leave? I tried everything I could think of but could achieve no connection.

Marge sat on the end of the couch further away from me than usual that day. With ten minutes left I asked her if I could sit on the couch with her for a few minutes, thinking that perhaps that might help. She assented with some faint signs of life. A few minutes later, in desperation, I asked if it would help if I put my arm around her. She thought she might like that and shortly perked up enough for me to let her leave safely. I have four children. I know what a father's reassuring arm can mean and what it feels like—and I swear to God that's the way it was. I also believe that was the way she received it at the time because we seemed to connect and she took heart. We continued therapy for some months and Marge began to get better, to relate to people more, and to take night classes.

To make a long story short, her husband lost his job, her insurance ran out, and I drastically cut my fee so we could continue meeting. After some months, the financial situation was getting even worse so she decided to stop seeing me, but the door was left open for her to continue her therapy at a subsequent date. Several years later I closed my practice entirely and left the clinic where I had been seeing Marge to take a full-time job for a managed care company. She wanted to be seen again and found out how to contact me. I explained to Marge over the phone the reasons why I could not continue working with her; at that point I had no office, no malpractice insurance, no setup in which I could see her. She was enraged. I had always promised to love her and to see her no matter what, she claimed. She wrote a threatening letter to the director of the clinic where I had worked. He asked if we three could meet together. She was insinuating I had behaved inappropriately with her, had hugged and kissed her and made all manner of promises to her – none of which was true. All of it was apparently fabricated from that one incident and my lengthy commitment while working with her. This meeting with the clinic director settled her down a bit and she recanted the things she had said in the letter. He tried to arrange for her to see another therapist, which she refused to do. Shortly thereafter she caught her husband in what she was sure was a lie about some woman he was involved with at work. Again she demanded to see me. I spoke with her on the phone, and tried to assuage her rage that I would not see her. She was in a tirade over how I was abusing her. By this time she had been in an incest survivors group for a while and she had gained plenty of validation for her rage at her parents, and so was much freer to rage at me. I gave her appropriate referrals.

The next thing I knew, an armed investigator from the state licensing board showed up at my work with an attaché case and a lot of questions. Marge had written a letter alleging sexual misconduct. I was not allowed to see the letter. You know we have no civil rights in administrative proceedings. We are presumed guilty until proven innocent. But I did discover that she accused me of making love to her on my couch for a whole hour, promising her unending love and devotion, and then making her promise not to tell. The "promise not to tell" part clearly linked her current accusation or delusion to her childhood molestation.

Whatever she told the licensing board, my attorney tells me I am in deep trouble because I'll never be able to prove it didn't happen. I have some notes but ten years ago we didn't keep many notes so I don't know what good they will do. And anyway I don't keep notes on things that don't happen. I'm told I may lose my license to practice psychotherapy. And if she wins at this level there's a million dollars in malpractice settlement money

waiting for her to go after. I'm really worried. I have a good job
and a family to support. If charges of sexual misconduct are made
I could lose my job and everything I have trying to defend myself.
We were doing good work and we both knew it. We got to
many of the really terrible things that happened to her in
childhood. I had her on her feet and moving in the world again
and I think I could have gotten her out of her deep and life-long
depression and low self-esteem if the insurance money hadn't run
out. But now this.

I came to see you because when I read your paper, "In Praise
of the Dual Relationship," and I got to the part about the
psychotic transference, I suddenly saw what had happened. You
said something to the effect that the tragedy is that the therapy
has succeeded in mobilizing deep psychotic anxieties in the
transference. But then reality testing becomes lost and the
therapist is confused in transference with the perpetrator of the
past. That really happened. We were never taught about such
things in school. Do you have any ideas about how I can get out
of this jam?

Commentary

The most dangerous thing a therapist can do when working
with an organizing transference is to connect successfully to the
person without adequate working through of the resistance to
emotional connection. Yes, this man saved the day and didn't
have to hospitalize his patient. He succeeded in calling her back
from the brink. But he is deluded in thinking that connection is
experienced as good by people living organizing experience. I
think she never forgave him for approaching and connecting
when she wanted distance and that he then became fused into
her psychotic fantasies as yet another perpetrator. Her distress
that she cannot have him further fuses him to the image of the
perpetrator. Also, physical touching for the purpose of providing comfort or reassurance is never a good practice. Because
if it's not misunderstood as a seductive invitation, it will surely

be seen as a replication of an abusive penetration. I do see one certain, carefully defined potential use for interpretive touching in work with organizing or psychotic transferences. But interpretive touch is a carefully calculated concretized communication given at a critical and anticipated point in time when the person is having a hard time sustaining a connection and clearly understands the communication (Hedges 1994c). The error that the licensing board will have no way of understanding is that the therapy was going well until outside forces interrupted, plunging Marge into despair, with which her therapist successfully connected. The psychotic transference then operated to fuse his contact with that of childhood abuse.

Case Consultation Two: Louanne (with a male therapist, twenty years experience)

A middle-aged, childless professional woman came to me twice weekly for about six months. She had been to dozens of therapists all of her life and had taken various psychotropic medications for years. She had a psychiatrist who was giving her antidepressants at the time. She had a well-developed mimical self so she could talk well about all kinds of things at work and home. I began to sense that she had come to me because her husband of ten years was pulling out of the relationship emotionally. But she said nothing directly to that effect, nor had he. They were constantly fighting but that was the way it had always been between them and that was the way all relationships were for her. In a variety of ways I gingerly began to ask if maybe her husband was distancing himself from her, but she couldn't tolerate any such suggestion. Meanwhile she was getting more frantic at work. She was in trouble with her supervisor for inefficiency and chronic severe tardiness. She couldn't get out of bed in the morning. She spent hours in bed masturbating and was horrified that the fantasy that sexually satisfied her was nursing on a woman's breast. She was terrified this might mean she was a lesbian, another totally intolerable idea. She demanded reassurance from me that she was not. I spoke of how despairing she was about her husband's lack of responsiveness, about the increased fragmentation she was experiencing at home and on the job.

She frequently indicated that there was only one way out but had no plan, no fantasy, only a wish to escape from pain or to hurt her husband. The idea of a hospital stay appealed as a place to be taken care of, but she adamantly refused it because that would be the last straw and her husband might divorce her.

Louanne enjoyed seeing me for the most part and I attempted some interpretation of the nursing fantasies as pictures of the kind of care and nurturance she wished for from her husband and from me. Her medication had to be increased. But she began spending whole days in bed after her husband started talking about getting an apartment. She hired a detective to be sure he wasn't seeing anyone. Apparently, he was out of patience—ten years of nothing but anger and depression with no relationship and no sex. Although he claimed he loved her, he was fed up with her manipulations.

She began talking about the physical abuse her mother had given her throughout her childhood and on one fragmented occasion remembered with horror how her father and both brothers had molested her repeatedly throughout her growing-up years. She said she had never told anyone this before. She was so damaged I had no special reason not to take her memories at face value, except that the memories appeared during a period of severe fragmentation and at a time when she was experiencing harsh rejection from her husband. She begged and pleaded for him not to leave, but he had by now found an apartment and would be moving out in six weeks.

On the evening that later came into question, she had a session with me in which she was no more depressed or obsessed than usual. In fact, she seemed a little more intact and oriented than she had been for some weeks. She left my office, swallowed a bottle of her husband's sleeping pills in the car on the way home, and collapsed in her husband's arms. The gesture was clearly a last-ditch manipulation to get him to say he loved her (which he did) and that he would never leave her. He knew it was a manipulation and was so angry he later confessed to me that he seriously considered letting her die. She came to one last session the following week. Now that she was getting divorced she said that she couldn't afford to see me (which wasn't true; they were quite wealthy).

All efforts then and in follow-up calls and letters to persuade her to resume her therapy fell on deaf ears. It seemed clear that I had failed to help her save the one relationship in her life that had been nourishing. Her husband was a good man and despite her "illness" and "manipulations" he did care about her and had stood by her through a series of crises.

A year later, both her psychiatrist and I were sued for failure to hospitalize. She had a long list of damages that she had suffered because we had failed to provide proper care and holding while the world at work and home battered her. We both had adequate records. Expert witnesses reviewed the case and rendered testimony that validated that we had upheld a proper standard of care and that there were no immediate indicators for hospitalization. Even her husband testified that we had responded well but happened to be "in the wrong place at the wrong time."

Now the attorney for the malpractice company has proposed a hefty settlement. Depositions have taken two years and I have spent a considerable sum consulting with experts and with my own attorney. He says I could refuse to settle so as not to have the settlement on my record, but the estimates of cost in terms of the time and money involved are staggering. The same insurance company canceled the coverage of a friend of mine shortly after a settlement for far less than the sum they are offering her. I tell you it's all insane. If insurance companies keep settling for large amounts every time a person with a psychotic transference sues, we soon won't be able to afford the premiums. Besides, everyone involved in this case knows it's wrong. I'm convinced even *she* knows it's wrong. But she knows she can get away with it, and she needs the money now since she was fired from her job. I feel morally obligated to stand up and fight it. But I also have a life to lead and a family to care for. It would take every penny of what my wife and I have saved for years to keep this wrong thing from happening. And the insurance company doesn't care. They want to avoid the high costs of deposing dozens of therapists she has seen over the years, having to fly them all here from Miami.

There may not be much you can help me with at this point, except to not feel guilty for throwing in the towel. But how does one avoid such circumstances in the future? Shall we stop seeing borderline psychotics altogether in order to be safe?

Commentary

When dozens of others have failed before you, do not assume it's because they were incompetent and you will be the first therapist to really help. People with psychotic or organizing transferences have had, at some point in their infancy, the experience of having to fight to stay alive. Despite their frequent suicidal threats they are, in fact, survivors who have had to work harder than most of us just to pass as normal in a social world full of relatedness complexities they have no way of understanding. Survival and desperation they do understand, and consideration of others has no importance when psychic death threatens. Yes, there are many people with primitive anxieties we should not be seeing in our private practices—or at least not without an involved case monitor (see Hedges 1994c). Such people can be referred to public nonprofit clinics where the liabilities to the treating therapists are not so great.

Case Consultation Three: Edward (with a female therapist, fifteen years experience)

My ex-client grew up in poverty, never being cared for or having anything. His earliest memories are starving in a crib with no one to feed or change him. He remembers scavenging in garbage cans and begging for food in the slum of a large Eastern city. By six he was selling newspapers on the street. Soon he was a newspaper distributor, then he got his own newsstand, and onward and upward, defying every obstacle all the way to the top of a major international corporation, finally becoming a wealthy man. But of course, he was only 4 months old inside. He could mimic, but he had no idea how to relate emotionally to himself or anyone else. He could put on elegant appearances, but it was the infant that showed up in my office.

I won't go into details of the treatment. Suffice it to say that I saw him as often as possible, sometimes several hours a day trying to contain him before some big meeting or business confrontation. He pleaded with me on several occasions to meet him for sessions in distant cities so he could be with me in advance of important deals and I went. The therapy was going well. It all centered around supplies: never having enough, being afraid of dying of starvation, and a veritable frenzy of concern and grasping at everything in sight – all of these clearly wounds from a neglectfully abusive infancy.

His concerns sooner or later came up in terms of preoccupation with body parts. He had dozens of doctors and literally hundreds of medications of all sort. After I became more secure in my position I sent him to a good doctor who could follow him regularly and arranged to have all of his pills taken away except those this doctor prescribed. He had a psychiatric consult with a top psychiatrist who I thought might try an anti-psychotic or lithium, but instead started him on Xanax, which he later became addicted to. There were many beautiful and grasping women, deceitful business colleagues, and greedy family members, all of whom wanted a piece of him. But he slowly learned to limit the demands and at times even to say "no" to outlandish requests. I became his sounding board, his source of reality testing, and practically a business and relationship consultant.

It was difficult trying to give him as much time and support as he wanted and it was tricky trying to stay in the role of therapist because he was so emotionally needy. It was clear he felt that he had never had a single human being in his life who cared for him and who wasn't out to exploit him. But the long and short of it is that there was a financial disaster in his corporation with everyone blaming everyone. There were lawsuits, scandals, the whole bit, and he was effectively financially wiped out. I couldn't hold onto him. I called for another psychiatric evaluation, which he refused. I spoke of possible hospitalization so he could get some rest time, but he refused that also. He was fragmenting severely from the stress. It was the worst I ever saw him.

Then he disappeared completely. He locked himself up in a hotel room without coming out until he was found a week later. He had starved himself. It was a luxury hotel with all kinds of services but he holed himself up, a fragmenting mess totally isolated from humanity, popping pills and drinking. He was located when a concerned housekeeper alerted her supervisor, who consulted the manager. He was found in terrible condition. He had turned away from everyone and everything—even me. He would not respond to my page with our secret code. I left messages everywhere. I searched everywhere, had the police out and everything. He had become a basket case—paranoid and suicidal.

When the authorities found him and hospitalized him, another psychiatrist got hold of him. He was diagnosed as bipolar and put on lithium. He had a loyal manager at the corporation who had held onto as much as he could and salvaged something—enough for him to still be well-to-do. But by now he had experienced starvation and I was his neglectful mother. There was nothing I could do. For months I left phone messages, sent cards and letters and even some flowers to cheer him up.

Some time later I heard from his lawyer. By the time the case shaped up with his crooked attorneys and psychiatrists he wanted millions in damage because I diagnosed him as lower borderline, hypomanic, and prescribed psychotherapy, soaking him with excessive expensive treatment when I should have seen that he had a bipolar biological disturbance and should have put him on lithium from the beginning. Of course his former doctor and psychiatrist are named too. But aside from the scam involved from a desperate man seeking to rebuild an empire, he said some really horrible things to me in our last phone call. He was dazed and confused and his basic message was that I wasn't there when he needed me, that I never helped him, never gave him anything, that I forced him into a fraudulent position by not giving him enough, by not containing him sufficiently.

I gave that man everything I had to give – and I'm a pretty good nurturer too. But an external disaster intervened before we got over the hump where he could trust. Maybe he's incapable of trusting. *He* certainly was never to be trusted in his business dealings. I was frequently revolted by the ruthless things he did to people. But I understood that he had no capacity for empathy. All of my expenses – which were many – are being investigated. He was so demanding that of course he paid for a considerable amount of my time. I kept hoping, truly hoping he would some day be able to emotionally connect. We were close, but it never happened. So his new empire will have a shot in the arm with a sizable settlement – his attorneys will stop at nothing. Their Mafia connection reputation has the insurance company intimidated.

This man so needed to be regarded as a person, to feel like a human being. He was kind of a Howard Hughes type, and just as pathetic and as exploited. I did my best, but now I'm seen as one of the many exploiters. They are even claiming that my bills for services are fraudulent, that he was charged for services never rendered. It's all so bizarre and untrue. How will I ever recover from reaching out so far to this pathetic human being and in the end having a starving mad viper hissing and snapping at me?

I know you speak about psychotic transference and I understand it intellectually. I could even understand how it operated when I would be five minutes late with a phone call and he would fly off the handle. But I could always somehow soothe him. We could talk about what it meant, about how the infant inside simply can't tolerate delay and how sorry I was to cause him such pain. All of that was okay, was manageable. But when the fragmentation leads to rage and realistic destruction of these proportions. . . . How will I ever feel safe with a fragmenting patient again? I repeatedly went beyond the call of duty in every possible way to accommodate this man. He has left me severely damaged, disillusioned with the human race, despairing about treatment, and questioning if it can ever really work. When I feel discouraged, I even question my competence as a therapist.

Commentary

Giving more doesn't cure psychosis. When you begin thinking that you are the only human this person has ever been able to deeply address, and you are the only person so desperately needed by this client to overcome horrible deprivation and/or abuse in childhood, perhaps you need to back off and examine the psychodynamic basis of your altruism. This is not the only case where a fluke in reality turned an otherwise good psychotherapy sour. This patient is a life-long expert at grasping and clawing when the odds are against him. Most therapists are naïve amateurs in survival skills and have no way to anticipate what such desperation might look like.

Case Consultation Four: Horace (with a male therapist, twelve years experience)

We finally reached the psychotic transference. I had been trying unsuccessfully for months to bring some deep abuse into focus. But he had a business presentation to make the next day and he was terrified of the challenge. It would be a reach for him and he might be questioned on some difficult issues. He didn't know if he could maintain. He was afraid. He went numb on the couch—had actual body paralysis for fifteen or twenty minutes. Had this not been a gradual descent into the psychotic pocket I had been hoping to explore, I might have been alarmed for medical reasons. In fact I did check with him to be sure he thought everything was okay. While he was in the trance he experienced severe blows to his face and head accompanied by loud, startling, and frightening yelling. They came suddenly out of nowhere. He had never been able to cry, never been able to raise his voice in pain. Now he knew why. It seemed certain that his father had abused him as an infant for being a needy baby, for whimpering and crying. He was feeling whimpery and needy that night with me because of the presentation the next day that I had been encouraging him about. In transference he experienced me as abusing him for being needy.

He now suddenly knew where his own sense of violence came from. He had always known that his taciturn father was a harsh man, but by the time he was old enough to remember in pictures, his father had withdrawn from emotional relationships in the family in order to contain his rage. This paralyzing insight into himself, his infantile rage, and the abusive humiliation he had suffered as an infant for feeling needy explained how he had come to believe himself defective and incapable, and had forced him "to fake his way" through most of life. He was terrified to have to feel the full impact of his psychotic core in this dramatic total body paralysis. He was deeply shaken and traumatized by having touched this primitive transference.

That night his therapy basically ended. He ran a fast retreat from that frightening place that he never wanted to be in again. He had been running from this terrifying body memory and the total agony it represented to him. Retrospectively, I see that his setting me up began at that point. He began needing a great many concessions and unusual arrangements in our work, which I did my best to accommodate. These seemed interpretable in a variety of ways within the context of his life history. But it turns out he was working behind the scenes collecting a list of variations in his professional relationship with me that could later be distorted in court to look as though they were inappropriate.

He terminated his work with me without ever successfully bringing the primitive transference into the analysis. When a subpoena for my records arrived I was in a state of total shock. His manner of turning against me when I was least expecting it — harsh blows coming out of nowhere — replicated what I had seen him experience on the couch. He never wanted to go there again and shockingly arranged to turn the tables so that it was I who felt like a fool for trusting.

Commentary

Never trust that someone in depth therapy will not attack you ragefully and mercilessly when the psychotic transference has been mobilized. Primitive transferences know no limit. Trusting that this person would never sue you is to be a fool about the very thing your therapy seeks to bring out—madness, desperation, and sociopathic manipulations.

Case Consultation Five: Jeffrey (with a female therapist, twelve years experience)

I see this young man four hours a week and we are in our fifth year. Because he had a mild learning disorder, he early on fell into bad company and spent most of his youth as a tough guy. His mother is seductive and intrusive, and I was slowly able to move him away from the overindulgent relationship he had with her. Father continues to bail him out of all kinds of trouble and to sponsor him financially so he never has incentive to achieve for himself. In the course of time I have largely been able to get him to back away from accepting so much from his father and to begin modest achievement on his own. We get along very well.

I want to talk to you about Jeffrey because I have read your work on countertransference and I have recently had a strong erotic countertransference reaction to him. I am a happily married woman and I have good boundaries so I'm not worried that anything would ever happen between us. After I helped him see how psychotic his last girlfriend was so that he finally got rid of her, he began making it better on his own doing some casual dating. He was planning to spend some time with an older woman over the weekend.

On that weekend I became sexually preoccupied thinking about him. I don't know exactly what I was thinking and I don't remember my fantasies, but I know my husband enjoyed how sexual I was. The following week he didn't mention his date until the third hour. He said he did not want to upset me by talking about sex. He had a wildly erotic story, however, about which he spared no details. I wasn't sure if he was trying to excite me or make me jealous. But his conscious accent was on trying to make me proud of him for having picked someone to spend time with who had some substance and sanity for a change. I don't know where all of that's going but we have a good relationship so whatever happens I'm sure we can talk it out.

But there's this other thing that started happening. He would begin to fall asleep in hours. I spoke with several consultants who interpreted it as his feeling safe enough to trust himself with me or that he experienced the interpersonal stimulation as so strong that he needed to pull away at times. But Jeffrey would awaken from these naps with dreams that we could then use to help us understand where he was with me and in our work together. In fact, some of the best material we have ever worked with has come from these dreams. Six months ago Jeffrey asked about hypnosis. He asked what it was and if I would hypnotize him so we could find out what is really going on "down there" that he avoids by sleeping, but then has access to in his dreams. I have never been trained in hypnosis but I said I would do this for him. So I have since taken a number of workshops in hypnosis and have a consultant I expect to use when we finally do try it. It was around the time I was beginning to think about starting some hypnosis with him when I felt the erotic counter-transference. But trying to deal with the erotic element slowed me down.

Commentary

When you find yourself wanting to do special things to accommodate your patient, be suspicious that there are some invisible dimensions operating. Here the mutual sexual excitement reaches a weekend peak when you are considering what it may mean to penetrate his consciousness with hypnosis. Recall that this man had both a mother and a father who intruded with good things so extensively that he failed to thrive academically and socially. Of course he yearns for helping support from his therapist, but the direction you are going runs the danger of replicating the destructive intrusiveness of good-intentioned parents. It further suggests that good-intended but destructive

intrusion may be an erotic scenario, which matches his history
of sadomasochistic love relationships.

Whenever we pride ourselves on being someone special for
our clients, a red flag should go up. What kinds of psychic
representations might appear to signal an infantile molest that is
being psychotically fused with the benevolent intrusiveness of
the therapist? Erotic transference and countertransference certainly occur and can be useful informers about the therapeutic
process. But when they are simply taken in stride, especially after
just getting rid of a psychotic girlfriend and just when hypnosis
is about to begin, they seem like warning signs to be reckoned
with.

Case Consultation Six: Matthew (with female
therapist, twenty years experience)

I know you basically know it all by now. You've heard it from my
patient when he came to you for consultation. I sent him to you
because I knew you could help him without encouraging anything destructive. I should have come to you myself months ago,
and it's stupid that I didn't. In a way I saw it coming. And in a
way I didn't. But if I'd talked about it, a lot of grief could have
been avoided. It's stupid that I didn't open up to some of the
people in my office. They've known me for years, they love me,
they would have understood. I knew you wouldn't judge me. I
knew they wouldn't judge me. But it was a stupid mistake and I'm
out of it by the skin of my teeth – at least hopefully I'm out of it.
The therapy was going well. Matthew was very intense from the
beginning and soon began feeling emotions for the first time in
his life. He had never emotionally connected with anyone
before. He's very bright, witty, and he always showed a great deal
of concern about how I was doing with the things he had to tell
me.

Meanwhile I was in this really awful place with my husband
that I won't even talk about now. It was a really horrible

breakup. I was fragmented and lonely. I called my client on impulse to have a drink. And that was really all that happened. But you know, sometimes a drink isn't just a drink. I could imagine situations where a chance encounter with a client or ex-client might spontaneously lead to a brief friendly exchange and a drink together. Not that I would recommend it to anyone. But I could imagine circumstances where it might be okay. Well, this wasn't okay and I knew it. I was clearly needy and turning to him for some consolation. I knew it was wrong and I even felt it coming up in all of my distress. If I had just said something to Becky or Bob, my office partners, they would have understood. They would have talked some sense into me. They would have pulled me back from the brink. But it was a fatal attraction. And this is a powerfully seductive man, as you know.

I really wanted to tell you about this. Because do you know what the worst part of this is? It's the stupid shame. Shame that I would be attracted to a client. Shame that I would want to be seen and liked by him. Shame that I didn't rely on my friends when I felt this happening to me. Shame that I didn't call you and ask for help. It's true he loved my personal involvement and couldn't understand why I felt I had violated his trust and couldn't continue seeing him professionally. To him, I was the first person in his life who had ever seen him, who saw how wonderful he was, who knew how he felt. Our sessions were magical—I'm sure he told you. It was like we were right together all the time. He loved it and he loved that I really cared for him. And I did. That part can't be wrong. It's not wrong to care for a client, even to love a client. That's happened many times in twenty years of practice and it's been beautiful and enhancing to the work.

But here I don't know what happened. Except that I really liked him and I was really feeling needy and vulnerable. You know, this is not the sort of thing you imagine happening to yourself. And, in fact, nothing really happened. It's not like we even kissed or held hands—we didn't. It was simply two people meeting for a drink. But a man's therapy was ruined.

Please tell the people you teach. Please write about it in your books. No one should be allowed to say "It can't happen to me." You now tell me that when you saw him, you saw a psychotic core, a manic frenzy to seduce the nurturing mother so he wouldn't die. And I fell right into that! If I hadn't been such a mess at the time, would I have been so enthralled by him, so pulled in by him? I honestly don't know. But it's a lesson in humility. And a lesson in false pride—as though I'm too good to make a mistake, too good to be tempted, too sane to get my thoughts all fucked up. I can't believe I'm even saying all of this. I hope others can learn from my mistake. I lost a good client.

And now you even suggest that I'm a fool to think I'm protected from his taking legal action because he's not litigious and because he has caring feelings for me. I guess I don't know enough about the power or unpredictability of the psychotic transference. Even though I've seen some pretty horrible things in other situations, I got to believing I knew what I was doing and it would all be okay. Is mania contagious?!

Commentary

It's not discrete behaviors, what we do or don't do, that count in protecting the therapy situation from overstimulation. But it's the spirit of the relatedness involved that defines the personal boundaries. Furthermore, we are always in trouble when we think we know for sure what we are doing, especially if we think we're safe from the unpredictability of the psychotic transference or from our own psychotic anxieties. We have to be free to turn to colleagues when we feel shaky. If we don't seek consultation in time, the power of the hidden psychosis can overtake us. She's right—it's false pride that makes fools of us all.

Case Consultation Seven: Trula (with male therapist, twenty-two years experience)

I know I did wrong and the worst part is that I knew it was wrong while I was doing it. It was uncanny. It was like a part of me was up on the ceiling looking down watching and knowing what I was doing was wrong.

We had worked well together for three years but the challenge of a major promotion at work that was just beyond her grasp set off a major regression with fragmentation and depression. She became increasingly desperate and wanted to stop coming to see me. Finances were an issue. I insisted we couldn't stop this way. I lowered my fee, and after some weeks of watching her desperately floundering just beyond my reach, I couldn't stand it any more. I moved toward her, I embraced her to protect and reassure her. I held her and I gently kissed her.

A part of me for a long time hoped she would sue me. Being punished would have been sweet relief. Instead, I had to experience the most agonizing regression imaginable in my own therapy.

My own mother was gravely disabled and couldn't care for me when I was born. I grew up in foster care and remember endless painful Saturdays waiting on the porch steps for her to come. Sometimes she would, sometimes she wouldn't, but I waited all day anyway, hoping. Even as an infant I must have somehow known she was fragmented, hurting, desperately needing help and reassurance. When my client entered this same despairing, unreachable place I could not bear it. I moved to rescue her, to try to give her the love, the containing, the touch she so desperately needed. And my client did respond favorably at the time. She pulled herself together and made a great success of her promotion. But when a devastating personal tragedy later hit her I succumbed to financial blackmail to avoid public embarrassment.

Commentary

The psychotic transference always hooks us deeply. As the analytic speaker continues to pull away we are in danger of reliving our own infantile organizing period and feel the desperation that we may die if we cannot find mother. It is the successful connection with the organizing transference that produces terror—replicating the original terror that the infant somehow experienced that foreclosed the possibility of an emotional bonding experience.

There is one last aspect to this problem of people reaching out to find one another that I would like to illustrate. A surprising feature of the analytic speaker's reaching often makes the psychotic transference difficult to detect, much less to respond to creatively and safely.

LUNACY AT THE SUSHI BAR: MORGAN

Not long ago I was working late on a rainy night and stopped by a local Japanese restaurant, The Mikado, on the way home. At the sushi bar I chanced to sit next to a pleasant-looking young fellow with dark hair, glistening eyes, a close-trimmed mustache, and tight-fitting Western clothes and boots. While I was scanning the menu selections, his tuna rolls arrived and he offered me one while calling for a second sake cup for me. We quickly lapsed into a fascinating conversation that lasted until the bar closed.

Morgan was a friendly and good-natured fellow. But as soon as he began to talk, I could see he was a strange enough person that most people would have quickly and politely moved away. Whether it was because I was tired and needed to unwind, or because he was plainly inviting, or because the sake went to work so quickly—I found myself interested and engaged. We talked about the weather, the recent disastrous fires, the unfortunate people spending this rainy night in tents after the devastating earthquake, and the many among us dead and suffering from the AIDS epidemic. Morgan's eyes filled with tears as he told me about his lover who had passed away almost a year ago—a loving man who had taken him under his wing and cared for

him for many years. We linked arms in traditional Japanese
fashion and lifted our sake cups in memory of his lover.

Then came crab, swordfish, shark, California rolls, and
more sake. We talked about the colleges we had gone to, the
fraternities we had belonged to, and what we were doing now.
When Morgan discovered I was a therapist, he explained he had
seen many counselors through the years since he was twelve. He
liked counselors and wondered if I knew this one or that one.
Then began a sequence that kept me spellbound for over an
hour—partly because Morgan was so sincere, so innocent, and
so intense; partly because I was genuinely enjoying him; and
partly because I was seeing in pure culture a spontaneous,
unadulterated version of an instantly formed organizing or
psychotic transference operating freely before my very eyes. I
couldn't help but play into it.

Morgan leaned forward in an intimate fashion. Though
quite masculine, he seemed like a soft and affectionate teddy
bear who could easily melt into a gentle cuddle. In contrast to
this bodily yearning and reaching out for contact, for human
warmth and affection, as he addressed me Morgan's eyes opened
widely and dilated as though he were startled or terrified. "I
could really tell you some things you wouldn't believe," he
challenged. I took the bait. The sequence started off with mildly
unbelievable, "new age" styled quasi-mystical events. Without
flinching I nodded in assent to his "amazing and unbelievable"
experiences, expressing surprise that he did not expect me to
believe him. I spoke in favor of trusting our own experiences,
even if others might not be able to follow them. There surely are
uncanny happenings in the universe that many people would
find difficult to believe. The illusions, delusions, and hallucinatory stories then began escalating with Morgan continuing to
lean forward affectionately with those same widely terrified
eyes—a posture simultaneously begging for connection and
challenging me to reject him by disbelief. Not to be easily
thrown over, I firmly maintained my position that while many

might indeed doubt what he had seen or heard, I saw no reason for him to doubt his own experiences.

The sushi, the sake, the recounting of psychic events, and the challenging engagement drew Morgan's bar stool closer to mine. I could clearly see something through Morgan that I had long intuited from experiences in the consulting room. But it was so much clearer, so much more vivid and real in this setting. I was witnessing his life-long investment in seeing to it that no interpersonal connection could possibly be made. That is, he was certain that it would only be a matter of time before I began to question, to doubt, to turn away, to see him as crazy, and to shrink away from him in fear or disdain. But alas, Morgan had met his match! There was nothing he could say that could possibly make me turn from his penetrating terrified gaze, from his soft affectionate approach, from the stories he told with hallucinatory vividness.

The climax finally came in a story about his mother, Laverne. One night some years ago, shortly after his father died, he was at Laverne's house having a smoke on the patio. At the time, she lived on the outskirts of a small town in Arizona. The desert behind the house stretched miles into the night to the high mountains barely illuminated by the summer skies. Suddenly, the heavens begin to fill with an intense iridescent blue light. Spellbound, Morgan watched as a giant craft silently and gently descended to the floor of the desert and as small aliens appeared, scouting the surrounding territory. Morgan wondered who they were, where they came from, and what they were there for. He felt afraid. Perhaps they wanted him. He ran to get his mother. He wanted to show her the great blue light and the strange night visitors. Laverne was irritated at having her television program interrupted, but she reluctantly followed him out onto the patio. Would you believe she could see nothing? No blue light, no aliens? She said he was crazy, that he was seeing things. But they were there. He was sure of it. He didn't know why Laverne couldn't see them. Morgan was leaning forward on his bar stool clutching my arm, terrified eyes searching my face. I was sure to doubt, sure to raise questions, sure to pose alternative explanations, sure to somehow challenge his sense of what was real, to echo Laverne's pronouncement that he was crazy. I would certainly not be able to believe what he had seen when even his own mother didn't believe him when the evidence was plainly before her eyes!

Not to be undone at such a critical moment, I asked Morgan why it even mattered to him what his mother thought. It was silly to worry about what other people believed, I said. He saw what he saw, experienced what he experienced, and if she couldn't deal with it, that was her problem, not his. Morgan turned into a statue before my very eyes, frozen in fright that I had heard him, had connected to him. He looked as though he anticipated my suddenly hitting him. Morgan was thrown into a state of total terror and confusion by our connection. He had spent a lifetime developing a technique to ensure that his desperate need for warmth, for loving reception, would be thwarted by the other's turning away in fear, horror, or disdain. *The internalized break in contact was skillfully incorporated into Morgan's way of reaching toward me, into his very way of being in the world. The internalized breach of connection with the other was already woven into, already implicit in, already ensured by the very way he approached me.*

I suddenly realized how many people live this way. The infantile trauma they have suffered and their primordial way of limiting the overstimulation, have become internalized in such a way that the very manner of approach for contact itself forms a social demand that assures that the other will reject connection.

I also understood in a flash that had I simply reached out toward him by naïvely "validating" the truth of his experience, Morgan would have known that he had found a kindred soul — someone else who was also terrified of connections and who managed in the world by issuing interpersonal invitations to have deep yearnings responded to.

But Morgan was foiled in his encounter with me. For some reason I liked him very much. I enjoyed his manly softness and his desperate search for nourishing touch. I felt compassion for his terror and I connected deeply with his pathos. In me he momentarily touched the mother he longed for and she had tenderly touched him back, throwing him into a state of terrible confusion and sudden fear of some sort of abuse. For a horrible moment that must have seemed like an eternity to Morgan, external reality was not matching internal reality. We sat together for a while in silence.

The sushi bar was closing. Morgan and I passed through the lobby, past cherry blossoms and a great golden dragon breathing fire, through the red lacquered doors, and into the crisp air of this strange California night. The rain had stopped and the skies had cleared. Before we headed our separate ways, Morgan and I shook hands. Then we embraced—two strangers having achieved a rare moment of intimacy laced with fear. The full moon rose above the temple gate of The Mikado.

The emergence of organizing or psychotic transference momentarily places the crucible of a person's life in a delicate balance. The traumatic reality of the primordial past is emotionally and powerfully pitted against the reality of the potentially satisfying intimacy of the present relationship. And ten thousand years of human experience says the deck is stacked against us—that craziness is intractable and untreatable, that in time we can expect that the power of the infantile past will inevitably reassert itself in a delusional way, and that we can expect the potentially curative present moment of relatedness will be forsaken or renounced in such a way that the therapist will be held responsible for the deep sense of trauma. At this critical moment of transference experiencing the affective past is fused with the present, and the power of the infantile trauma totally eclipses the transformative possibilities inherent in the present intimate relationship. The peril inherent in the psychotherapeutic relationship is not caused by the recent widely publicized recovered memories controversy. The problem of transference psychosis has always been with us. It is real. It is dangerous. It is universal. And it isn't going away. Our task is to find creative ways of meeting and working through the organizing experience.

References

Alexander, F. (1961). *The Scope of Psychoanalysis*. New York: Basic Books.

Allison, R. (1974). A new treatment approach for multiple personality. *American Journal of Clinical Hypnosis* 17(1):15–32.

American Psychiatric Association (1952, 1968, 1980). *Diagnostic and Statistical Manual* I, II, III (respectively). Washington, DC: American Psychiatric Association.

Balint, A. (1939). Mothers and motherhood—object love (infants). *International Journal of Psycho-Analysis* 20(3, 4):223–230.

_____ (1943) On identification. *International Journal of Psycho-Analysis*, 24:97–107.

Beahrs, J. (1982). *Unity and Multiplicity: Multilevel Consciousness of Self in Hypnosis, Psychiatric Disorders and Mental Health*. New York: Brunner/Mazel.

Bion, W. R. (1962). *Learning from Experience*. New York: Basic Books.

_____ (1963). *Elements of Psycho-Analysis*. New York: Basic Books.

_____ (1977). *Second Thoughts.* New York: Jason Aronson.

Bollas, C. (1979). The transformational object. *International Journal of Psycho-Analysis* 59:97–107.

_____ (1982). On the relation to the self as an object. *International Journal of Psycho-Analysis* 63:347–359.

_____ (1987). *The Shadow of the Object.* London: Free Association Press.

Bowlby, J. (1969). *Attachment and Loss: Separation Anxiety and Anger,* vol. 1. New York: Basic Books.

Braun, B. (1984). Uses of hypnosis with multiple personality. *Psychiatric Annals* 14(1):34–40.

Braun, B. G., and Braun, R. E. (1979). *Clinical aspects of multiple personality.* Paper presented at the annual meeting of the American Society of Clinical Hypnosis. San Francisco, November.

Brazelton, T. B., and Barnard, K. E. (1990). *Touch: The Foundation of Experience.* Madison, CT: International Universities Press.

Cameron, N. (1963). *Personality Development and Psychopathology.* Boston: Houghton Mifflin.

Caul, D. (1984). Group and videotape techniques for multiple personality disorder. *Psychiatric Annals* 14(1):43–50.

Eissler, K. R. (1953). The effect of the structure of the ego on psychoanalytic technique. *Journal of the American Psychoanalytic Association* 1:104–143.

Ekstein, R. (1979). *Narcissism and the psychopathology of the self in childhood.* Lecture delivered to The Child Psychiatry Service–Tufts University of Medicine.

_____ (1984). *Prolegomena to the study of the languages of psychoanalysis and psychotherapy.* Lecture delivered at the Newport Center for Psychoanalytic Studies, Newport Beach, California, October.

Ferenczi, S. (1912). Transitory symptom-constructions during the analysis (transitory conversion, substitution, illusion, hallucination, "character-regression," and "expression-displacement"). In *First Contributions to Psycho-Analysis,* compiled by J. Rickman, pp. 193–212. New York: Brunner/Mazel, 1952.

——— (1919). On the technique of psycho-analysis. In *Further Contributions to the Theory and Technique of Psycho-Analysis*, pp. 177–189. London: Hogarth Press, 1950.

——— (1952). *First Contributions to Psycho-Analysis*. Compiled by John Rickman. New York: Brunner/Mazel.

——— (1955). *Final Contributions to the Problems and Methods of Psycho-Analysis*. New York: Brunner/Mazel.

——— (1962). *Further Contributions to the Theory and Technique of Psycho-Analysis*. New York: Brunner/Mazel.

Fingarette, H. (1969). *Self-Deception*. New York: Routledge & Kegan Paul.

Fraiberg, S. (1982). Pathological defenses in infancy. *Psychoanalytic Quarterly* 51:612–635.

Freud, A. (1951). Observations on child development. In *Indications for Child Analysis and Other Papers*, pp. 143–162. New York: International Universities Press, 1968.

——— (1952). The role of bodily illness in the mental life of children. In *Indications for Child Analysis and Other Papers*, pp. 260–279. New York: International Universities Press, 1968.

——— (1958). Child observation and prediction of development. In *Research at the Hampstead Child-Therapy Clinic and Other Papers* (1970). pp. 102–135. Taken from Khan, M. M. R. (1974). *The Privacy of The Self*, p. 57. New York: International Universities Press.

Freud, S. (1895a). Project for a scientific psychology. *Standard Edition* 1:283–388.

——— (1895b). Studies on Hysteria. *Standard Edition* 2.

——— (1900). *The Interpretation of Dreams*. New York: Avon Books.

——— (1912). Papers on technique: the dynamics of transference. *Standard Edition* 12:92–108.

——— (1914). Recollecting, repeating and working through (further recommendations on the technique of psycho-analysis II). *Standard Edition* 12:145–156.

——— (1915). Observations on transference love (further recommendations on the technique of psycho-analysis III). *Standard Edition* 12:159–171.

——— (1918). An infantile neurosis. *Standard Edition* 17:1–124.

_____ (1920). Beyond the pleasure principle. *Standard Edition* 18:3–64.

_____ (1923). The ego and the id. *Standard Edition* 19:3–68.

_____ (1926). Inhibitions, symptoms and anxiety. *Standard Edition* 20:75–175.

_____ (1933). New introductory lectures on psycho-analysis. *Standard Edition* 22:1–184.

Ganaway, G. K. (1991). *Alternative hypotheses regarding satanic ritual abuse memories.* Presented at the ninety-ninth annual convention of the American Psychological Association, San Francisco, California, August.

Giovacchini, P. L. (1975). *Psychoanalysis of Character Disorders.* New York: Jason Aronson.

_____ (1979a). Countertransference with primitive mental states. In *Countertransference*, ed. L. Epstein and A. H. Feiner, pp. 235–265. New York: Jason Aronson.

_____ (1979b). *Treatment of Primitive Mental States.* New York: Jason Aronson.

Glover, E. (1932). Affects, instincts, ambivalence, depressions, stress, tension, sadistic "aphanisis." In *A Psycho-Analytic Approach to the Classification of Mental Disorders.*

Green, A. (1986). The dead mother. In *On Private Madness.* London: Hogarth Press.

Greenacre, P. (1958). Towards the understanding of the physical nucleus of some defence reactions. *International Journal of Psycho-Analysis* 39:69–76.

_____ (1960). Further notes on fetishism. *Psychoanalytic Study of the Child* 15:191–207. New York: International University Press.

Greenson, R. (1965). The working alliance and the transference neurosis. In *Explorations in Psychoanalysis*, pp. 199–225. New York: International Universities Press, 1978.

Grotstein, J., ed. (1981). *Dare I Disturb the Universe?* Beverly Hills, CA: Caesura Press.

Hammett, V. B. O. (1961). Delusional transference. *American Journal of Psychotherapy* 15:574–581.

Hare, D. (1983). *Plenty.* New York: Penguin.

Hedges, L. E. (1983a). *A listening perspective for the organizing personality.* Cassette lecture distributed by The Newport

Center for Psychoanalytic Studies, 1439 E. Chapman Ave., Orange, California 92666. Presented June 5, 1983.

———— (1983b). *Listening Perspectives in Psychotherapy*. New York: Jason Aronson.

———— (1992). *Interpreting the Countertransference*. Northvale, NJ: Jason Aronson.

———— (1994a, in press). *Strategic Emotional Involvement*. Northvale, NJ: Jason Aronson.

———— (1994b, in press). Taking recovered memories seriously. *The California Therapist*.

———— (1994c). *Working the Organizing Experience*. New York: Jason Aronson.

———— (1994d, in press). *In Search of the Lost Mother of Infancy*. Northvale, NJ: Jason Aronson.

Hedges, L. E., and Coverdale, C. (1985). *Countertransference: the royal road to the merger experience*. Videotape cassette lecture distributed by the Newport Center for Psychoanalytic Studies, 1439 E. Chapman Ave., Orange, CA 92666. Presented October 27, 1985.

Hedges, L. E., and Hulgus, J. (1991). *Working the organizing experience: a cutting edge approach to work with psychotic, schizoid, autistic, and organizing states*. Seminar filmed at Charter Hospital of Mission Viejo, September 20, 1991 (four hours).

Hilton, V. W. (1994). The devil in America: the end of the millennium. *The California Therapist* 6(1):37–41.

Holmer, N. M., and Wassen, H. (1947). *Mu-Igala or the way of Muu, a Medicine Song from the Cunas of Panama*. Goteborg: (Quoted in Lévi-Strauss 1949.)

Jacobson, E. (1954). The self and object world: vicissitudes of their infantile cathexis and their influence on ideational and affective development. *The Psychoanalytic Study of the Child* 9:75–127. New York: International Universities Press.

———— (1964). *The Self and Object World*. New York: International Universities Press.

Kafka, F. (1926). *The Castle*. New York: Schocken Books.

———— (1937). *The Trial*. New York: Vintage Books.

———— (1979). *The Basic Kafka*. New York: Pocket Books.

Katan, A. (1969). *The Therapeutic Nursery School*. Edited by R. Furman and A. Katan. New York: International Universities Press.

Kernberg, O. F. (1975). *Borderline Conditions and Pathological Narcissism*. New York: Jason Aronson.

_____ (1976). *Object-Relations Theory and Clinical Psychoanalysis*. New York: Jason Aronson.

Khan, M. M. R. (1963). The concept of cumulative trauma. *Psychoanalytic Study of the Child* 18:286–306. New York: International Universities Press.

Kitchener, K. (1988). Dual relationships: what makes them so problematic? *Journal of Counselling and Development* 67:217–221.

Klein, M. (1937, revised in 1975). *Love, Guilt and Reparation and Other Works*. New York: Free Press.

_____ (1952). Some theoretical conclusions regarding the emotional life of the infant. In *Developments in Psycho-Analysis*, ed. J. Riviere. London: Hogarth.

_____ (1957). *Envy and Gratitude*. New York: Basic Books.

Kluft, R. P. (1979). *Epidemiology of multiple personality*. Paper presented at the annual meeting of the American Psychiatric Association, Chicago, May.

_____ (1984a). An introduction to multiple personality disorder. *Psychiatric Annals* 14(1):19–24.

_____ (1984b). Aspects of the treatment of multiple personality disorders. *Psychiatric Annals* 14(1):51–55.

Kohut, H. (1971). *The Analysis of the Self*. New York: International Universities Press.

_____ (1977). *The Restoration of the Self*. New York: International Universities Press.

_____ (1981). Summarizing Reflections at UCLA Conference on "Progress in Self Psychology," October 5, 1981.

_____ (1984). *How Does Analysis Cure?* Chicago: University of Chicago Press.

Kosinski, J. (1970). *Being There*. New York: Harcourt, Brace, Jovanovich.

Kris, E. (1951). Some comments and observations on early autoerotic activities. *Psychoanalytic Study of the Child* 6:95–116. New York: International Universities Press.

_____ (1956a). The personal myth. *Journal of the American Psychoanalytic Association* 4:653–681.

_____ (1956b). The recovery of childhood memories in psychoanalysis. *Psychoanalytic Study of the Child* 11:54–88. New York: International Universities Press.

Lacan, J. (trans. 1977). The function and field of speech and language in psychoanalysis. In *Ecrits: A Selection*. New York: W. W. Norton, 1953. (*Ecrits*. Paris: Sevil, 1966.)

Lévi-Strauss, C. (1949). The effectiveness of symbols. In *Structural Anthropology*, vol. 1, pp. 186–205. New York: Basic Books, 1963.

Little, M. (1957). 'R': the analyst's total response to the patients needs. *International Journal of Psycho-Analysis* 38:240–254.

_____ (1958). On delusional transference (transference psychosis). *International Journal of Psycho-Analysis* 39:134–138.

_____ (1960). On basic unity. *International Journal of Psycho-Analysis* 41:377–384.

_____ (1981). *Transference Neurosis: Transference Psychosis*. New York: Jason Aronson.

_____ (1990). *Psychotic Anxieties and Containment: A Personal Record of an Analysis with Winnicott*. Northvale, NJ: Jason Aronson.

Loftus, E. L. (1993). The reality of repressed memories. *American Psychologist* 48:518–537.

Lowen, A. (1971). *The Language of the Body* New York: Collier Books.

_____ (1975). *Bioenergetics*. London: Penguin Books.

_____ (1988). *Love, Sex, and Your Heart*. New York: Macmillan.

Mahler, M. (1968). *On Human Symbiosis and the Vicissitudes of Individuation, vol. 1, Infantile Psychosis*. New York: International Universities Press.

Marmer, S. S. (1980). Psychoanalysis of multiple personality. *International Journal of Psycho-Analysis* 61:439–459.

McDougall, J. (1989). *Theatres of the Body*. London: Free Association Press.

Milner, M. (1952). Aspects of symbolism in comprehension of the not-self. *International Journal of Psycho-Analysis* 33:181–195.

Modell, A. H. (1976). "The holding environment" and the

therapeutic action of psychoanalysis. *Journal of the American Psychoanalytic Association* 24:285–308.

Natterson, J. (1991). *Beyond Countertransference. The Therapist's Subjectivity in the Therapeutic Process.* New York: Jason Aronson.

Putnam, F. W., Post, R. M., and Guroff, J. J. (1983). *100 cases of multiple personality disorders.* Paper read at the annual meeting of the American Psychiatric Association (New Research Abstract #77), New York, May.

Reider, N. (1957). Transference psychosis. *Journal of Hillside Hospital* 6:131–140.

Rosenfeld, H. (1954). Considerations regarding the psychoanalytic approach to acute and chronic schizophrenia. *International Journal of Psycho-Analysis* 35:135–140.

Russell, J. M. (1978a). Sartre, therapy, and expanding the concept of responsibility. *American Journal of Psychoanalysis* 38:259–269.

———— (1978b). Saying, feeling and self-deception. *Behaviorism* 6(1):27–43.

———— (1980). How to think about thinking. *Journal of Mind and Behavior* 1(1).

Ryle, G. (1949). *The Concept of Mind.* New York: Barnes and Noble.

Sandler, J., and Rosenblatt, B. (1962). The concept of the representational world. *Psychoanalytic Study of the Child* 17:128–145. New York: International Universities Press.

Sanville, J. (1992). *The Playground of Psychoanalytic Psychotherapy.* Hillsdale, NJ: Analytic Press.

Sartre, J.-P. (1956). *Being and Nothingness.* (Trans. Hazel E. Barnes). New York: Washington Square Press.

Schafer, D. (1984). *Recognition and treatment of multiple personality.* Lecture given at the Brea Neuropsychiatric Hospital, Brea, California, June.

Schafer, R. (1976). *A New Language for Psychoanalysis.* New Haven: Yale University Press.

Schreiber, F. R. (1973). *Sybil.* Chicago: Henry Gegnery.

Schwaber, E. (1979). *Narcissism, self psychology and the listening perspective.* Pre-presentation reading for lecture given at the

University of California, Los Angeles Conference on the Psychology of the Self-Narcissism, October.

_____ (1983). Psychoanalytic listening and psychic reality. *International Journal of Psycho-Analysis* 10:379–391.

Searles, H. F. (1960). *The Nonhuman Environment*. New York: International Universities Press.

_____ (1979). *Countertransference and Related Subjects: Selected Papers*. New York: International Universities Press.

Spence, D. (1982). *Narrative Truth and Historical Truth*. New York: Norton.

Stern, D. N. (1985). *The Interpersonal World of the Infant*. New York: Basic Books.

Strachey, J. (1934). The nature of the therapeutic action of psychoanalysis. *International Journal of Psycho-Analysis* 15:117–126.

Suskind, P. (1986). *Perfume*. New York: Washington Square Press.

Tausk, V. (1919). On the origin of the influencing machine in schizophrenia. *Psychoanalytic Quarterly* 2:519–556.

Taylor, W. S., and Martin, M. F. (1944). Multiple personality. *Journal of Abnormal and Social Psychology* 39:281–300.

Thigpen, C. H. and Cleckley, H. A. (1957). *The Three Faces of Eve*. New York: McGraw-Hill.

Tomatis, A. A. (1991). *The Conscious Ear: My Life of Transformation through Listening*. New York: Station Hill Press.

Tomm, K. (1991). The ethics of dual relationships. *The Calgary Participator: A Family Therapy Newsletter* 1:3. (Reprinted in *The California Therapist*, Jan./Feb., 1993.)

Tronick, E. and Cohn, J. (1988). Infant–mother face-to-face communicative interaction: age and gender differences in coordination and the occurrence of miscoordination. *Child Development* 60:85–92.

Tustin, F. (1972). *Autism and Childhood Psychosis*. London: Hogarth Press.

_____ (1981). *Autistic States in Children*. London: Routledge and Kegan Paul.

_____ (1986). *Autistic Barriers in Neurotic Patients*. New Haven: Yale University Press.

Van Sweden, R. (1994). *Regression to Dependence: A Second Opportunity for Ego Integration and Developmental Progression*. Northvale, NJ: Jason Aronson.

Wallerstein, R. (1967). Reconstruction and mastery in the transference psychosis. *Journal of the American Psychoanalytic Association* 15(3):551–583.

Wilbur, C. (1984). Treatment of multiple personality. *Psychiatric Annals* 14(1):27–31.

Winnicott, D. W. (1949a). Birth memories, birth trauma, and anxiety. In *Through Paediatrics to Psycho-Analysis*, pp. 174–194. New York: Basic Books, 1975.

—— (1949b). Hate in the countertransference. *International Journal of Psycho-Analysis* 30:69–75.

—— (1952). Psychoses and child care. In *Through Paediatrics to Psycho-Analysis*, pp. 219–228. New York: Basic Books, 1975.

—— (1953). Transitional objects and transitional phenomena: a study of the first not-me possession. *International Journal of Psycho-Analysis* 34:89–97.

—— (1954). Metapsychological and classical aspects of regression. In *Through Paediatrics to Psycho-Analysis*, pp. 278–294. New York: Basic Books, 1975.

—— (1958, revised 1975). *Through Paediatrics to Psycho-Analysis*. New York: Basic Books, 1975.

—— (1960). The theory of the parent–infant relationship. In *The Maturational Process and the Facilitating Environment*, pp. 37–55. New York: International University Press, 1965.

—— (1965). Birth memories, birth trauma and anxiety. In *Through Paediatrics to Psycho-Analysis*, pp. 174–193. New York: Basic Books, 1975.

—— (1971). *Playing and Reality*. London: Tavistock.

—— (1974). Fear of breakdown. *International Review of Psycho-Analysis* 1:103.

Wittgenstein, L. (1953). *Philosophical Investigations*. (Trans. G. E. M. Anscombe), New York: Macmillan.

Credits

Index